To Cindy & Paul

Viki McCabe

Coming to Our Senses

"McCabe has given us a wise and timely book that applies cutting-edge thinking from perceptual psychology and from the analysis of complex natural systems to many contemporary social problems. The work is both fascinating in its presentation and important in its implications."

—Harry Heft, Professor and Chair, Psychology Department, Denison University, and Author of *Ecological Psychology in Context: James Gibson, Roger Barker, and the Radical Empiricism of William James*

"Reality, we generally think, is a simple thing, and yet, different people constantly come up with conflicting and often troublesome views. Viki McCabe offers an important, thoughtful, and thought-provoking perspective on why this happens and what we might do about it. Enhance your reality, and give it a read!"

—David P. Barash, Professor, Psychology Department, University of Washington, and author of *Homo Mysterious: Evolutionary Puzzles of Human Nature*

"A wonderful read that clarifies the role of perception, information, and complex systems in understanding and dealing with world problems."

—Reuben M. Baron, Professor Emeritus and Senior Research Scientist, Department of Psychology, The University of Connecticut

"Viki McCabe breaks boundaries by writing a book that expands our awareness of complex systems on which our health and survival depend. She directs us to trust the intelligence of our senses as a path away from illusory theories and the damage that they wreak. Rarely is a book so compelling and significant in its message as well as its structure. People of all professions need to hear and heed this book's message."

—Louise Chawla, Professor, Environmental Design Program, University of Colorado

Coming to Our Senses

Perceiving Complexity to Avoid Catastrophes

VIKI McCABE

OXFORD
UNIVERSITY PRESS

OXFORD
UNIVERSITY PRESS

Oxford University Press is a department of the University of Oxford.
It furthers the University's objective of excellence in research, scholarship,
and education by publishing worldwide.

Oxford   New York
Auckland   Cape Town   Dar es Salaam   Hong Kong   Karachi
Kuala Lumpur   Madrid   Melbourne   Mexico City   Nairobi
New Delhi   Shanghai   Taipei   Toronto

With offices in
Argentina   Austria   Brazil   Chile   Czech Republic   France   Greece
Guatemala   Hungary   Italy   Japan   Poland   Portugal   Singapore
South Korea   Switzerland   Thailand   Turkey   Ukraine   Vietnam

Oxford is a registered trademark of Oxford University Press
in the UK and certain other countries.

Published in the United States of America by
Oxford University Press
198 Madison Avenue, New York, NY 10016

© Oxford University Press 2014

Library of Congress Cataloging-in-Publication Data
McCabe, Viki.
Coming to our senses : perceiving complexity to avoid catastrophes / Viki McCabe.
pages cm
Includes bibliographical references and index.
ISBN 978–0–19–998858–7
1. Perception.   2. Perception (Philosophy)   3. Reality.
4. Knowledge, Theory of.   I. Title.
BF311.M4276 2014
153.7—dc23
2013025381

1 3 5 7 9 8 6 4 2
Printed in the United States of America
on acid-free paper

To the Bainbridge Island and Kitsap Regional Library
Outreach Librarians, especially Bonnie McKernan

Table of Contents

Acknowledgments

I OWE THE greatest debt to those who read, reread, and critiqued the entire manuscript—my patron saint, Letitia Anne Peplau, emeritus professor at the UCLA psychology department, for being there through thick and thin with astute comments and unfailing encouragement; my life companion, Doug Tanaka, who took the greatest burden off my shoulders by dealing with e-mails; my dear friend, Mikki Townshend, for understanding everything I wrote no matter how convoluted; almost everybody's favorite professor who we all miss sorely, Tom Wickens, emeritus professor at Berkeley, who from the beginning to the very end kept telling me, in distinction to everyone else, that the world would catch up to how I saw things; my amazingly astute reviewer, Harry Heft at Denison University, for championing the book and convincing me to add material at the last minute that was critical; and Robert Laughlin, Nobel Laureate and professor of physics at Stanford University and Evelyn Fox Keller at MIT, for reading portions of the manuscript. Far from least, I want to thank my dear friend Gerow Reece, as well as Jennifer Hager and Diana Somerfield, for making excellent suggestions and attempting to keep my endlessly embedded clauses within the confines of the *Chicago Manual of Style*. I also owe an enormous debt to the UCLA Psychology Department for their generous provision of a visiting scholar position with all its attendant privileges. For help along the way, I want to thank Pat Greenfield, Robert E. Shaw, Steve Braddon, Bob Katz, and a mentor who is sorely missed, Mike McGuire.

Although they have no idea how helpful they have been through the books they have written that helped lead to this book, I want to acknowledge Benoit Mandelbrot, Brian Goodwin, Peter Stevens, Michael Gazzaniga, Phillip Ball, John Barrow, Marcia Bjonerud, Heinz von Foerster, Edward Lorenz, Stuart Kauffman (the biologist), John Briggs and David Peat, Harold Morowitz, Nassim Taleb, John Gribbin, Ilya Prigogine, Henri Poincaré, Konrad Lorenz, Irenaüs Eibl-Eibesfeldt, Michael Pollan, Paul Ekman, Robert E. Shaw, John Bransford, Frantz Fanon, Steven Strogatz, James Austen, Ernst Cassirer, D'Arcy Thompson, John Archibald Wheeler, Elinor Ostrom, Christopher Alexander, Thomas McMahon and John Tyler Bonner, Edward O. Wilson, Karl Von Frisch, Charles Wohlforth, François Jullien, David Bohm, Michael Polyani, Nikolaas Tinbergen, Richard E. Nisbett, Alfred North Whitehead, Maurice Merleau-Ponty, David Meyers, Thomas Kuhn, Marjorie Grene, Agnes Arber, Andy Goldsworthy, Janine Benyus, Per Bak, Susan Oyama, Graham Collier, evolutionary biologist Sean B. Carroll, Wendell Berry, J. E. Gordon, Eric Beinhocker, Tristan Gooley, Barry C. Lynn, Jeremy Rifkin, James Gleick, J. A. Scott Kelso, John Lanchester, Maya Lin, Tony Judt, the scholars at the Santa Fe Institute, and all the others I forgot. I owe special thanks to James Gibson and Gunnar Johansson, whose work opened my eyes.

Introduction

> *To represent something symbolically, as we do when we speak or write, is somehow to capture it, thus making it our own. But with this approximation comes the realization that we have denied the immediacy of reality and that in creating a substitute we have spun another thread in the web of our illusions.*
>
> —HEINZ PAGELS

DESPITE A DECADE of superb books devoted to exposing Wall Street malfeasance, escalating temperatures, alarming increases in inequality, and the insidious privatization of the commons, all these problems have increased to epidemic proportions. These books were carefully researched, have been read by many thoughtful people, and have generated considerable discussion. Yet their words have produced little measureable change. Ironically, the lexicon we use to write and talk about such problems and the theories we construct from our words are not equipped to tell the whole story. Words categorize and minimize. Theories often add to the confusion by reframing reality to reflect our interpretations and biases. Neither can encompass the complexity of reality because they prune what is happening on the ground into parts to make it mentally manageable, not better understood. But the Earth is not composed of separate parts, nor is anything on it. Instead, our world is filled with multicomponent, complex systems, from cells to cities, that do not take well to being partitioned (nor do they reveal themselves in our symbol systems). Yet, we live our lives supported by these systems—the ecologies and economies in which we are embedded, the neural networks, and the vascular organizations and skeletal and muscular arrangements that make us who we are. And when we function well, it is not because of our verbal descriptions or mental theories of such systems, it is because we evolved to directly perceive a somewhat overlooked form of information: *the structural organization that brings each system into existence, makes it what it is, determines its functions, and reveals its properties.*

This book argues that the information that reveals these systems is structural rather than symbolic and comes packaged in dynamic spatial configurations that echo each system's organization. Thus, we can parse both natural and human-made systems as disparate as economies, neural networks, river deltas, and communities by perceiving their *branching layout*—the geometry that promotes their function as distribution systems. In like fashion, tornadoes, whirlpools, and hurricanes are perceived as their *spiraling configuration* harnesses the makings of turbulence, and the cells of our immune system communicate with one another and lay down memories using their own unique *geometric signals*. In short, *form not only follows function, it doubles as accurate and comprehensive structural information.*

But let me be clear: Structural information is not our creation. It reflects universal forms that emerge far from the confines of our minds, as the laws of gravity and electromagnetism, in league with evolutionary processes and least-energy-use, parcel out the structural organizations that support real-world operations. This same basic structuring process works with all creatures and all senses. For example, vibrations become auditory patterns that echo their source. Odors produce geometrically deployed volatiles that rise into the air and allow us to judge the bouquet of wines, while creatures such as ants and termites use chemical signals called pheromones to communicate with one another.

We can watch as individual ants coalesce to make cooperative decisions using the informative geometry of their volatile pheromone messages. They self-organize into a multicomponent complex system and, without a prior plan or a construction boss directing their enterprise, they act in tandem to build their residential hills. Each ant simply relies on structured chemical signals to sense and imitate the actions of its close-by cohorts. The ants' interactions are local, but their results are global. Their collective behavior produces an intricately tunneled and seamless hill that houses the entire colony. In a similar way, one of your mother's fertilized eggs replicated into many cells. Those cells interacted and self-organized into your interdependent yet differentiated organs, nerves, bones, and vascular systems, and they extended this process until a larger complex system called "you" emerged and became recognizable from your whole structure rather than a catalogue of your separate features.

If, however, one of your components, even a single cell, mutates and turns rogue as in cancer, or is infiltrated by a virus, your entire system can be at risk. This shows that systems and their components have a reciprocal relationship that cannot be breached without courting harm to both. In complex systems, parts and wholes are two sides of the same coin, and if we break that symmetry, we can compromise or destroy this inherent partnership (as has happened in systems such as the U.S. economy and our global climate).

The question is can we know the world directly, or are we predisposed to creating theories in order to make sense of things? Because their theories have stood the test of time, the best people to ask would have been Darwin and Galileo, who proposed the theories of evolution and the movement of the Earth around the sun, which many consider to have reached the status of fact. The interesting thing about Darwin and Galileo's theories is that they are both based on repeated observations or perceptions of the real world—Darwin of the different beaks of finches, Galileo of the moons of Jupiter. So, which came first, the observation or the theory? Clearly with Darwin and Galileo, it was their observations. For Galileo it was what he saw through his telescope that confirmed Copernicus's theory and contradicted what was written in Scripture—an unsubstantiated theory of geocentricity whose origins came from authority, not from observations, and which has been proven wrong. I do not know whether we have a predilection to create theories. Theories are typically about the world, which is itself a far more reliable source of information. It would seem that if we do have that predilection, it does not support either acquiring knowledge or survival and instead must be in the service of something else. I do suspect that if we have a need to make sense of the world and do not do so by observing it, we can easily default to making up theories. In chapter 7, I describe how research into our embrace of theories points not to our need to make sense of the world, but to our need to be right, because by using theories to prove we are right we can influence others, whether we are actually right or wrong. Unfortunately, this strategy leaves the world, and what is actually happening on the ground, out of the equation.

When we ignore the complex systems we perceive, however, and instead rely on words to label and mentally separate things that cannot be separated in the world and still retain their purpose, we obscure the way complex systems function. If we add theories to the mix, we can easily retreat further from reality and into a parallel world of our own inferences and assumptions. Consider what happened to a riverside ecosystem in Yellowstone National Park when, on the basis of an unsubstantiated theory, the rangers removed one of its linchpin components. Goaded by local ranchers, whose theory was that "eliminating the wolf from Yellowstone would ensure the safety of their cattle," the government removed this one species from the park. With their main predator gone, the elk population burgeoned and stripped the leaves off most of the trees along the riverbanks. Without their leaves the trees died. Because the living trees necessary for their dams were gone, the beaver population disappeared. Without the beaver dams and the riverside tree roots to retain the riverbanks, they eroded, floods followed, and new trees could not grow in the floodplains. Without trees there were no leaves and the elk population died of starvation. Before this debacle, the wolves had killed very few domestic animals. Why would they? They were part of an ecosystem that included elk. By removing one of the riverside's critical components, an entire ecosystem was destroyed.[1] However, "it is often much easier to conserve states than to restore them. . . . failing to maintain intact food webs can lead to degraded, alternative states that are not restored quickly, simply, and easily."[2,3]

Despite such successes, we often override our direct perceptions with our theoretical conceptions, and when we fail to check back with the world and instead, believe our own inventions, we ensnare ourselves in unworkable webs of self-deception. To wit: Wall Street's theory that "markets regulate themselves," which invited fraud and melted the global economy; Army engineers' "no-outlet levees," which first undermined the Mississippi Delta ecosystem and then triggered the levee's collapse, submerging New Orleans; nutritionists' well-meaning theory that "eating fat will make you fat," which increased sugar consumption exponentially and helped inflict obesity and type II diabetes on eight-year-olds; or perhaps the most insidious theory of all, the misrepresentation by some business interests that "global warming does not exist," while in the real world, temperatures rise, glaciers melt, and deserts encroach.

A dangerous theory hatched in someone's mind can escape and, like an alien virus, lay siege to other minds and ultimately to the physical, economic, and ecological systems of our world. Many scientific theories have served us well, but very few people would dispute the fact that other theories that once guided our behavior have been bereft of worthy intelligence. Few past supporters of such theories still believe, for instance, that the world is flat or that stress causes ulcers (since the discovery that *Helicobacter pylori* is the culprit). Not many today would buy into the theory that "Iraq had weapons of mass destruction" or that banks are "too big to fail" (they failed *because* they were too big). Hindsight, however, is rarely theoretical. It comes from finally seeing the pertinent evidence that was always there.

Since information specifying the world originates in the world and not in our minds, consider why we fail to look before we leap into acting on untenable theories. One reason is that our perceptions typically occur below the level of our conscious awareness and unless we trust our "intuitions" (which are simply our perceptions of structural information), we can easily default to acting on a theory. A second reason is that we cling to the notion that we are rational creatures despite our bouts of "irrational exuberance" and as a result, we give our "higher mental processes" and the theories they produce undue credit. In doing so, *we overlook the fact that our "rational" processes are locked into windowless skulls with no direct access to the world except through our senses.* At the same time, the collective "we" assumes that our senses and the information they access tend to be unreliable. If that assumption were true, it would be a miracle that we know anything at all. But it is understandable considering that we perceive such information subliminally. A third reason is that we confuse our conceptual interpretations of the world with the world itself without realizing that our bent to categorize and label has more to do with our reliance on language and our need to have simple ways of communicating, than on what it is we actually know.

There are, however, very good reasons why we evolved to act on subliminal perceptions. To focus on one reason: In emergencies that require rapid responses to ensure survival, it takes too long for what we see to be sent off for the mental processing required for conscious awareness. The information we perceive must go directly from our eyes to our motor centers if we are to respond in time to avoid disaster. In such situations, our conscious awareness is irrelevant because it occurs after the fact and takes too much time. As neuroscientist Michael Gazzaniga points out, if you touch your nose with your finger, you are conscious of a single event in that you experience your finger touching your nose and your nose being touched simultaneously. But the neural connection between your nose and the area of your brain that processes that information is three inches long, while the neural connection from your finger to that area is three-and-a-half feet long, and the impulses from your finger take longer to get there. Your conscious experience of simultaneity is actually a memory that is assembled in your brain after all the pertinent information is in and has been sorted and constructed into a credible mental representation of the situation. If you had touched a hot stove instead, you would have pulled your hand away before you were conscious of feeling the heat because your subliminal perception–action response system acts before you are aware of what you are doing.[4]

This is where a new view of information, perception, and knowledge acquisition enters the picture. Consider again that our senses provide our sole contact with the world. Then consider that because we coevolved with and adapted to a world of complex systems in which we participate, our senses evolved to parse the structural information that specifies the properties of those systems. Given, however, that we are not as rational as we would like to think, and that we tend to reframe and often distort such information when we make decisions, an important question remains: How is it that our species came to know the world with enough precision to avoid extinction while being able to achieve such extraordinary feats as landing on the moon and sequencing our genome—both of which required us to look carefully at what we were doing? In other words, there is another, less familiar side to our information-gathering skills.

This book tells the untold backstory of how the world's structural information, its "language of phenomena," underlies our ability to comprehend the complexities of the universe and thus accomplish such amazing feats as unpacking the genome and walking on the moon. Even more important, I suggest that if we attend to the world and the structural information it displays, that instruction can help point the way out of the global and local holes that we and our propensity to act on unsubstantiated theories have dug ourselves into. As a cognitive psychologist alarmed about the future of our planet's fragile systems and vulnerable populations, I feel compelled to tell that backstory.

This tale is atypical because, unlike most books about cognition and perception that focus primarily on us—what we think and how our brains work—*this book takes its lead from the world itself*, a state of affairs aptly described by Francis Bacon:

> The contemplation of things as they are…without substitution or imposture, is in itself a nobler thing than a whole harvest of invention.[5]

To add to its contrarian nature, I will not contrast and compare the various ideas that have led up to my conclusions because *this book is not about us and our ideas; it is about the world and the structural information its complex systems display, which stand alone without human interpretation or analysis*—a subject that seems to have fallen through the cracks of our tendency to cut the world into parts to further our own agendas. A wise Zen master, Dainin Katagiri Roshi, made this very clear when he asked his student whether she wanted to be an "artist," or whether she wanted to drop herself and devote her life to creating art.[6] *This book asks if you want to continue to approach the world solely through the interpretations and theories that the professions, alliances, or belief systems you have adopted offer, or if you also want to know the world itself, the place upon which the survival of all of us depends.*

That world keeps turning on its axis and displaying information that emerges from its many interdependent, multicomponent, complex systems. Because we coevolved with, adapted to, and participate as components of those systems, it seems reasonable to consider that we are reciprocally structured to resonate to and understand the structural information that reveals their ways. Consider the following example of how one of those systems—our bodies—provides us with that information.

I first discovered structural information when I was a student at the University of California, Los Angeles and saw an astonishing film on biological motion that completely changed my understanding of the type of information we use to know the world around us.[7] To get a feeling for what I saw, picture a screen, totally black except for sets of tiny lights that resemble stationary fireflies. As the film progressed, the lights began to move and, as if by magic, coalesced into the twinkling perimeters of continually transforming geometric configurations. The film offered no clues to the source of these seemingly abstract, content-free configurations, yet as soon as they started to move across the screen, a wave of gasps rippled through the audience. Viewers knew immediately and without any doubt that what they were seeing was not abstract at all; it was concrete adult men and women who were walking, dancing with one another, and then dropping to the floor and doing push-ups. Given that there was nothing on the screen except moving configurations outlined by tiny lights, the effect was stunning. But even more amazing, if the viewers already knew the people who were performing these activities, they recognized who they were!

The secret behind such unexpected revelations is refreshingly simple. The lights were reflective bicycle tape that was affixed to the six major joints of each of the film's performers. As these actors cycled through various activities, the reflective tape on their joints outlined the movements that emerged from their underlying muscular-skeletal structure. Because each actor's structure was unique, the configurations his or her movements produced reflected those differences. As a result, each seemingly abstract configuration revealed the identity of that actor as well as his actions. One might ask how it was possible to acquire this knowledge when each actor was continually moving and continually changing his or her configurations? The answer is that each actor's unique structure was composed of invariant proportions, and those proportions remained constant across his or her movements and lifespan even as other bodily characteristics changed. Although we are conscious of seeing people move, we are not typically aware of the informative configurations their movements produce. In this film, however, the reflected lights acted as signposts that directed information that we typically would detect subliminally into our conscious awareness. In contrast to the verbal descriptions, theories, or pictorial images that provide the content of the information that our minds rely upon, it was structural information that organized that content and made it what it was.

As another example, take the information we require to recognize other people. If someone asks us to describe a particular person, we typically offer a list of that person's features—hair, eye and skin color, and the shape of their nose. But that is not how we actually recognize others. We recognize people from their facial structure.[8] A person's features are the content of their face just like words are the contents of a poem. But it is the structure of their face that makes it a face, just like the structure we call *poem* makes it a poem.

Because we see the world through our mind's eye as made of separate, nameable parts, we have developed methods of assembling those parts into mental representations. But in the real world, things are not assembled from parts. They self-organize into complex systems, and the information that specifies those systems is produced by the interactions of all the components that make up that system, not by a subset that we arbitrarily choose. Representations lack the structure that actually specifies a system, and we are left with mental forms that at best contain a fraction of the actual content of that particular system. Throughout this book, I will compare the real-world outcomes—from financial meltdowns to escalating obesity—of using mentally abstracted and reassembled content information (e.g., theories about the world) to the outcomes of using directly perceived structural information that specifies a complex system in the world.

Several recent books have catalogued many more of our cognitive and perceptual shortfalls—our irrational decisions, our inability to grasp probability, and even our failure to see men in gorilla suits wander onto basketball courts when we are otherwise occupied.[9,10] While all these unwanted outcomes occur, they do not reflect the larger problem discussed here—that there are widely accepted, if misguided theories about how our minds work that distract us from seeing the world as it is. I recently read a book that asserts such theories. It claims, and I quote, "all our perceptions must be considered illusions. That's because we perceive the world only indirectly, by processing and interpreting the raw data of our senses. That's what our unconscious processing does for us—it creates a model of the world."[11] The author reports that he came to these conclusions based on considerable research into cognitive science (a field that investigates how our perceptual and mental processes work), plus a hair-raising experience he had in Israel's Golan Heights. While hiking just after the Yom Kippur war, this gentleman saw an interesting bird in a fenced field that warranted a closer look. The fence was posted with a sign in Hebrew that he had trouble reading but that nevertheless made him feel uneasy and, in his own words, made him think that he "should stay out."[12] Although he was not consciously sure what the sign said, he had some familiarity with Hebrew and inferred that "the usual message would have been 'No Trespassing.'" On that basis, his "conscious deliberative mind, said, *Go ahead. Just be quick.* And so I climbed the fence."[13] But as he walked into the field, a man on a tractor started gesticulating wildly and yelling at him in Hebrew. Despite the hiker's limited Hebrew, he "realized that I did recognize those Hebrew words. The sign said, "Danger, Minefield!' "[14]

But why did it take a while for him to become aware of this critical information? The answer is that the seeming time lag applied only to his conscious awareness. He actually knew what the sign said immediately, or he would not have felt uneasy. However, this warning bypassed his conscious awareness and was probably relayed straight from his eyes to his danger-sniffing emotional center; it did not stop off for contemplation because the situation was dangerous enough to require a rapid response.[15] Informed by the structural information that he had perceived, his emotional center—policed by two almond-shaped structures, one on each side of his brain, called the amygdalae—triggered his feeling of uneasiness and thus warned him to be careful. Because dangerous situations up the ante on our reliance on structural information, our interdependent perceptual and body-information signaling systems often "know" a great deal more than our rational minds. This may explain why these systems typically bypass our theory-driven conscious processes that, given their willingness to rationalize taking lethal chances such as walking into minefields, are not always reliable guides.

That leaves us with the question of how this gentleman deciphered the sign with his limited Hebrew. Because all languages are organized by syntax—the structural property that determines the way letters, words, and sentences fit together—as long as we have some familiarity with a given language, we can make very educated guesses of the meaning of particular words from their own structure as well as how they fit into the structure of a sentence. This is how I manage to finish the *New York Times* crossword puzzle even when it contains words that I've never heard of, and this is probably how the hiker deciphered the sign: by using structural information about Hebrew. Even though we do not keep the rules of syntax in our conscious awareness, they are not unconsciously manufactured models. Although not everyone agrees with his analysis, MIT emeritus professor and

Nobel Prize–winning linguist Noam Chomsky holds that the rudiments of syntax are hardwired into our brain.[16]

Current theories of brain organization suggest that we are hardwired to respond to the structural information that specifies many worldly phenomena, especially those that are critical to our survival. For example, the fusiform gyrus area of our brain is specialized for recognizing faces.[17] Harvard University researchers Alphonso Caramazzo and Jennifer Shelton "claim that animate and inanimate conceptual categories represent evolutionary adapted domain specific knowledge systems that are subserved by distinct neural mechanisms."[18] Neuroscientist Michael Gazzaniga at the University of California, Santa Barbara puts our brain's innate abilities in perspective—"domain-specific knowledge systems aren't actually the knowledge itself, but systems that make you pay attention to particular aspects of situations, and by doing so, increase your survival chances." Gazzaniga suggests that we may be hardwired to pay attention to certain aspects of biological motion that trigger a fear of predators, such as the slithering of snakes.[19] Gazzaniga's proposal is backed by research into domain specificity—the idea that the real estate of the brain is divided into separate areas for different competencies.[20] From face recognition to motion perception, we seem to be innately structured to detect the dynamic configurations of structural information that provide the basis of our knowledge of the world.

The hiker's story illustrates this book's primary yet rarely considered points: *We evolved to perceive and comprehend the structural information that specifies worldly phenomena and is critical to our survival. Yet despite its availability, our conscious minds often ignore the information we perceive and default to theories we have conceived, which lead us astray.* If the man on the tractor had not been there to bring the hiker back to reality, he could have died from following the dictates of his conscious mind, which would have led to an exploding landmine. We all tend to use this default option to overlook many real-world situations, such as global warming if we want to continue to drive gas-guzzling combines or SUVs, or our empty bank accounts if we want a collateral-free loan that we cannot repay to buy a house that we cannot afford. This is why the alternative of relying on structural information is so critical.

Still, naysayers who believe that we cannot know the world without mental mediation point out that our perceptions cannot be counted on because we are susceptible to illusions. Yet such illusions exist mostly in books and make minimal appearances or have any effect on our daily lives.[21] Instances when our perceptions do seem to fail, such as when we see a straight stick as bent when it is partly underwater, are easily checked, in this case by moving the stick or ourselves to see it from another viewpoint. Some theorists also question our perceptual acumen by conflating the software of our decision processes with the hardware of our visual system. They cite factors such as the blind spots in our eyes where the optic nerve is attached, or the fact that our retinal images are often blurry. But structural information is not affected by such technical glitches. For example, we recognize the letter A (and the rest of the letters in the alphabet) from its basic structure, regardless of the font, lighting, or context in which we see it, because an *A* retains the structural properties that make it an **A** across all these different conditions. An ⟨A⟩ does not become incomprehensible until is it so degraded that it is unreadable, and that occurs because of the state of the ⟨A⟩ itself, not because of the state of our retinal images.[22]

The Source of Common Sense: Our Senses

> *Everyday reality is a collective organizational phenomenon.... The most important effect of...organization is that it causes objects to exist.*
>
> —ROBERT LAUGHLIN

The Anglo-American tradition that is alive and well in traditional perceptual theories harbors a belief that reason should rule and our senses are unreliable. But no one seems to ask *where the supposedly reliable information comes from that we are reasoning about.* After all, our senses are our only direct connection to the world and our sole conduit for worldly information. Blaming our "out of control" emotions for the purported errors of our senses begs further questions. Our emotions are part of the early warning system that evolution devised to help us notice danger, when an attractive mate is present, or when we have gone off course. If someone has a strong emotional reaction to a benign situation for which such a response is unwarranted, it could be because that information has a similar structure to that of a dangerous situation, such as when grass moves in the wind as if a snake were weaving through it. Or, more probably, the person's mistake results from a wrong interpretation, such as misjudging that someone looks angry when they have a stomachache. Despite the prevailing theory that our senses and the information they access are unreliable, the claim I make in this book is that we can both see and understand structural information without mental augmentation, and that theories claiming otherwise suffer from at least five misconceptions.

The first misconception is that our senses cannot be trusted because they are subjective. If our senses were subjective, we would all see, hear, and smell a different world. Clearly this is not the case. Even as newborns, without any prior experience, we are all equipped with the same ability to perceive structural information. If an adult sticks their tongue out at a two-hour-old newborn with no prior experience, the baby, with as far as we know virtually no rational processes, is likely to imitate what she sees and stick her tongue out at the adult. We may make perceptual errors such as confusing one identical twin for another, but in our daily lives, most of us manage to navigate the physical world without falling into manholes or retrieving the wrong children from preschool despite the fact they are all dressed alike. Our eyes are not subjective, if for no other reason than they lack the capacity to have opinions.

While most people seem to believe that everyone sees a different world, this is not actually the case. This notion confuses seeing with selecting. If two friends go shopping together one day and one is hungry, she will be aware of restaurants while her friend, whose shoe is damaged, will be more aware of shoe repair shops. If their needs are reversed the next day, so will what they report perceiving. Different people have different motives and needs, and they attend to the things that meet those needs—and this holds true for the same person at different times. We perceive the array of sensory information in front of our noses, but we discard what fails to interest us before it makes it into our conscious awareness. Later, we claim those things weren't there at all, and are amazed when they resurface in our consciousness years later when a similar situation triggers their retrieval.

A second misconception is that the world is too complex for our senses to comprehend. Creatures ranging from bacteria to ants operate well enough to find each other, form quorums, make group decisions, locate food, and live in complicated communities that act in unison to build complex structures using their chemical senses. Why, then, would primates like us, with far more numerous and sophisticated sensory receptors for gathering information, be less capable of dealing with the world's complexities? It may be that our mental habit of partitioning the world into an infinite number of sections leads us wrongly to conclude that it is impossible for us to keep track of so many things. But because the structural information we perceive is so efficient that it simultaneously specifies whole systems and their components in a single configuration, we can easily avoid the perceptual overload that endless numbers of separate parts would generate.

A third misconception about our senses is based on the belief that because brain lesions can impair comprehension, comprehension takes place in our brains. Since patients with cerebral lesions can often no longer identify what they see, and the lesion that causes this condition is in the brain, it is easy to conclude that our perceptions are controlled by the area of the brain where the lesion is located. But a great deal of sensory processing operates on autopilot, and patients who claim they do not see something are often able to pick that item up when asked to do so.[23] Brain lesions can certainly interrupt our conscious awareness of something, but not necessarily our sensory intake or our under-the-radar comprehension.

A fourth misconception about our senses is rooted in a belief that since neurons in different sections of our brains all fire when we see a particular item, we must use mental processes to connect those separate firings into a mental representation in order to know what we have seen. Ask yourself how it is possible to reconstruct a mental representation of something in your head from widely deployed, single neuron firings if you do not already know what that something is. If you already know what it is, you must have had prior access to information that specifies that whole item rather than a set of separate neural bursts. The notion that separate neuron firings require top-down central management to organize themselves (rather than being self-organizing) can also be traced to our atomistic worldview. Even though our brain operates as a complex system, many of us still falsely believe that since neurons are separate items, they need an outside orchestrator to get them to respond in unison. Recent findings in evolutionary biology on self-organization would dispute that view because neural networks tend to fire in unison.[24,25]

A fifth misconception can be traced back to the declaration of the Greek philosopher Democritus that our world is made of atoms. We have generalized his atomistic assertion to everything in our terrestrial world and concluded that they, too, are made of separable parts that our cognitive processes assemble into comprehensible phenomena. This did not work for Humpty Dumpty and it will not work for us, because such a faculty would have to know the basis upon which to assemble a bunch of parts into a functioning whole. This job is done by bottom-up, self-organizing systems that manage to accomplish this task without calling in outside help.

Compelling evidence for our perception of structural information is that our visual and auditory experiences of the same event may seem different on a conscious level, yet the structural information we use to comprehend both sensory experiences is the same. For example, if you were to draw the branching configuration of a lightning strike and compare it to the auditory pattern of sound vibrations of the thunder that follows, you would find that the spatial configuration of both the visual and the auditory versions of that event's physical specifications, as well as its mathematical equations, are identical.[26] Recent research on language acquisition in infants has shown that when babies begin to babble, they do not listen to the talkers as much as they watch their lips and imitate the configurations the talker's lips form when uttering particular words.[27] We also recognize others by detecting their patterns of movement, configurations such as the figure eight that emerges from their yoked skeletal and muscular structures and that oscillates around their belly button as they walk toward us.[28] Our perceptual skills for gathering accurate and comprehensive information go far beyond our daily lives. Pathologists diagnose rare cancers by observing the aberrant structure of particular cells. Inupiaq whalers have shown research scientists how to track global warming by observing the changes occurring in the structure of sea ice.[29] On a more amusing level, Supreme Court Justice Potter Stewart in *Jacobellis v. Ohio* concluded that although he could not define pornography in words, "I know it when I see it."[30]

In sum, the phenomena of the world do not reveal themselves using the words, pictures, and theories that we use to communicate with one another, to create mental images, and to think about things that are no longer in evidence. Instead, each phenomenon displays the emergent structural information that reveals its own inner workings. That information is what our perceptions parse to know the world. Everything else is hearsay.

The following chapters are filled with compelling, research-backed true stories that serve as universal joints to turn our attention 180 degrees from the reality-distorting content that our minds produce to our direct perceptions of the world that instead reveal reality. In this way, the text gets down on the ground, takes the overlooked structural information on which our survival depends out of the closet, unmasks our own and others' hostile mental takeovers, and brings us back to our senses.

To recap: This book interweaves three major themes. The first is that the Earth functions as a set of multicomponent, self-organizing, self-sustaining, yet interdependent complex systems (e.g., cells, brains, people, economies, trees, ecologies, climate, and cities) that cannot be partitioned and continue to operate successfully. Each system's organization brings it into existence, determines its function, and produces the emergent structural information that specifies its identity and properties. Thus a phenomenon's form not only follows its function, it creates it, and then doubles as its specifying information. We evolved to directly perceive, comprehend, and act on such information (often with scant awareness), which is why we avoid walking into walls, recognize our friends, and ultimately are able to function and evade extinction. The challenge we face is to use perceptual learning to bring this subliminally accessed instruction into our conscious awareness, increase the accuracy and comprehensiveness of our knowledge of the world, and make more informed decisions.

The second theme concerns the loss of information and the addition of interpretations that we incur when our minds translate the structural information we perceive into a mentally manageable form that converts easily into our symbol systems. Our conceptual/theorizing processes typically partition such information into mentally abstracted parts and then, often infiltrated by our existing preconceptions and beliefs, they assemble those parts into simple representations, theories, and ideologies. By ignoring the information we perceive and acting largely on the information we conceive, we take our representations for reality and become pawns of the flawed theories that have guided us into the global and local catastrophes we now face.

The third theme concerns the acumen of our perceptual systems. As we coevolved with the Earth, these systems were reciprocally structured to recognize the various forms of organization that bring Earth's phenomena into existence and that produce the informative configurations that make those phenomena knowable. Yet a problem remains. Because we buy into the belief that our direct perceptions and the structural information they access are unreliable, we too often consider the world to be ambiguous, a mystery to be theorized about and solved. This is certainly the case some of the time. But the world is typically an open book, written in the language of phenomena that we neglect to read. Instead, we act on unsubstantiated theories that lead us astray. As Proust wrote, "The real voyage of discovery . . . consists, not in seeking new landscapes, but in having new eyes."[31]

PART ONE

On the Nature of Information

I

The Structure of Reality

Only when the human organism fails to achieve an
adequate response to its situation is there material
for the processing of thought.

—L. L. WHYTE

Theory Promotes Disaster

At 9:54 a.m. on July 3, 1988, the U.S. Navy cruiser *Vincennes* mistakenly shot down Iran Air's Flight 655, killing all 290 people on board.[1] It was the ninth worst incident in aeronautical history and to make it even worse, the decision that led to these deaths was based on a theory of the situation rather than on supporting evidence.[2] Here is a very brief recounting of how our mind can reframe reality.

When this incident began, the *Vincennes* was in Iranian territorial waters in violation of international law and had been mixing it up with several Iranian gunboats. At 9:47 a.m., a distant blip—an airplane lifting off from Bandar Abbas airport—was picked up by the *Vincennes'* radar, whose crew responded immediately with a standard Identification Friend or Foe (IFF) query. They received a Mode 3 Commair response, which indentified the plane as a commercial airliner. But during the gunboat fracas circumstances on the *Vincennes* had become chaotic, and in the confusion the crew ended up providing mixed messages—one speculating that the blip could be an enemy F-14 fighter jet and another insisting the blip was a civilian plane.

"In the cramped and ambiguous combat environment of the Persian Gulf...the captain chose to rely on his own judgment."[3] He reportedly ran a *simulation of the situation* in his mind where he tried "to imagine what the pilot was thinking, what the pilot's intent was."[4] His belief—that without direct evidence, we can nonetheless deduce what someone whom we do not know and cannot see is planning to do—could qualify as magic thinking. Yet without checking further, the captain developed the theory that the plane was an F-14 fighter and that it was diving directly at the *Vincennes*.[5]

A simulation is not the situation itself. It is only a theory of the situation. A key point is that no one else actually saw this theorized threat. In fact, a crewmember standing right behind the captain later "testified that he never saw indications that the aircraft was descending."[6] Further, the commander of a nearby frigate, the *USS Sides*, reported that his radar showed an ascending, not a descending plane. That plane was not only much larger than a fighter jet, but it was also flying in Iranian airspace over Iranian territorial waters on its regularly scheduled twice-weekly flight from Tehran, Iran to Dubai, United Arab Emirates via Bandar Abbas, Iran. The radar-tracking systems of the *Sides* and the *Vincennes* both covered that same airspace.[7] When the record of the *Vincennes'* tracking system was later reviewed, the information it showed was found to be identical to the one from the *USS Sides*.[8] How was it that the captains of these two ships reported seeing such different situations?

One clue was that each man approached the situation he was in very differently, which in turn influenced what they saw, or thought they saw. By creating a mental simulation, the captain of the *Vincennes* approached the situation through the filter of a theory he had constructed in his mind, while the commander of the *Sides* responded primarily to the information that he perceived on his radar screen. Of interest as well is that the commander of the *USS Sides* reported that in the week before the incident, "the actions of the *Vincennes*, which was equipped with the sophisticated and costly Aegis air defense system, were 'consistently aggressive.'"[9] In addition, in his *Newsweek* article, "Sea of Lies," John Barry wrote that the *Vincennes* had deliberately instigated the earlier skirmishes with the Iranian gunboats despite the fact that "this was her first time in combat" and she was breaking "international rules of war."[10]

Since the *Vincennes* was acting illegally, it's hard to imagine what her captain was thinking when, without provocation, he chose to confront Iranian gunboats. But, it is even harder to imagine what he was thinking when he mistook a large, Airbus passenger plane that was ascending for a much smaller, sleeker F-14 jet fighter that was diving, and shot it down. However, one thing was clear: What he thought he saw did not come from his direct perception of the situation at hand. It had to have come from the theory he had created in his mind. In this sense, the descending jet was simply part of the captain's theory of the situation, not a component of the situation itself. Since he was instrumental in shooting this purported jet down, it is not difficult to conclude that this theory also implied that the *Vincennes* was about to be attacked by an enemy plane, and that an immediate defensive response was required. Again, there was no evidence to indicate that these imagined circumstances reflected the reality at hand.[11] Yet due to that theory, the passengers on Iran Air Flight 655 never reached their destination or lived out their lives.

The only way for this situation to have been assessed accurately was to carefully observe the radar screen and to track the location and activity of any planes in the area. At the very least, that information would have shown whether a plane was in military airspace and could be a fighter jet, or whether it was in civilian airspace and was likely to be a harmless passenger or cargo plane. The fatal error was the failure to pay sufficient attention to the information the radar revealed, and instead to reframe reality using an unsubstantiated theory of being under attack.

In this book, the term *theory* has broad applications. *It refers to ideas about the world that originate in someone's mind, rather than from observable evidence.* Recall also, that in the Introduction a distinction was made between the *structure* of a phenomenon, which reveals who or what it is and what it is doing, and its *content,* which consists of a narrative description of that phenomenon that we create from a mentally abstracted subset of its parts and assemble into a representation. The perceivable structure of the *Vincennes* incident and the information that specified it was the tracking configuration on the radar screen that showed where and when the blip appeared. But the captain's version of this event was a story in which he switched the components of that configuration to match his misconceived theory that the *Vincennes* was in danger.

University of Michigan psychologist Richard Nisbett testified before Congress that both the *Vincennes'* captain and his crew suffered from "expectancy bias."[12] Expectancy bias occurs when people expecting something to happen allow this to distort their view of what is actually happening to match their expectations. Nisbett proposed that because the *Vincennes'* crew believed the blip was a hostile plane, they failed to see the ascending Airbus. Instead they apparently imagined a descending enemy fighter. But expectations, like simulations, are similar to theories. All three are mental versions of situations as opposed to perceptions that reveal the situations themselves. In other words, by pointing the finger at the people involved and their possible propensities to see what they expected to "see" instead of what was actually there, Nisbett overlooked the more basic role that substituting a cognitive for a perceptual process— a theory for actual evidence—played in promoting this event. We often forget that our cognitive processes lack windows on the world. They receive their information about what goes on outside ourselves from our perceptual systems. They then translate that complex intelligence into simpler symbolic forms that are often influenced by our preconceptions, theories, beliefs, and general worldview. Without such a theory to set the stage, the captain's and the crew's expectancy bias would have no ground upon which to play out.

The Navy compounded the situation by creating false videos to cover up what actually happened.[13] The Iranians were enraged at such a maneuver and accused the United States of a "barbaric massacre" and "vowed to avenge the blood of their martyrs."[14] There have been unconfirmed rumors that to retaliate, the Ayatollah Khomeini retained a hit man who, on December 21, 1988, blew up Pan Am Flight 103 over Lockerbie, Scotland. On November 16, 2003, the International Court of Justice concluded that the actions of the *Vincennes* in the Persian Gulf were unlawful. The most important fact to take away from this dismal tale is that the outcome would have been very different if the captain and crew of the *Vincennes* had simply put their theories aside and paid more attention to the information on the radar screen. That information revealed the true structure of this complex event in which the location of the blip, the commercial airspace on the radar, and the ascending Airbus in the sky were linchpin components.

This situation was particularly tragic, but not that surprising. Because we are easily seduced by words and the simpler narrative explanations, simulations, and theories we create in our minds, they often override and suppress the complex systems we perceive in the world. Our tendency to privilege our mental over our perceptual processes often distracts our attention from our direct experience. This mental bias is aided and abetted by our tendency to create and keep our theories on the ready in our conscious awareness—a state of affairs that can easily lead us to jump to conclusions—while the structural information our perceptions access often remains below our own radar.

It is not that we do not continually perceive and use structural information to guide our behavior, it is that we often remain consciously unaware that such information exists. For example, we can easily recognize a friend who is walking toward us from the configurations produced by their movements, but those configurations rarely surface into our conscious awareness. If we were asked how we knew who that person was, we would likely come up with a list of their separate features—blue eyes, red hair, and freckles—but we would be wrong. As I discussed in the Introduction, even though we are conscious of people's individual features, research shows that recognition is not based on features. It depends on our perception of facial structure.[15]

Ironically, the *feature information we are aware of* and consciously abstract from phenomena is often unreliable, leading us to make uninformed, error-filled decisions, while the *structural information that we are largely unaware of* is far more precise and supports more informed and accurate decisions. Fortunately, this curious situation does not affect most of our behavior, even though 95% of our actions are guided by such information, because they also occur on autopilot; but serious problems can arise when we make conscious decisions based on cognitively distorted information. A true story in chapter 2, for example, shows how using facial features as evidence rather than facial or body structure resulted in a case of mistaken identity that sent an innocent man to prison for life. In such instances, facial features can best be characterized as the misused content of facial structure.

To recap, recognition is a direct perceptual act that relies on structural rather than content information. In contrast, abstracting features from a person's facial structure is a cognitive act because abstraction requires agency (who chooses?) and choice (which features?). While our senses are reciprocally structured to detect the information that is there, they are not equipped (as our cognitive processes are) to add their two cents to the mix. Further cognitive processes such as abstraction and theorizing are easily influenced by our resident biases, which then override our more veridical sensory experience. When we do have such biases, it is difficult for us to give them up. Instead we tend to rationalize and defend the theories and decisions they promote as if they were part of us.[16,17]

In fact, at a project at the U.S. Office of Naval Research that analyzed the *Vincennes* incident for the Navy, the participants produced an elaborate explanation of what happened that in effect rationalized the decision to shoot down the Iranian Airbus. To their credit, however, in a write-up of that project they did note that "many have claimed that there were clear flaws or biases in the decision making of the crew of the *Vincennes*."[18] Post hoc explanations such as the one put forth by the Office of Naval Research can be bent in one direction or another depending on which components of a complex event such as the *Vincennes* incident one includes. But one factor is not at issue: where evidence comes from. It comes from the world, not from mental simulations or theories. In this case, the only evidence that was actually perceived by several different people, including the commander of the *Sides,* was the fact that the plane in question was ascending in commercial airspace.

What is so peculiar about making up our own version of a situation in our minds is that, in most cases, all the information we need to make an accurate decision is visible from the situation at hand, as it was on the *Vincennes'* radar screen. A bit further on in this chapter, I recount a parallel true story with one difference: the radar reader acted on the structural information he saw, not on content information he theorized. As a result, he saved the USS *Missouri* and her entire crew.

The key point to take away from this analysis is that the structural information the world displays and our content-driven representations of that information are considerably different. While our conscious thought processes rely on the content that we abstract from the world and assemble into representations that can be infiltrated by our preconceptions and biases, the real world was created by the syntax of space and time and the grammar of gravity. Because the world and the complex systems that constitute it are under constant transformation, the information it displays does not come packaged as static assemblies of features and parts from which we construct theories. Rather it reveals itself in dynamic configurations that emerge from the self-organized interactions of each system's constituent components. In this way, the pattern of information on a ship's radar screen emerges from the interactions of the planes or missiles flying over the area with the time and location at which they appear on the screen.

The Origins and Nature of Structural Information

> *There is nothing in the world except empty curved space. Matter, charge, electromagnetism, and other fields are only manifestations of the bending of space. Physics is geometry.*
> —JOHN ARCHIBALD WHEELER

In the beginning of our universe, the curving physics of space-time produced a dynamic, generative geometry that constrained the visible structure of all material phenomena within its jurisdiction,

including those on Earth. This overarching geometry was adminis-
tered by a persuasive force field called gravity that attracted cosmic
particles to coalesce into stars and planets and determined how this
cosmic real estate and its various components were structured. By
harnessing the demands of gravity, making allowances for electromagnetism, and adhering to the rule that the least energy possible
be expended, space limited the structure of everything on Earth
(including ourselves) to a set of reusable structural arrangements,
plus their variations, permutations, and combinations. The restrictions imposed by these force fields ensured that worldly things
would function efficiently and not disintegrate, implode, or collapse. Residency permits were restricted to those items that developed according to one of gravity's approved plans. We are conscious
of seeing some of these plans, such as the spiral geometry of galaxies, tornadoes, and fiddlehead ferns, and the branching of trees
and vascular systems, but we typically call them natural patterns.
We seem unaware that such patterns are the most profound and
comprehensive form of information we have, because they reveal
the basic organization of our world's complex systems. Because the
bulk of our behavior operates on autopilot, our lack of awareness
of this structural information may stem from the fact that we typically detect such spatial organization subliminally. Consider the
biological motion experiment described in the Introduction: it
took reflective tape attached to the actors' joints—which made the
configurations produced by their movements super-visible—to
bring this structural information to our conscious attention.

While gravity constrains the structure of Earth's complex systems, it is only one component in the production of structural
information. For living things, regulator genes that sequence each
creature's morphological development are stirred into the mix. The
result is that, within these constraints, each of Earth's complex systems adopts its own variation of one of gravity's functional layouts.
We can see that trees, river deltas, and vascular systems all *branch*,
and each one branches in its own way; whirlpools, chambered nau-
tilus shells, and hurricanes *spiral*; and rivers and even our brain's
gray matter fold into *meanders*.

Thus, gravity's organizing layouts, plus the laws of organization that create complex systems, constitute a building code that sets the structural standards for survival and the perceptual standards for comprehension. Comprehension itself is an interactive process between the structural configurations we see and our responsive neuron networks that mirror these configurations and then reorganize as new information arrives. Although our neural networks are in many ways already organized when we are born, they continually reorganize themselves in response to what we see and do. The more we attend to in the world around us, regardless of whether we can describe our experiences or even be aware of them, the more complex brains we build, the more we know. The world itself is knowable largely because it is organized, and we know the world because our neural networks are organized to resonate to and comprehend the various types of organization that it displays as structural information.

One way to look at why we evolved to perceive structural information is to examine our adaptation to the physics of light. As physicist Gerald Huth suggests in his controversial *Primer on Geometry and Vision,* "the structure of the eye evolved in consonance with the physical principles of the refraction of light."[19] Huth explains that the eye's structure is "pure physics, not biology." He outlines the visual process and makes a case for the geometric or configured nature of the sensory information we detect on the nanometer, femtosecond level. In his paper, "A New Explanation for Light Interaction With the Retina of the Eye and the Vision Process," Huth further asserts that "the retina of the eye should be visualized as a logically spaced array of wave-to-particle transition sites.... moving through a sea of electromagnetic energy and geometrically extracting three specific Wavelengths.... to form what we perceive as the visual image."[20] Instead of the words that we use to name things or the pictorial images we draw to represent things, our planet's lexicon of structural forms reveals, identifies, and explains things, and it does so with extraordinary parsimony. *What is most important to consider is that we cannot think about things without first seeing the information that specifies them.* As creatures that coevolved with our world, we come equipped with senses that are reciprocally structured to be part of our complex perceptual systems, not separate operations that require mental mediation.

A supporting hypothesis on the terrestrial level comes from mathematician and complex-systems analyst Herman Haken, emeritus professor at the University of Stuttgart. Haken proposed that perception "is a self organizing, pattern-formation process, hence the duality between principles of pattern formation and pattern recognition."[21] Scott Kelso, director of the Center for Complex Systems at Florida Atlantic University, adds, "Self-organization is the way components cooperate to form coherent patterns. Self-organization provides a paradigm for behavior and cognition, as well as the function of the nervous system."[22] Again, the self-organizing neural networks that activate when our perceptual systems detect something of interest to us reorganize themselves and incorporate its specifications, thus expanding our knowledge of, and ability to respond to, the world around us.[23] What is difficult for us to understand is that we do this even though we are not necessarily aware that we are doing so. Our lack of awareness comes from the fact that self-organizing systems act on their own without instructions from a central command center.

The USS Missouri: *Saved by Structural Information*

You can observe a lot by looking.

—YOGI BERRA

At 5:01 a.m. on February 24, 1991, while monitoring the airspace off the coast of Kuwait for the allied fleet during the Gulf War, Lt. Commander Michael Riley of the HMS *Gloucester* also saw an ambiguous blip on his ship's radar screen. While the setting and situation was very similar to that of the *Vincennes*, the strategy that Riley used was not. He relied on his eyes, not his mind, to provide the information he needed. As a result, he brought about a very different outcome. Although Riley could not identify the blip and had no conscious knowledge of what the screen revealed, he nonetheless kept his focus on it, later reporting that he from what he saw, he just "knew" that the blip spelled danger.[24]

Riley had less than a minute to decide what to do. On one hand, the blip might be a friendly American A-6 bomber flying back to its aircraft carrier from Kuwait. But on the other hand, the blip could be an enemy Silkworm missile aimed directly at the *USS Missouri*. If it was an A-6, Riley had no way of contacting the crew because their pilots turn off their radar on the return flight to minimize detection by an enemy. But the blip was traveling at Mach 1, and time was running out.

For the next forty seconds, Riley's eyes never left the screen as he attempted to find some small piece of evidence that would help him identify exactly what the blip was. He was never conscious of having seen such evidence. The only thing he had to go on was his pervasive feeling that something was very wrong. On the basis of his "intuition," Riley ordered two Sea Dart surface-to-air missiles released to intercept the source of the blip and shoot it down. As soon as the Sea Darts made contact, the blip disappeared. Whatever it was that the missiles hit fell into the ocean just 700 feet short of the *USS Missouri* and her full complement of crew. If the blip was a missile, then Riley had saved the *Missouri* and her crew. If it was an American plane, he had killed its two pilots.

Over the next four hours, Riley waited in a state of panic while a team went out to investigate the site. The wreckage showed that that Riley's intuition had been right. The blip was an enemy missile. Out of curiosity, the *Gloucester's* captain asked Riley how he was so sure that the blip was not an American plane. Riley again replied that he "just knew." A more formal analysis by the Royal Navy after the war ended found nothing on the *Gloucester's* radar tapes to explain Riley's decision. Since his response to the blip was never explained, some attributed it to a lucky guess, and others attributed it to intuition or to chemical signals from dopamine molecules in his brain that responded to danger.

It is difficult to understand how Lt. Commander Riley's intuition or his dopamine molecules became so well informed on their own. Where did the information that triggered their emotional response come from? This mystery disappears if one credits two critical factors with providing the information he used: the actual situation in the world, and his senses' ability to access that information. From the point of view of this book, his intuition was simply the gut feeling all of us get when we perceive the structural information that specifies and summarizes a complex system or event. As a result of that perception, we "know" exactly what is going on, even though we are not consciously aware of the information that triggers our feeling of knowing. This is simply a case of knowing something without knowing how we know. The mystery is how did Lt. Commander Riley know that the blip was a Iraqi Silkworm missile and not an American A-6 plane?

One answer was put forth in 1993 during a review of this event at a workshop at the Defence Research Agency in the United Kingdom.[25] The participants at the workshop knew that Riley had been looking at the blips that American planes made on his radar screen for months. What no one realized, however, was that because of these repeated perceptions, Riley actually knew where and when those A-6 planes appeared on the screen—just as the hiker in the Golan Heights in the Introduction knew more Hebrew than he thought he did. The critical information was that American A-6s flew at 2,000 to 3,000 feet, while Silkworm missiles flew at 1,000 feet. The plane flying at 3,000 feet could be spotted during the first or second radar sweep, while the missile at 1,000 feet would not appear on the screen until the third radar sweep, because on this particular radar screen, it was obscured for a longer time by the ground. The result was that the A-6 blips would show up on the screen before a missile. In the forty-second-long tape, the missile blip appeared on the third radar sweep—perhaps eight seconds after the American planes always appeared. The explanation of Riley's intuition that came out of the Defence Research Agency's workshop involved a complicated theory in which Riley's feeling that the blip was a missile came from his misperception that the track on the radar screen was accelerating. Since nothing was actually accelerating, but the altitudes of the missile and the plane were different, they deduced that he had confused acceleration and altitude.[26] Regardless of the theory the workshop constructed, the only available evidence was the time and location that the blip appeared on the radar screen. Consequently, a simpler explanation is that Riley already "knew" where and when the planes appeared on the radar, and the missile had appeared at a different time and place. Even though the structure of this event never made it into Riley's conscious mind, his perception of its visible configuration on the screen triggered his conclusion that the blip was a missile. This explanation may not match Riley's memory that he knew the blip was dangerous in the first five seconds of seeing it, but memory, especially of a difference of seconds in stressful situations, may not be completely reliable.

Certainly, Riley was afraid. He was looking at what he knew "in his gut" could, if not deflected, kill the *Missouri's* entire crew. His emotions and their associated dopamine molecules told him he was scared and helped him make his decision, but the structural information he saw told him what he was looking at, why that information scared him, and ultimately what he should do about it. Without that information, neither his molecules nor his cortical decision processes would have had a clue. Simply put, Riley relied on the world as depicted on his radar screen for his information and made an accurate decision, while the captain of the *Vincennes* ignored the evidence the world offered, defaulted to the contents of his mind, and made a disastrous one.

A Contrasting View: Signal Detection Theory

The juxtaposition of established signal detection theory models of perception and the more recent claims about the encoding of uncertainty in perception is a rich source of confusion.

—WEI JI MA

The analyses of the *Vincennes* and the *Gloucester* decisions contrast with a more traditional method—signal detection theory (SDT). This book argues that we evolved to perceive and make decisions based on the largely unambiguous information that the world displays, while SDT assumes that the world is always somewhat ambiguous and thus we typically make our decisions under conditions of uncertainty. SDT divides that uncertainty into two parts. The first is the quality of the available information, its clarity and sensitivity to the situation under scrutiny; and the second is the degree of competence, the level of bias, and the state of the person making the decision at that time.[27] In the *Vincennes* case, the fact that different crewmembers had different interpretations of the situation made it seem as if the information the blip provided was uncertain or at least unclear. But a closer look at the chaotic conditions aboard the *Vincennes* would augur more for the possibility that no one looked carefully at the radar screen. What was pertinent to SDT is that the *Vincennes'* captain's behavior showed a high degree of "response bias," the predilection to respond in a particular way regardless of the evidence available. His confrontational tendency lowered his criterion for responding to what he considered to be threatening situations. This made him more likely to shoot first and ask questions later.

But the fact that biases compromise a decision does not necessarily mean that the situation itself is ambiguous, or that the information available is unclear or uncertain (as signal detection theory assumes). In this instance, that same radar signal was perfectly clear and comprehensible to Captain Carlson on the USS *Sides*, a boat very near the *Vincennes*. Recall that Carlson saw an ascending passenger plane, not a descending fighter jet, on his radar screen, and the same information was later recovered from a radar tape from the *Vincennes*. Even more to the point, using nothing more than the information on his radar screen, Lt. Commander Riley made an accurate decision that saved the *USS Missouri*. Characterizing the cause of Riley's decision as a "feeling" or an "intuition" confuses the issue. His feeling was merely his body's clever device to bring the accurate structural information that he had perceived on a subliminal level to his conscious attention. *Intuition is simply the act of directly detecting structural information on a subliminal level.* If, however, viewers bypass the structural information they see and act instead on what they think they see, they have clearly introduced uncertainty into the equation.

Our Complex Perceptual Systems and Structural Information: J. J. Gibson's View

One sees the environment not just with the eyes, but with the eyes in a head on the shoulders of a body that gets about. Perceptual seeing is an awareness of persisting invariant structure. Knowing is an extension of perceiving.

—J. J. GIBSON

Along with signal detection theory, other traditional theories such as "information processing theory" cannot easily account for Lt. Commander Riley's so-called intuitive rout of the missiles that threatened the USS *Missouri*.[28] This is the case because those theories mandate mental mediation, while Riley based his decision on information that he perceived directly from the world. Traditional theories typically assume that worldly information is merely "raw data," which enters our eyes as sensations and is at best incomplete, and at worst incomprehensible. Most traditional theorists carve our perceptual activity into sensory input and motor output, both of which, they claim, are integrated and made comprehensible by some higher order mental process. They argue that mental mediation is required to "process" these "impoverished" sensations into credible perceptions.[29,30] The flaw in this reasoning is that if we have to rely on our minds to create credible perceptions then we must have pre-existing knowledge of the world in order to know what to do. If the information that the world displays is incomprehensible, then this requirement leaves us with the question of where such pre-existing knowledge might come from. Perceptual psychologist J. J. Gibson points out that "knowledge of the world cannot be explained by supposing that knowledge of the world already exists."[31]

If traditional views of perception are accurate, then we are left with the following problems: First, *on what basis does our mind connect our continually changing sensations into a constant, credible perception?* This is a constancy problem. Second, *how do we decide which of the enormous number of sensations we continually receive are relevant?* This is an assembly problem. In 1785, Scottish philosopher Thomas Reid provided us with a partial answer to the first question. He argued that sensations and perceptions are two different processes that make up our visual experience and that they play different roles: "The external senses have a double province; to make us feel and to make us perceive."[32] Reid's analysis was based on everyday common sense for how things had to be in order for them to function. As a result, he was able to dispense with both the constancy problem of the first question and the assembly problem of the second by proposing that there was no need for our minds to engage in either activity, because our senses were naturally constructed to do double duty—not only to respond to light, but also to provide us with the accurate and comprehensive information we need.[33] Reid's analysis that our native sensory equipment would yield such informative direct experiences, however, had little effect on the more influential theories of his British empiricist colleagues (John Locke, Bishop Berkeley, and David Hume), or on the current perceptual theories that follow in these philosophers' footsteps.[34] Ironically, the empiricists' view, with its insistence on mental mediation, marginalized the importance of the environment, despite the fact that this is where the evidence valued by their enterprise is supposedly located.

A sharp contrast to traditional views of perception can be found in the work of J. J. Gibson and the field he founded, ecological psychology. Gibson expanded Reid's world-bound analysis. He was also influenced by the radical empiricism of William James, which holds that our direct experience is not meaningless but is full of connections, as well as the work of the gestalt psychologists, who argued that we see things as wholes, not as assemblies of separate parts that require mental assembly.[35] Gibson's most original, and as yet largely unacknowledged, contribution is that he analyzed perception not as a separate faculty or mechanistic act, but as a complex system. In bypassing the empiricist view, Gibson reconnects the senses, the body, the mind, and the environment. He shows that such a complex system operates in real time, in the real world, and provides the ground for the direct perception of the structural information that specifies our environment's complex systems.[36] Rather than creating causal theories of how the brain constructs a perception from the linear inflow of sensations, as traditional theories propose, Gibson's view of perception can be seen as a complex system that operates by a circular causality. He proposes that our eye-head-brain-body perceptual system, including the neural networks from the eyes to the brain, resonates to and perceives information that specifies the environment from the *invariants in the structure of ambient light*.[37] The term *invariant* is borrowed from mathematics. It refers to the properties of a phenomenon that remain the same as its other properties change. Proportions or ratios, for example, are invariant properties that stay constant across a person's lifespan. Because a person's proportions are unique, they also preserve identity over time. In contrast, separate features such as noses and hairlines often remodel and change as we grow from children to adults and then again as we age, making them poor choices to explain our ability to recognize a person over time.

But what does Gibson mean when he cites the structure of ambient light? Before we continue, it will helpful to distinguish between three types of light: (1) light as unstructured radiant energy from the sun that lands on and illuminates objects in the world, (2) unstructured light that stimulates vision and produces sensations, and (3) light as a medium that is structured by items in the environment and carries that structured information to our eyes. Light as structural information is an unfamiliar category with an unfamiliar name, but it works as follows. When radiant light lands on and illuminates an object, it takes on that object's invariant properties. It is this structured form of light that is reflected from that object. In sum, structured, reflected light is the ambient medium that carries structural information from the environment to our receptive eyes. Counterintuitive as it might seem, in this view, we do not know what an object or a system is, or how it functions, because we have mentally assembled and interpreted a representation such as a pictorial image. Rather, we know things because we directly perceive their invariant structural configuration, such as the movement patterns discussed in the Introduction, that specify our identity, properties, and actions simultaneously.

Gibson clarified Thomas Reid's analysis by pointing out that "light as energy is necessary if the photo-chemicals in the photo-receptors of the retina are to react, but light as a structured array is necessary if the visual system is to pick up information about the world."[38] To recap, from Gibson's view, the act of perception involves "picking up" information that specifies real-world items directly from the structured light these items reflect. That reflected light is in the world to be seen, not in our minds to be interpreted.

The way all this happens is that, as we move through our environment, we bring different aspects of things into view, and when we turn our heads to examine those aspects more closely, we perceive that certain properties of things remain the same regardless of our viewpoint. In fact, as we see objects from varying views, we perceive that their "underlying invariant structure has emerged from the changing perspective structure....Perceptual seeing is an awareness of persisting invariant structure."[39] For example, faces typically appear quite different from the front view than they do in profile. Yet we continue to recognize people regardless of the aspect from which we view them. This is because the information we use to recognize people is not their features, which do look different from the front and the side. Rather, it is the invariant proportions that constitute their facial structure. Those proportions remain constant over our changing viewpoints. Again, the fact that we see structured reflected light rather than the item that reflects that light is because our eyes are designed to respond to light, not to things. If we see light, not things, then the question becomes how we come to know what those things are. The answer is that the light we see that is reflected from an object has been structured by the invariants that constitute that object, and those invariants constitute the information that specifies that object and thus allows us to know it.

Gibson's work takes perception out of our heads and brings it back into the world. Indeed, he says "we must perceive in order to move and move in order to perceive," and our environment provides the structural information that allows us to do both.[40] Building on both Gibson's research and that of Swedish psychologist Gunnar Johansson, this book adds that we not only perceive the world directly, but we perceive the structure of phenomena, not their content, in order to understand what they are and how they operate. It also adds that we resonate to and incorporate the information that specifies those phenomena directly into the neural networks that our perceptual systems activate. This process changes us. As Gibson noted, we are no longer our old self that has simply added another item to our archive of retrievable information. By incorporating new structural information directly into our appropriate neural network, we become a new, reorganized self that knows better and responds accordingly.[41] This process is called *perceptual learning*. In *The Necessity of Experience*, ecological psychologist Edward Reed, whose work was influenced by Gibson, makes the important point that this type of learning is very different from book learning because the firsthand environmental information that fuels perceptual learning is inexhaustible, while the secondhand information we find in books and other archival sources is necessarily limited.[42,43] Reed makes an excellent case for why we need more opportunities for direct experience, especially in education, in order to gain a better understanding of the complex world we live in.

Although Gibson died just before the field of complex systems was formally established, his work clearly shows that each of us, and our environment, are all functional complex systems, and that these two systems are inextricably interconnected by our interactions into one larger system. Reed compares this view with the traditional view, which holds that

the nervous system is a machine for carrying out instructions…from the environment, or from "the genes," or from some "executive system" in the mind. But the nervous system is nothing of the sort.…From an ecological point of view [it] is not a commander of the body nor a storehouse of ideas; it is

something much more amazing: a system that serves to maintain an animal's functional contact with its surroundings.[44]

Gibson's and Reed's views are supported by Columbia University
neuroscientist Gerald Edelman's assertion that the nervous system is
organized to select, not to be instructed.[45]

Complex Systems and Structural Information

Who has seen the wind? Neither you nor I:
But when the trees bow down their heads
The wind is passing by.
—CHRISTIANA ROSSETTI

The various winds of our world and the patterns they each produce
are examples of emergent complex systems and the information
that specifies them. Like all such systems—from cells to brains to
economies—their simultaneously interacting components self-
organize "into a collective whole that creates patterns, uses information, and in some cases evolves and learns."[46] As maps of our
world's winds show, each type of wind has its own configuration as
well. When, for example, one component of an emergent wind—
the air—is very still, another component—say, a high-pressure
system that builds up over the Great Basin of the Western states—
begins to interact with a third component—a low-pressure system
over the Pacific Ocean. This three-way interaction compresses and
thus heats the air as it flows from higher to lower elevations and
kicks up the hot, dry Santa Ana winds that blow across the desert,
where a fourth component—the topography of the land—funnels
that wind through the canyons of the Southern California coastal
range, and blows hot, smog-laden inland air over the ocean.[47] On
its way out to sea, that wind hits a wall of giant red gum trees, with
their crowns of weeping branches, that line the top of the palisades
above the Pacific Coast Highway. Because the wind is blowing
hot and dry from the inland desert, those variables influence the
way the form of its force bends the gum tree branches toward the
sea and produces the signature configuration of a Santa Ana. In

contrast, a different configuration emerges when a cool, offshore breeze coming off the ocean interacts with and lightly bows the gum trees' branches toward the land.

In stark contrast, hurricane winds produce their own configuration. Their spiral form emerges "as the storm crosses the ocean, water evaporates into it, condensing to produce towering clouds. Condensation releases latent heat, warming the air and making it rise further. Evaporation and condensation supply the energy to drive the storm."[48] Evaporation and condensation, combined with the Coriolis effect (which deflects winds according to the Earth's direction of rotation in that hemisphere), whips the air into turbulence, which produces the spiral configuration that characterizes such storms. Each type of wind has a signature configuration that emerges from its interactions with more stable components in its environment. At the edge of the sea, the gum trees are to the wind as the reflective tape was to the actors' illuminated movement configurations, as described in the Introduction. Both the trees and the tape make configurations that we typically perceive subliminally visible to our conscious awareness.

If we want to truly understand information, it is important to distinguish between the configuration that organizes a particular entity that constitutes information, and the entity that we conceptualize and describe in words, which is a representation. We do not perceive things. We perceive the structural information that reflects an entity's organization and reveals multiple layers of information. This distinction is even more important when there is information that specifies something that we cannot actually see. For example, if you have ever gone fishing on a lake or pond, you might have noticed that every so often ripples appear on the surface of the water. What you probably do not know is that those ripples are the surface configuration caused by a fish that is moving about below the surface. Just as the configurations made by our body movements can reveal our identity, the ripples on the surface of the water can reveal what kind of fish is swimming below the surface, because those ripples are produced by that fish's movements. Different fish make different ripple patterns, and since they also are fond of different types of bait, this information can be valuable to a fisher set on catching dinner.

You can also watch where a fish goes by watching the trail of ripples it leaves in its wake.

Wave watcher Gavin Pretor-Pinney has characterized waves of all sizes, including ripples, not only as moving energy (which they are) but also as information. If he sees ripples when he is fishing, he says, "It's a real giveaway. Watching the surface of the water is just like watching a radar screen."[49] Whether the complex system of interest is a ship-to-air event such as the *Vincennes* incident, or a fishing event involving components such as a fisher, a lake, a bait choice, and various fish species, the information that specifies the fish as a component of that complex system is the configuration that organizes the system, not the specific fish itself. Even if we perceive that fish itself, the information by which we know it is still the configurations it produces as it flips its tail, swirls around, and swims away.

The current focus on complex systems in many disciplines signals a paradigm shift in science. As Stanford University physicist and Nobel laureate Robert Laughlin noted:

> Science has now moved from an Age of Reductionism to an Age of Emergence, a time when the search for the ultimate cause of things shifts from the behavior of parts to the behavior of the collective.... The reason our minds can anticipate and master what the physical world does is not because we are geniuses but because nature facilitates understanding by organizing itself.... In passing into the Age of Emergence we learn to accept common sense, leave behind the practice of trivializing the organizational wonders of nature and accept that organization is important in and of itself—in some cases the *most* important thing. The laws of quantum mechanics, the laws of chemistry, the laws of metabolism, and the laws of bunnies running away from foxes in the courtyards of my university all descend from each other, but the last set are the laws that count, in the end, for the bunny.[50]

Systems are not complex simply because they have a great many components interacting simultaneously, but because their complexity is organized. And its organization is displayed as structural information. But what happens when we ignore the sensory information we perceive and default to the preconceptions in our minds?

Seeing What We Believe: How the Mind Hijacks the Senses

The healthy human brain is not a veridical recorder of events, but rather a meaning machine that fills in gaps, rearranges time and space, delays conscious experience, and generates false explanations via available cultural theories. To confabulate is human.

—THALIA WHEATLEY

In the 1940s, Harvard psychologist Gordon Allport conducted an experiment with his student, Leo Postman, showing how we can unwittingly override what we see with what we believe.[51] He showed people pictures of a white man holding a knife talking to a black man and asked them to relate the scene to someone else who had not seen the pictures. In explaining what they saw, the participants in this study unconsciously switched the knife from the white man's hand to the black man's. Even though those viewers actually saw the knife in the white man's hand, they blocked out this visual information with what turned out to be their belief that black men were naturally violent, and so the black man had to be the culprit. These biased believers used the cognitive process of abstraction to switch two features from the actual event: skin color and a knife. They then assembled those switched features into a representation of the scene that matched their expectations rather than what had actually occurred.

As neuroscientist Michael Gazzaniga points out, "A vast amount of research in cognitive science clearly shows that we are conscious only of the content of our mental life, not what generates that consciousness."[52] The result is that both experts in cognitive science as well as the rest of us *tend to blame our accurate and realistic senses for our mistakes when we actually make those errors with our opinionated, often biased cognitive processes.*

To illustrate this tendency, chapter 2 demonstrates that when we are called to give eyewitness testimony in court, we may believe we are recounting what we consciously saw, but we are actually defaulting to our mental representations of that event. Eyewitnesses are typically unreliable because they rely on content information in the form of separate features that they mentally abstracted from the person they saw at the crime scene, rather than the invariant structural information that preserves a person's identity.

2

Perceiving Structure

Perception is identical to its object.
—ARISTOTLE

ON DECEMBER 15, 1997, the prime-time news in Philadelphia reported that a tiny baby had been killed by a fire as she lay sleeping in her crib.[1] They were misinformed. The real story was far more intriguing and also put a human face on our ability to perceive structural information.

Fast-forward six years to when Luz Cuevas, the baby's mother, went to a birthday party at a friend's house and saw a little girl who stopped her in her tracks. Like Lt. Commander Riley, Luz just "knew" that this six-year-old child was her lost infant daughter, Delimar Vera, who was supposedly consumed in a fire when she was only ten days old. Luz never saw her baby after that night, but since no remains were found, she never believed that her baby was dead. And now, six years later, Luz was positive that this girl was her baby grown into a child. Although Luz was not aware of how she knew this (she attributed it to the child's dimples), her certainty actually came from recognizing the unique structural configuration of Delimar's face. While many facial features change and remodel over time, facial structure has invariant proportions that are conserved over the human lifespan. Those proportions are unique to that person, and thus they preserve their identity and provide the structural information that we rely on to recognize them.

Luz's "vanished" child came to the party with one Carolyn Correa. Correa was a distant cousin of Luz's husband and had visited the Cuevas home the day before the fire. She returned the following night ostensibly to retrieve her purse from an upstairs bedroom. Right after Correa left the house that night, the baby's room erupted into flames. Because the firemen found no remains, they concluded that the tiny baby burned up in the fire. Officials attributed the blaze to an extension cord that overheated while connected to a space heater. The firefighters never considered arson.

When Luz saw the little girl at the party, she was beside herself. She was sure that Correa had stolen her baby and set the fire to cover her tracks. To prove this, Luz approached the child and on the pretense of removing some bubblegum from her hair, took several strands. Luz then went through a tortuous process of attempting to get a DNA test of the child's hair. She barely spoke English, and had no connections in the institutional world where DNA tests are done. The police turned her away, telling her that they did not do such tests at that station. Finally Luz contacted Angel Cruz, a Pennsylvania state representative who agreed to help. Cruz obtained hair samples from both Luz and the child and took them to the police for DNA analysis, along with Luz's accusation that Carolyn Correa had stolen her baby and set her house on fire to cover the kidnapping. The DNA results proved that Delimar was indeed Luz's daughter. Correa was arrested. On September 25, 2005, Correa received a nine-to-thirty-year sentence for kidnapping. Delimar Vera was returned to her family and is now at home with her mother.

The intriguing question is, what type of information gave Luz the certainty that a six-year-old she had not seen since infancy was her missing daughter? When Luz first recognized Delimar, no DNA tests had been done. The only evidence she had was the child herself. But many children look like other children. They often have very similar facial features, the same height and general form. How did Luz know that this child was her daughter and not another youngster who bore a family resemblance? The information Luz needed had to be specific to Delimar and to her alone. It could not be her features, because they had changed in size and shape during the intervening years. The information Luz used to recognize Delimar also had to remain constant over those six years—and it did. It was Delimar's unique facial proportions, such as the ratio of the space between her eyes to the span between her ears that scaffolded the structural configuration of Delimar's face.[2] From ages one to three, Delimar's structural development, like other toddlers, had been isometric, or roughly proportional for both her body and head. From three to six it became allometric, which means that the size of its parts increased relative to her growth as a whole. Her body grew faster than her head, but it still grew according to the universal laws of growth that preserved her unique structure. In fact, as human beings develop, their body height grows proportionally to the cube of their head size. Although her face had grown larger and transformed over the years, and her features had changed and been remodeled, her cranial/facial structure retained the basic proportional relationships that were in place when she was born; those relationships continued to reveal her unchanging identity. Such spatial relationships (mandated by biomechanical forces that follow physical laws such as gravity), in league with Delimar's regulator genes (which turned the growth trajectory of her skull bones off and on), created the unique facial structure that Luz knew on sight belonged to her long-lost daughter.

Because each person, even an identical twin, develops somewhat differently, the proportions that constitute his or her physical parameters are unique. Something as simple as each twin's different position in the womb and each one's access to nutrients can set them on different developmental paths. In sum, a person's proportions and their resulting overall structure are the products of their self-organizing developmental processes dutifully following the laws of biomechanics.[3] These factors operate within the constraints of the regulator genes that pace their growth and the contexts in which they develop.

Recognition and Structural Information

The more things change the more they stay the same.
—FRENCH MAXIM

Have you ever come across a puzzle where you match the baby and adult photographs of famous people? This may seem like a simple parlor game, but it actually sheds light on how structure, and the information that specifies structure, develops. As you grow from infancy to adulthood your structure transforms. You grow larger, your baby button nose turns into a prominent Roman edifice, your wispy blonde hair becomes chestnut, and your blue eyes turn brown. Yet in spite of these measureable changes, you continue to look like you. For the purposes of recognition, these individual and seemingly defining characteristics can be considered the changeable content (as opposed to the structure) of your face. When you become an adult, friends who never knew you as a child can still pick your baby picture out of a pile of other infant photographs because your facial proportions have remained constant over the years.

Recall that one problem we have in understanding this type of information is that, while we perceive and use it, we often do so on a subliminal level; we are not always aware of doing so because our conscious mind is busy focusing on our facial content and partitioning us into parts. As I discussed in the section on J. J. Gibson in chapter 1, while our individual features change, our proportions remain constant both over time and under changing conditions such as different types of lighting and various viewpoints. Consider again how different your nose looks from the front than from the side. In mathematics, persistent measurements such as proportions are called invariants, which (as mentioned in chapter 1) simply means that they remain constant even as other properties change. To recap, your proportions scaffold your structure, and your structure which comes about through the interactions of all your components gives rise to the structural information that specifies your identity.

Attempts have been made using computer technology to duplicate our ability to recognize faces and we are making some progress. But because our faces are actually multicomponent complex systems that we perceive under different conditions in multiple environments, most computer strategies cannot handle that variability to say nothing of the confusion that is added by different facial expressions, age, or the angle from which a person is seen. These factors make the same person appear different under varying conditions. University of Glasgow psychologists Mike Burton and Rob Jenkins managed to reduce that variability by creating a single image of a well-known person by merging a host of different images that they had stockpiled over time from many sources.[4] In effect they created the "average face" of that person by merging photographs taken from many different viewpoints. By combining these numerous views, Jenkins and Burton captured the invariant properties embedded in all the images and washed out much of the variability.

Altering Facial Proportions Disrupts Recognition

The aim of science is not things in themselves … but the relations among things; outside these relations there is no reality knowable.

—HENRI POINCARÉ

Research using the photographs of well-known people such as President Clinton showed that if everything in these pictures was kept the same, except for the distances between their features, people who viewed these photographs no longer recognized who they were looking at, even though these celebrities' unaltered pictures constantly appeared daily on television and in newspapers and magazines.[5] This was the case even though their facial features themselves were not altered. The same lack of recognition occurred when researchers simply raised the level of Clinton's eyes while keeping everything else constant.[6] If, however, the researchers raised only one eye above its normal position, viewers could still recognize the person in the photo, because with only one eye displaced, the person's normal proportions—the information specifying their identity—was still visible on the unaltered side of the face. But with two eyes displaced, the structural relationships within the face were too compromised for them to be recognizable.

In a more radical test of our response to compromised structural information, experimenters cut photographs of celebrities' faces in half and combined the upper half of one face with the lower half of another to yield a newly minted face.[7] The result was that viewers of these fused photographs could not recognize either of the two original faces. This is not surprising, because the proportional relationships that produced the structure of the original faces had morphed into totally new relationships when the halves of the two different faces were merged. When, however, the two halves of these same composite faces were not aligned directly with each other, but were offset a bit and presented again, the original relationships were partially preserved in each half-photo, and the participants' ability to recognize both people from only half of their face improved.

The proportional relationships exhibited in half of a person's face provided the information for recognizing the whole face because a person's proportions are all related to one another, and you can make approximate predictions of one of their proportions from the parameters of the others. What this means is that if someone's eyes are a particular distance apart, the distance between their nose and lips is more likely to fall within a related range, and therefore is more predictable. The upshot of the relationship among proportions is that, if you know someone, you can often predict a person's identity from seeing just a small part of them (as forensic anthropologists and paleontologists often do when reconstructing shattered skeletons).

Caregiving by Configuration

Baby face, you've got the cutest little baby face.
—HARRY AKST AND BENNY DAVIS

From infancy to maturity, the structural information that specifies human age level is the changing proportion between our cranium and our face. This ratio starts out in babies as a large cranium and a tiny face. As we grow older, that ratio slowly reverses, marking each subsequent age level with a slightly smaller cranium and a longer face. The result is that, as adults, the size of our foreheads is much smaller compared to the size of our face. This proportional configuration is critical to the continuation of our species because it provides the structural information for age level that we rely on to make wise caregiving decisions for our young.[8] Ethologist Konrad Lorenz named this infantile facial layout the *kinderschema*. It is the structural configuration that underlies looking "cute." Lorenz speculated that it is this configuration that trumps the wailing, pooping, spitting up, and sleepless nights that adult caregivers encounter by seducing them into wanting to protect these tiny people.[9] The cranial/facial proportion comes about as gravity's progeny—compression, shear, and strain—form an unseen diagram of pressures that orchestrate our facial remodeling procedure.[10] Although our bones continuously adjust to meet gravity's constraints, the structural layout of our faces retains its invariant properties, and those properties double as the information that reveals our identity, characteristics, and age level.[11,12] On rare occasions, however, structural information can be physically accurate yet carry the wrong message. Children whose cranial/facial proportions are more mature than their chronological age often do not receive the care they need and are expected to act older than they are because they look older. In some cases, because these youngsters do not live up to their caregiver's expectations, they are more subject to physical abuse.[13]

Facial Structure

Information is meaningful and specific to the dynamic patterns that biological systems produce.

—J. A. SCOTT KELSO

Although you might suppose that your facial structure rolls right out of your genes (after all, you look just like your mother), this is not exactly the case. As Sir D'Arcy Thompson speculated decades ago, every creature's structure develops according to the physical stresses imposed upon it by mechanical and gravitational forces. In effect, biological forms grow and remodel within the invisible but compelling diagrams that such compression, tension, and shear manifest and impose on all physical entities. In the end we all become incarnate echoes of those diagrams.[14] Such structural layouts provide the underlying organization of each of Earth's structures, including ourselves, and that organization also provides the information we rely on to recognize them.

Thus, facial structure and the structural information it displays develop from infancy to adulthood though a progression of fits and starts that include multiple internal interactions among many different body systems—skeletal, muscular, neuronal, soft tissue, and hormonal—all orchestrated by the biomechanics of bone development within the constraints on the growth of the entire head. This is why, even though you may look like your mother, your face has the same general form of all other faces. Your genes do not create your face; they simply regulate your facial development by turning your growth process on and off. Your resemblance to your mother (and not to your uncle Louie or a chimpanzee) owes a great deal to similarities in genetic pacing. If, however, your regulator genes are snoozing and your jaw keeps growing, you can develop a condition called acromegaly, where your jaw grows abnormally long and you end up looking a bit like a chimpanzee after all. In this situation, it is as if your regulator genes reverted to a long-lost ancestor's developmental trajectory.

Interestingly enough, the regulator genes that direct your bone growth are not located in your calcified bones themselves, but in the soft tissues and membranes that enclose each bone, showing how interrelated all body "parts" and processes are, and why chopping things up into parts to understand them is ill advised if you are seeking accurate information. In any case, you and your bones grow larger as pressure-sensitive crystals within growing bones are activated by the compressive forces of gravity on your soft tissue, and they continually restructure themselves along electromagnetic fields. All the tissues that touch a facial bone and impose pressure— the muscles, tongue, lips, cheeks, nerves, blood vessels, and brain mass—"provide information signals that pace bone development."[15] So once again, biomechanical forces within your body produce the information for your growth trajectory, and that trajectory ends up providing the information for your identity.

To accommodate your growth, however, your adjacent bones must first drift apart, which causes their relationships to one another to change. To retain your unique facial structure during this process, each bone then remodels itself to accommodate its new relationships with the surrounding bones and tissues.[16] In other words, two basic processes occur as faces grow: displacement, which is triggered by the compressive forces of the soft tissue growth around each bone combined with genetic regulatory processes that sequence the way bones move apart; and remodeling, which involves depositing and reabsorbing bone. Regardless of all these changes, Donald Enlow, consummate bone expert and currently an emeritus professor at Case Western University, pointed out that:

> Facial growth is a process that requires intimate morphogenic inter-relationships among all its components' growing, changing, and functioning soft and hard tissue parts. No part is developmentally independent and self-contained…that is the proportions, shape, relative sizes, and angles are not altered as each separate region enlarges. Thus the geometric form of the whole face for the first and last stages is largely the same; only the over-all size has been changed. Each sequential stage incorporates all the stages that preceded it.…Consequently, the same facial pattern is maintained throughout.[17]

As with all complex systems, that spatial pattern emerges from the interactions of all the components that produce the structure of the face. In other words, like everything else on Earth, your face is a dynamic complex system and your features are simply components of that system. In his discussion of facial development, Enlow emphasizes that this process occurs over time. Although at any one instant the structure of someone's face might seem to be static, this quiescent state is more an artifact of our perceptual threshold for detecting movement than it is of a face's static state. Nothing in the world is actually static. Even glass flows, as one can see in the windows of old houses, where the glass is measurably thicker at the bottom than at the top.

Face Blindness and Super-Recognizers
Have we met?

Although most of us recognize the people we know by looking at the structure of their faces, some people are born unable to see facial structure, and therefore cannot recognize faces at all, even the faces of their own children. It is as if their normal recognition processes have been turned inside out, because they can still recognize the component parts that constitute the facial complex. Chuck Close, a portrait painter who is face blind, has learned to use his cognitive powers to deduce people's identity from such parts. When Lesley Stahl in a *60 Minutes* interview showed him a picture of a famous person, he reasoned thus: This man has a moustache and no beard. Today, that is not common. He is black and he is famous. The photograph must be of Martin Luther King.

Oliver Sacks, professor of neurology at the Columbia University Medical Center and the author of several books on strange neurological properties, is also face blind. He found one day that he was apologizing to a man who turned out to be himself viewed in a mirror. To avoid a repeat of this incident, he decided to isolate his most salient feature, his large ears, and now he manages to recognize keep track of the fact that he is looking at himself by checking for ear size.[18] The interesting thing about face blindness from a recognition standpoint is that these unfortunate folks cannot perceive the structure of a face, yet they are aware of its content—the features—that our cognitive processes abstract from a face, name, and transmit into our conscious awareness. In fact, Jo Livingston, who cannot recognize her own daughter and is now a face-blind participant in psychologist Brad Duchaine's functional magnetic resonance imaging experiments at Dartmouth, stated, "I can describe anything that I can put into words" (words being the vehicle for cognitively modulated content information).[19]

On the opposite side of the coin are super-recognizers like Jennifer Jarett, who continues to recognize everyone she has ever seen in her life (which unnerves the folks that she knew years ago and still recognizes today, but who no longer recognize her).

Lesley Stahl showed Jarett photographs of famous people in which they barely look like they do today. Jarett identified each person in turn, from veteran *60 Minutes* reporter Mike Wallace (at four years of age) to David Letterman sporting a beard (which made him look exactly like an Amish elder). She instantly identified George Clooney, whose picture depicted him as a long-haired teenager with a goofy, identity-defying facial expression. Once Jarett identified one of these folks, most of the rest of us could see the resemblance immediately. We could now see how George H. W. Bush's childhood picture resembled a miniature of his adult face.

If one compares the face-blind person's inability to recognize facial structure and their ability to recognize facial parts (and to describe those parts using words) with the super-recognizer's skill at recognizing facial structure, one might consider the rest of us to fall between these extremes. We are born with the ability to recognize structure, but because we rarely use this faculty on a conscious level, it remains undeveloped. But as we shall see in the discussion of experts in chapter 5, this capacity can be measurably increased.

In sum, we know that a face is a face, and whose face it is, by its global structure, not by its separate features.[20] The structure of each face develops according to physical laws that preserve its invariant properties even as its individual features may change over time. Thus, the invariant structural information that specifies someone's face also specifies their identity.[21] Yet our cognitive habit of partitioning things into separate parts can interfere with our normal recognition process, leading us to mistake one person for another and possibly causing great harm, as the following story shows.

What's Wrong With Eyewitness Testimony?

The Whole is More Than the Sum of Its Parts.
—ARISTOTLE

On June 29, 1984, Jennifer Thompson-Cannino, a straight-A college student in Burlington, South Carolina, woke up as a man was raping her at knifepoint.[22] Her assailant took over her apartment, eating her food and going through her belongings. He kept her prisoner for several hours, and during that time, Jennifer's fear turned to outrage, and she reported deliberately studying her rapist's features to make sure she could identify him later. Unfortunately, like most of us, Jennifer did not realize that the features she consciously chose to remember do not provide the best information for recognizing and remembering. As we saw with Delimar Cruz, the information that reveals someone's identity is not their separate features, which change over time, but their facial structure, with its invariant proportions that remain constant over one's lifespan. Furthermore, abstracting a subset of features from a whole face requires choice, and choice requires agency, a cognitive rather than a perceptual process. Such choices are also vulnerable to the chooser's inadvertent biases, such as having recently seen people with similar features and confusing the two. Because different people often have similar features, relying on feature information to identify a particular person can lead to a case of mistaken identity.

Be that as it may, when her rapist was momentarily distracted, Jennifer ran out the back door and fled to a neighbor. Later that day, Jennifer "retrieved" the features she had deliberately etched into her memory to help a police artist create a composite sketch of her assailant. While at the station, she looked at police books filled with hundreds of examples of separate features—noses, eyes, eyebrows, hairlines, nostrils, and lips—and compared them to her memory of the features she had deliberately abstracted from her assailant at the time of the rape. This gave the artist an idea of what to draw. One problem with this strategy is that our memory is not a reliable recorder of reality; it tends to slot similar items into the same general category to reduce our information load. As a result, the features Jennifer had abstracted at the time of the rape commingled with features she had seen before. In that melding, her rapist's features lost some of their unique character and turned into prototypes that could reflect the faces of a range of people.

Despite these drawbacks, the composite sketch of the rapist was circulated in the community, and a local business owner saw the sketch, called the police, and told them he thought the drawing resembled his employee, Ronald Cotton. Cotton was picked up and photographed, and his picture was included in a series of mug shots for Jennifer to identify. Consider, however, that the drawing used to identify Cotton was not drawn from life. Instead, it was a representation in Jennifer's memory, assembled from a set of subjectively chosen features and archived for later retrieval. Based on this representation, however, Jennifer picked Cotton's photograph out of the group and also identified him during a live lineup. After he was indicted, she identified him again in court at his trial. In other words, even as Jennifer looked at him, she never saw Cotton as himself, only as she represented him in her mind.

Psychologist Elizabeth Loftus at the University of California Irvine has described eyewitness testimony as "among the most damning evidence that can be used in a court of law. When an eyewitness says, 'he did it. I saw him,' the case is as good as over. 'Cast-iron, brass-bound, copper-riveted, and air-tight' as one prosecutor put it."[23] Cotton was tried and convicted. At no time did Jennifer doubt her conclusion; she was absolutely certain that Cotton was her assailant. Her faith in her memory of Ronald Cotton never changed. It was not influenced by subsequent stories she read in the newspapers or news she saw on TV, even though that sort of material easily infiltrates and rearranges most people's ability to recall what they have actually seen. This was not surprising since she was comparing the Cotton she actually saw at these later dates with a representation that she had constructed herself. Considering her to be an eyewitness who has seen someone in person overlooks the fact that she was comparing the man she saw in court to her memory of that man (which is one reason that such testimony is so often wrong).

In fact, while in prison Cotton met Bobby Poole, who was serving a life sentence for multiple rapes, and who boasted that he had committed the rape that put Cotton behind bars. In addition, during the period when Jennifer was raped, there had been a similar break-in, rape, and robbery, and the victim of that rape had identified another assailant. On the basis of the other rape victim's conflicting testimony and Poole's boast to Cotton, Cotton's attorney appealed his conviction. In 1987, Cotton was granted a new trial. Unfortunately, the superior court judge assigned to the case refused to admit Bobby Poole's confession into evidence. The only new evidence for this trial was the other rape victim's testimony. By the time of Cotton's second trial, however, the other victim was influenced by what she had seen and heard in the media about the Cotton trial. She reframed her memory, changed her story, and identified Cotton as her rapist as well.

When Bobby Poole was brought into the courtroom for his second trial, Jennifer was again asked, "Ms. Thompson, have you ever seen this man?" She replied, "I have never seen this man in my life. I have no idea who he is." Jennifer again identified Cotton as her rapist, and he not only went back to prison, but he was also accused of and convicted of the second rape. He was given two life sentences plus fifty-four years. False memories based on unreliable "content" information had sealed his fate. A world expert on such testimony and its flaws, Loftus wrote, "Some reliable estimates of the number of wrongful convictions in the United States alone in a single year are staggering—exceeding eight thousand."[24]

In 1994, the chief appellate defender in North Carolina smelled something fishy regarding the Cotton case and ordered two new lawyers to take over Cotton's defense on the basis of inadequate appeal counsel. In 1995, Jennifer was asked to give a blood sample for DNA testing. That new DNA sample did not match the one taken from Cotton at the time of the rape, but it did match a sample taken from Poole. The 1995 DNA evidence proved that Poole was actually Jennifer's rapist. Ronald Cotton was exonerated and eventually released. Bobby Poole died in prison. Similarly, over 200 wrongly convicted prisoners have been released in the last few years based on DNA evidence obtained by attorney Barry Scheck's Innocence Project.

When Cotton's DNA evidence was revealed, Jennifer was horrified at the role she had played in sending him to prison. She reported feeling overwhelming shame and guilt and questioned everything she had once believed in. With the same zeal that she had focused on remembering his facial features, she set about trying to understand how she had made such a disastrous mistake and what she could do to prevent such a mistake from happening again.[25] Unfortunately,

Jennifer's error is all too common. On August 24, 1986, a young woman named Toni Gustus was raped by a drunken intruder. She also escaped.[26,27] Although at first she was not as sure as Jennifer was about her assailant's identity, nevertheless Toni made virtually the same mistake as Jennifer. She identified Eric Sarsfield as her assailant and, although he insisted that he was innocent, he was arrested, tried, convicted, and sent to prison. Like Jennifer, Toni had studied her rapist's features carefully and swore to herself that she would never forget his face. She went through the same identification steps as Jennifer. The police showed her mug shots, a composite drawing, even a videotape from a convenience store.

Fourteen years later, Toni received a letter from the district attorney of Middlesex County, Massachusetts, telling her that new evidence had surfaced in her case and requesting that she come in and talk about the matter. DNA evidence from a rape kit showed that Eric Sarsfield was innocent. Like Jennifer, Toni was also horrified at the mistake she had made. A year later, Sarsfield's attorney contacted her and asked whether she would like to meet his client. He assured her that Eric had forgiven her for mistaking his identity, and she agreed to meet with both Eric and his attorney. As soon as Toni saw Sarsfield, she realized that he could not have been her rapist. When she had consciously studied her assailant during the rape and chose features in order to remember him, she had not chosen his one feature that turned out to be critical. Her rapist had very even teeth, a feature that she had failed to include in her description. In contrast, Eric's teeth were crooked. If Toni had cited her rapist's even teeth as one of his defining features, Eric might not have been arrested.

Although Jennifer and Toni had both made a terrible mistake, did they have a choice? When Jennifer deliberately "studied her rapist's features," she tried her best to gather useable evidence that she would remember at a later time. When any of us looks at someone, we are typically conscious of seeing particular features— height, facial features, skin and hair color. Aren't those the attributes the police always ask witnesses about on TV police dramas? Yet, in Jennifer's case, the answers to those questions and the features she remembered led her to mistake Cotton's identity. But as

Elizabeth Loftus points out, "wrongful conviction caused by faulty eyewitness testimony shows how even good people with the best intentions can get things terribly wrong."[28]

The flaws in Jennifer's eyewitness testimony originated in the fact that she bypassed the structural information she detected with her sensory receptors during the rape and, instead, consciously gathered a subjectively chosen set of separate features. Abstracting certain parts of an event or features from a person is a mental process that, as we have seen, produces unreliable content information that is influenced by whatever other content is already lodged in one's mind. One clue that sheds some light on the mental nature of Jennifer's mistake is that even after the DNA evidence proved without a doubt that Cotton was innocent, Jennifer still consciously "saw" what she thought was Cotton's face. What she did not realize was that she was seeing his face in her mind's eye (not with her visual receptors) whenever she thought about or remembered the rape. She brought that false image into the courtroom, where it was used as eyewitness testimony that wrongly convicted Ronald Cotton. The question then becomes: Exactly what was Jennifer conscious of when she brought her memory of Cotton to mind, and why was the information she used to construct that memory so wrong? Let's unpack the flaws in the mental process that led up to Jennifer's identification of Cotton to see how and why it spun off the track.

Why Features Fail as Evidence

One of the most highly developed skills in contemporary Western Civilization is dissection: the split-up of problems into their smallest possible components. We are good at it, so good that we often forget to put the pieces back together again.

—ALVIN TOFFLER

As previously noted, when we are asked to describe someone, we typically default to lists of their features—for example, tall, slim, blonde and blue-eyed. Yet, because many of us belong to the same gene pool, different people who are not even related can have quite similar features, leading us to easily mistake one person for another. There is barely a baby born that is not immediately seen to look just like his uncle George, or to at least have his father Peter's nose and second cousin Louise's eyes. In fact, Ronald Cotton and Bobby Poole shared certain features. They were both big and black with similar hair and noticeable cheekbones. It is difficult to believe that the images of people that we have in our mind's eye are not the same as the ones we directly experience in real life. When we perceive an actual person in the world directly, we are not aware that we construct images of that person in our mind. To be more accurate, as I discussed in chapter 1, we do not actually perceive that person directly at all. We perceive the light that lands on that person and is reflected into our retinas. When light lands on something, it is, in effect, structured by that entity. In other words, what we actually see is the invariant structure of the person we are looking at, which in turn has structured the reflected light our visual receptors receive. In this way the structured light preserves the structure and thus the identity of the person (not their features) and that is the information that our perceptual systems perceive when we recognize someone.

In contrast, and counterintuitive as it might seem, it is possible that the feature-filled pictorial images that colonize our consciousness are actually just memories. This may be the case because it takes time for the information in the structured light to travel from our eyes to our brain's translating facility (where representations are constructed that are then transmitted into our conscious awareness). By the time we become conscious of seeing someone, that act of observation is in the past and the person, along with the world, has moved on. We are left with our recently encoded, feature-filled memory of what we already saw. What is most peculiar about this process (and our conception of it) is that the separate features we are conscious of seeing may have a different meaning once they are abstracted from the larger structures that provide them a home. For instance, the exact same nose would look different in the context of a different face. We do end up with a representation of someone's face, but one that has been interleaved with our memories of other faces and that does not necessarily match the one at hand (to say nothing of what we might make of a nose alone in the world with no face at all for its context).

If we use features as our primary source of information, our choices are also limited by our short-term or working memory. Working memory is restricted in both time and capacity. In a classic study titled "The Magical Number Seven, Plus or Minus Two," Harvard psychologist George Miller showed that, at the best of times, the number of separate items (such as the digits of a phone number) we can remember is typically limited to five to nine.[29] Under stressful circumstances, that number might be even smaller. The features we do remember are also suspect because we chose them subjectively. Since different people can easily choose a different set of features to focus on, one person's representation of someone can differ measurably from another person's representation of that same person, making such cognitive constructions unreliable.

Recall the case of Toni Gustus and Eric Sarsfield. Toni had studied her rapist's features carefully, and by the time she identified him, she felt 100 percent confident that she was right. But again, Toni was relying on the subset of features she had subjectively chosen from Sarsfield. One feature that would have cleared Sarsfield, his crooked teeth, never made it into Toni's working memory. If she had known to rely on Sarsfield's movement patterns to identify him, the feature-picking fiasco that landed him in prison might never have occurred. To make matters worse, as time passes, the memory of someone's features that were encoded at the scene of a crime becomes more entrenched in a phenomenon called freezing.[30] Each time witnesses like Toni and Jennifer repeat what they saw to police and juries, it strengthens their original memory regardless of whether it is subjective or false.[31] At every step of the way, Jennifer and Toni relied on the subjectively constructed representation of their rapist that they had encoded into their memory, and that representation finally nailed the lids of Cotton's and Sarsfield's convictions shut.

Recall that even at the trial, with both Bobby Poole and Ronald Cotton in the courtroom, Jennifer still identified Cotton as her assailant. Since Cotton was not actually her rapist, who was Jennifer "seeing" when she looked at him in the courtroom and made this wrong identification? She was obviously not seeing Cotton as he actually was; instead, she had to be seeing him through the flawed, feature-filled representation that she had consciously constructed, archived in her memory and retrieved for her testimony at the trial. It was that flawed representation that filled her conscious awareness each time she was called upon to identify Ronald Cotton. If this were not the case, as soon as she saw Bobby Poole walk into the courtroom, she would have seen that Poole's movement patterns (which she saw as he walked around her apartment) were those of the man who raped her, and she would have realized that she had made a mistake. But, since she still identified the wrong man when the right man was right in front of her, neither the real Cotton nor the real Poole made it through her entrenched mental representation.

It is as if we momentarily see the structural information that specifies what we are looking at, and then send it down subliminal neural paths to guide our automatic behavior. But as soon as we translate that real-world information into a representation, a switch is tripped and we are no longer aware of the world as it is. In other words, when we think we are aware of the world itself, we may only be aware of our representations of it. At the same time, our actual knowledge of the world remains subliminal and unused, or perhaps surfaces as gut feelings whose source is unknown, as it did with Lt. Commander Riley and Luz Cuevas.

The implications of the difference between our conscious and subliminal knowledge are startling and might simplify unanswered philosophical questions concerning consciousness. For example, what we call consciousness and what we call memory may be very similar and perhaps interchangeable. This means that when we are not careful to keep track of what our eyes see and our ears hear, our various mental processes (from constructed representations to invented theories) can hijack our sensory systems and lead our recognition processes astray.

From this view, except for the structural information that is currently in front of our noses that is relayed directly to our emotional

or motor faculties to guide our responses—what we actually see—
everything in our conscious awareness is a memory. This may be the
reason that Zen masters are always admonishing us to stay in the
present, the here and now, rather than the then and there. This is
because "now" is the only time we are in contact with reality, know
what is actually going on, and are truly able to make informed decisions (even if we are not aware of the information we are using). The
paradox is that although we are consciously aware of seeing someone's separate features, and can picture those features in our mind's
eye, unless we are dealing with Richard Nixon's nose or Jay Leno's
chin we do not use features to recognize someone. We rely on their
facial structure.

Our Atomistic Worldview Leads Us Astray

Nothing exists except atoms and empty space.
Everything else is opinion.
—DEMOCRITUS

Our current belief that the world is made of separate parts obscures
the reality that it is composed of complex systems. We would not
be here if our ancestors had not relied on the structural information that specifies those systems and that our senses evolved to
detect to understand the world. Yet eventually our own minds distracted us from that incarnate reality and into the ungrounded theories we construct in our own heads. One clue as to why this might
have occurred lies in the differences between the Western and the
Chinese worldview. The Chinese view is rooted in the natural world
and its ways. The Western view is rooted in theories put forth by the
Greeks, especially the philosopher Democritus, who first proposed
that the world was made of atoms. We generalized this theory of the
atomistic nature of matter to the nature of everything in the world.
This gave us the grounds for the worldview that now suffuses both
our culture and our brains—that the world is made of separate parts
instead of complex wholes. But because a parts-based perspective

is necessarily static and the world is dynamic, the realistic information we sense must not only be structural, but must also occur over time. Chapter 3 explains the dynamic aspects of structural information that we commonly call "body language," and how one person's perception of those continually changing biological configurations helped catch a child molester.

3

Perceiving Dynamics

*If intuition is immediate knowledge without rea-
soned analysis, then perceiving is intuition par
excellence.*

—DAVID MEYERS

ON JANUARY 15, 2006, Georgia resident Tracie Dean saw an old
man with a young girl in an Alabama convenience store, and her
skin began to crawl. Tracie felt that the child was afraid, and so she
followed the pair out of the store and watched them drive away in
a truck with Washington State license plates. As soon as the truck
was out of sight, she called 911, then the police and *America's Most
Wanted,* to find out whether a child resembling the one she saw had
been reported missing. After checking, the local 911 dispatcher told
her that the man was the child's grandfather and everything was fine.
But Tracie did not agree. She later told a sheriff's deputy, "My suspicion was that this young girl did not belong with that man," but
she could not explain why.[1] It seemed to be nothing more than an
"intuition." But what was an intuition beyond a word that referred
to her feeling of unease? That word said little about the information
that triggered that feeling.

Even though the bulk of child abuse is committed by close
relatives and friends of the victims, most people tend to think of
grandfathers as elderly men who supply children with ice cream
cones. They rarely think of them as pedophiles. Once the operator found out that the man Tracie saw was a grandfather, her

preconceptions about grandfathers blocked her ability to take Tracie's concerns seriously. Nonetheless, Tracie insisted that even if he was her grandfather, something was still very wrong in his relationship to the child. In the end, no one in any of the organizations that Tracie contacted would look into the matter and, very reluctantly, she went home to Atlanta.

But the memory of this child haunted her. She couldn't sleep. For a week she looked online for missing children, but found none matching the little girl. Then, unable to get the child out of her mind, she and two friends drove the 260 miles back to the convenience store in Alabama and asked to see the surveillance tape for the day she had been there so that she could review what she had seen. Sheriff's Deputy Bryan Davis of the Evergreen, Alabama police department happened by the store at that time, listened to her concerns, and agreed to look into the matter. The results of his investigation made the prime-time news.

Davis found that the old man Tracie had seen, one Jack Wiley, and his wife, Glenna Faye Cavender, were wanted in California on multiple counts of child abuse and arson. Wiley and Cavender had allegedly raped a three-year-old and were supposedly holding a seventeen-year-old boy in their trailer at the time that Tracie first saw them and called 911. The trooper sent the local police to Wiley and Cavender's trailer, where they found a teenage boy and the little girl that Tracie had seen in the convenience store. The police took both children into protective custody. The suspects were detained on January 20, 2006. On June 30, 2006, Cavender pleaded guilty to two counts of child sex abuse and was sentenced to two concurrent ten-year terms. In November 2007, Wiley was convicted of two counts of rape of the three-year-old girl and one count of sodomy with the seventeen-year-old boy. He received three consecutive life sentences.

Tracie knew nothing of Jack Wiley and his supposed grand-daughter before she saw the pair in the convenience store. How was she so sure that something was so wrong that she drove all the way back to Alabama to make it right? At one time or another, many people have a feeling that they know something for which they have no tangible proof. It might be a hunch that someone is lying, or the unsettling suspicion that someone who seems benign is actually dangerous. We call these hunches intuitions, but naming them does not explain their origin or, as in Tracie's case, help other people to believe such claims. Because we are not aware of the source of these feelings, they make us feel silly and we often put them aside. Yet, there it is, that niggling discomfort in our gut.

The question then becomes: Exactly what did Tracie Dean see in the relationship between Jack Wiley and the little girl that made her so sure that things were not as they should be? That question takes us behind the scenes of our conscious awareness to the sub-liminal relationship among the structural information our percep-tual systems detect, our emotional evaluation of that information, and the responses of our neural networks. I will cover these top-ics more extensively later in this chapter. For now, this is what Tracie saw: When the old man and child walked around the store together, their yoked movements revealed unspoken levels of ten-sion and fear that were unusual between a small child and a legiti-mate caregiver. It was as if Tracie could see into Jack Wiley's soul by watching him move.[2] But how could someone's movements reveal their intentions?

Dynamic Structural Information

We must seek knowledge that is neither of actors or actions but of which the actors and actions are a vehicle. The knowledge we can acquire is knowledge of a structure or pattern contained in the actions.

—SIR ARTHUR EDDINGTON

The last section ended with the question of how it could be that peo-ple's movements held the key to revealing their intentions. Consider that each of us develops as a multicomponent complex system whose components—skeletal structure, emotional center, senses, neurons, muscles, hormones, cerebral networks, organs, and vascular sys-tems—interact with and influence one another, and make us who we are. More transient states such as our emotions and intentions are components that, when present, are diffused throughout, and therefore influence the state of our whole system, including our visible movements. Tracie perceived Jack Wiley's tension and the little girl's fear in the informative configurations their movements produced. In short, what we feel or intend becomes part and parcel of the dynamic structural information we display—the body movements, hand gestures, and facial expressions that constitute our non-verbal communication system.

For example, we tend to recognize how other people feel by simply looking at the configurations produced by their facial movements. Just as we label our feelings "intuitions," we label such configurations "facial expressions," but these labels fall short. They only refer to what is happening with us and tell us nothing about what we perceive in the world (which may have convinced the authorities to investigate Tracie's claims). Words are only placeholders that obtain their meaning from our direct experience of the structural information we perceive. That information is packaged as perceivable configurations that summarize a person's current state. We have no language for most of these configurations.

Thus, Tracie's intuition that there was something very wrong with the old man and the child in the convenience store came from simply seeing the configurations they produced as they walked. The old man's intention to control the child, his emotional tension at being in public, and the child's fear of him were all revealed in the relationship between the interdependent patterns their bodies and gaits displayed. The problem with such situations is that although Tracie "knew" that the old man posed a threat to this child (and was later proved right), there were no adequate words that explained that situation to those who either did not see it themselves, or, if they did see it, failed to pay attention to its perceivable parameters. This example clearly illustrates the abyss that exists between language and knowledge. As long as we fail to acknowledge the disjunction between the symbolic and the actual, and continue to replace our direct experience with verbal descriptions, we will lack the knowledge necessary for true understanding and be unable to make realistic decisions.

We do not, however, have to depend solely on anecdotal reports such as Tracie's experience to believe that the structural information that specifies what is happening around us exists. The biological motion study outlined in the Introduction showed that we perceive other people's identity, characteristics, and actions from such configurations. These informative forms were isolated in a seminal study done by perceptual psychologist Gunnar Johansson at Uppsala University.[3] Recall from the Introduction that upon seeing a film composed of nothing more than seemingly abstract, content-free configurations, viewers knew immediately that these configurations were actually adult men and women who were walking, dancing, and doing push-ups. Johansson had borrowed the idea for this study from a Czech ballet company that staged their dances in the dark and illuminated the dancers' movements by attaching lights to their joints. Although Johansson's study did not test whether emotions and intentions could be discerned from these illuminated configurations, his students, Sverker Runeson and Gunilla Frykholm, adopted this paradigm and did several studies that tested this. They found that in addition to perceiving permanent characteristics such as sex and age level, humans are able to directly perceive periodic ones such as intention from these same abstract configurations.[4] In the first part of Runeson and Frykholm's study, the obscured actors did various tasks while pretending to be the opposite sex. In the second part, the actors pretended that the boxes they were lifting were very heavy when they were actually very light. In both parts, the audience immediately knew—simply from viewing the movement configurations that each set of actors produced—that they were neither the opposite sex nor lifting heavy boxes. In other words, the viewers easily perceived that the actor's *intention* was to deceive them. In fact, our ability to detect deception often occurs without our necessarily knowing how we do so. Many of us have perceived such attempts written across our children's faces when they insist that they were not the ones who emptied the cookie jar, or that they did not crawl out their bedroom window to meet their friends on Saturday night. Because we are not typically aware of how we appear, deception, like other human behavior, is often difficult to hide. Unless we are trained mimes like Marcel Marceau, it is virtually impossible for us to completely conceal how we feel from people who pay attention to what they see. However, since we are typically influenced by the words people use, we often ignore the evidence their faces reveal and accept what they say instead. Advertising and public relations firms depend on our susceptibility to words and contrived images, which makes the fact that Gunnar Johansson's studies brought structural information out of the closet and into our conscious awareness critical. By illuminating people's movement patterns, Johansson revealed that information comes in a much more accurate and comprehensive form than can be carried in words. In doing so, he showed that despite our subliminal access to such intelligence, what we see is nonetheless etched into our knowledge base and is available to us when we make decisions. In addition, by rendering the actors in his film virtually invisible, Johansson also relegated the feature information discussed in chapter 2 that typically distracts us to the blacked-out background, allowing us to focus on the structural information we actually need.

Although these two studies do show that we perceive structural information, we are not home free. Even though structural information is critical to our ability to function and know the world around us, when it comes to the conscious decisions we make, we too often revert to the mental concepts and theories that we couch in words and that often lead us astray. Because we can name and describe separate features and then construct theories from these features, it is easy for us to fall into this verbal trap. Our mental processes typically rely on language. Because the features we abstract have names, they are easy to anchor in our memories and even easier to communicate to others. These factors give words an edge and help to further obscure the structural information we perceive. Again, because Tracie detected the state of the old man and the child on a nonverbal and subliminal level, it was well-nigh impossible for her to explain her conclusion to others, and she herself was not conscious of the information she was using to come to that conclusion.

But all is not lost. Consider that we live most of our daily lives by subliminally accessing and relying on structural information.

We jump out of the way of an oncoming car as soon as we see it (because its moving configuration expands as it progresses toward us in a "looming" effect that signals danger). We would not respond so quickly to this type of danger if we did not directly perceive the meaning of its nonverbal configuration. But regardless of whether we are conscious of what we know or not, one lesson that biological motion research teaches is that structural information is available, and if we focus on the world around us, and like Tracie take our conscious experiences and verbal descriptions with a grain of salt, we can start to improve our ability to trust our perceptual acumen and the structural information we access. If we learn that our knowledge of things outside ourselves does not come from the parts and images we are conscious of and can name, but from the informative configurations we perceive under the radar, we can, in time, learn to distinguish between the contents of our minds and the reality of the world. Separating a person into parts is a conceptual act that is only useful when we want to compare one person to another on particular dimensions such as height or weight. But such dimensional comparisons do not actually tell us anything about that person except how tall or heavy they are relative to each other.

If structural information can tell us anything, it is that acquiring comprehensive, accurate information requires direct experience. On the one hand, if that experience is translated into symbolic forms, much of that information is lost or distorted. On the other hand, to communicate what we know to others requires the use of words or images, which only represent things rather than duplicating them. But the knowledge we can communicate is still far less comprehensive than the experience itself and is often reduced to generalizations just as what occurred with the 911 operator who Tracie spoke to. That operator was bound by a general image of grandfathers that closed her mind to Tracie's report about a particular grandfather at that particular time with that particular child. But generalized grandfathers do not exist; they are a product of our cognitive bent to slot complex items into simpler categories on the basis of a few features. Symbolic representations such as names, categories, and concepts are necessary for communication, but if we don't constantly compare them with their more complex real-world counterparts, they can continue to misrepresent and misinterpret the reality we see and hear.

The same communication problem faced Luz Cuevas (in chapter 2) when she tried to tell the authorities that the child she saw at the party was her daughter. Luz had recognized Delimar's facial structure from the unique, invariant proportions that had remained constant over her lifetime and thus revealed her identity. But again, there are no words that could convincingly communicate this information. Fortunately, Luz obtained DNA evidence that revealed how Delimar's structure was related to her own, thus making a case that convinced the authorities. What Tracie and Luz's situations both tell us is that our sensory perceptions are critical to acquiring the type of knowledge that reflects reality.

This raises a question: If structural information is typically dynamic, how do seemingly static configurations such as facial structures qualify? As we saw in chapter 2, although the structure of Delimar Luz's face might seem to be static compared to the movement configurations we produce when we perform various activities, that stasis is an artifact of our perceptual threshold for detecting motion. It is similar to the fact that we cannot see our fingernails grow, yet despite our inability to perceive that growth, they need regular trimming. Delimar's face, while retaining the proportions that preserved her identity, was in fact remodeling imperceptibly daily as she grew older. Both Delimar's invariant proportions and the continual remodeling of her facial bones was visible in her facial structure when Luz recognized her as the child who, six years earlier, had been her baby. Psychologist Emily Grossman and her colleagues at the University of California, Irvine have performed neuroimaging studies showing that the networks of coordinated brain areas that respond to biological movements (in this case, dynamic configurations) also respond to size invariance (in this case, constant proportions), indicating that we continue to perceive invariant structural identity in the midst of evolving change.[5]

The Oscillating Figure Eight Reveals Identity

Matter is pregnant with its form.

—MAURICE MERLEAU-PONTY

Recognition information is not limited to perceiving people's faces. Recall that we can also perceive the figure-eight configurations that oscillate around people's belly buttons and reveal their identity.[6] Imagine that you are walking around the reservoir in Manhattan's Central Park, and far off in the distance you recognize a friend walking toward you. Even though you are not aware of the information you are using to make that identification, we know from Johansson's study that such a configuration emerges from the interactions of the components that comprise that person's core structure as they walk forward. Technically, this emergent geometric form is produced by the "displacements of a person's center of moment in three planes of space during a single stride."[7] This means that our bodies move up, down, back and forth, and side to side around our center of moment or central balance point. The location of our center of moment is largely a function of the ratio of our shoulder width to our hip width. Since no one else has the exact same ratios of limb length to body height or shoulder to hip width, each person's forward stride produces its own unique figure eight and reveals who they are.

As you watch your friend walking toward you, you recognize her immediately, even though the actual information you are using never surfaces into your conscious awareness. If, however, someone attached lights to strategic places on her body, as in Johansson's experimental paradigm, you would become conscious of seeing that figure eight. But the fact that you can recognize your friend without visible "cues" demonstrates our ability to perceive and comprehend the structural information that people display, regardless of whether we are aware of seeing those patterns or not. In fact, research shows that even two-day-old infants, given the choice, prefer to look at a point light display depicting biological motion (a walking hen) rather than a display of a rotating rigid object.[8] Companion research shows that infant brains are activated only by the dynamic facial configurations produced by point light displays, not by static ones.[9]

If Jennifer Thompson-Cannino in chapter 2 had focused on her rapist's underlying facial structure or the way he moved, or if she observed her assailant's facial layout carefully, she might not have mistaken Ronald Cotton for her actual assailant, Bobby Poole. But since she remembered the features she had chosen and not the identifying movements he made, she was locked into her conclusion by the unreliable processes of her own mind. Recall that Toni Gustus, the rape victim whose case was added to Ronald Cotton's indictment during his second trial, had not been as sure as Jennifer that she had identified the right man. One difference is that Toni had seen a videotape of her alleged assailant and had mentioned that the person on the tape exhibited the same body language as her rapist. Her doubts most probably came from her memory of her rapist's actual movements, while her subsequent change of mind and her accusation of Cotton during his second trial most likely occurred because of something she read or was told after the rape incident occurred but which nonetheless became interleaved with memories of her actual experience. Since we are able to recognize and identify people without error all the time, do we have and use memories of structural information that never surface into consciousness?

Few studies outside of sports psychology have been done that connect structural patterns to real-world knowledge acquisition. In fact, the figure-eight configuration was discovered inadvertently by orthopedic experts who design prosthetics, when they were attempting to produce the best fitting product for their clients. The motion picture industry has also contributed to this field via films such as *Avatar* by using "motion capture" techniques, which are used to map human movements onto nonhuman characters.

Do We Have Memories of Structural Information?

The human brain is fundamentally a pattern forming self-organized system governed by non-linear dynamical laws

—J. A. SCOTT KELSO

One finding that has emerged from neuroimaging studies of biological motion is that our perception of these dynamic configurations recruits a complex network of coordinated brain areas that have the capacity to support the layered information load that is embedded in such configurations.[10] As you perceive new input that is related to something you have seen before, the neural connections that resonate to that phenomenon rearrange and amplify to increase your perceptual reach. If you could see a video of such a neural network, you would see it continuously changing its connections and transforming its configuration whenever new, relevant information enters your visual field. The result of this continual remodeling procedure is that, without necessarily being aware of it, you are effortlessly and continually acquiring new knowledge that allows you to perceive more and thus know better in the future. Evidence supports this view; one study has shown how disturbances in brain connectivity in the right temporal cortex can lead to disintegration of the neural network that processes our perception of body motion.[11]

Our Brain–World Interface

The feedback between reality and the individual through perception of the physical world determines the interconnected structure of the brain.
—MITCHELL WALDROP

The claim made in this book is that our perceptual systems, in league primarily with our spatially adept right hemisphere, are structured to detect and comprehend the structural information that specifies the world with which we coevolved. A further claim is that this type of information triggers the reorganization of our neural networks to include the new information our senses access and deem relevant. But how does the actual spatial layout of a tree or a person's movement patterns make the journey from its worldly source to a memory that allows us to identify that source in the future? Frankly, we do not actually know. But recent research on the memory of sea slugs done by Dr. Eric Kandel at Columbia University may contain a clue. Kandel's work shows that "screwing a normal nerve cell protein into a distorted shape helps slugs, and possibly people, lock in their memories."[12,13] These sensitive proteins change shape in response to experience, and then transmit this shape change to companion proteins that carry that experience into long-term memory. When researchers blocked the protein's ability to change shape, no connections were formed and no memories were encoded. This research may be a first step in showing that living creatures can lay down structural memories based on shape-changing proteins. In the same vein, Kausik Si of the Stowers Institute for Medical Research in Kansas City, Missouri discovered that short-term proteins called CPEBs help to change the structure of synapses themselves and promote new synapses, which in turn help to form the type of strong neural connections in the appropriate neural networks that are needed for such long-term memories.[14]

The question then arises as to how shape-sensitive proteins might influence our ability to remember the "shape" of someone's movements and, more important, to discern what those movements mean. First, we all have neurons in an area of our brain called the right inferotemporal cortex that "are selectively responsive to the complex shapes that specify structural information such as facial expressions."[15] Furthermore, the selectivity for shape of these neurons changes with each new experience, and if those neurons are destroyed, we end up with severe deficits in our ability to recognize visual patterns. These findings tell us two related facts: First, we have synaptic protein molecules that respond to environmental input by changing both their own shape and the shape of their synapse; and second, those proteins team up with neurons within our cortex that are structured to continue this response and to form neural networks that reorganize in response to each new shape change.

As we see and react to the structures that constitute the world, our neural networks receive feedback from our own sensory-motor, synaptic, and neuron responses. The feedback from these various sources reorganizes our neural networks to accommodate new information, and in this way, the spatial and temporal structure of the world outside of us becomes enfolded within us. We rely on this sort of molecular computing to operate the entire communication network within our bodies. These signaling molecules provide the bases for the dendrites that branch off our neurons and reach out across our synapses to pass information on to their neighbors and eventually to the rest of our body. What is most important for our purposes here is understanding that this whole process relies on an information system based on configurations that allow these molecules to recognize one another and form coalitions that specify and allow us to understand the world within and around us. The studies described at the start of this section attest to our ability to run complex, biological systems such as our bodies using bottom-up processes that require little central control or advice. Our brains are wired together with 100 billion of these tiny computers. They recognize informative patterns by scanning their internal environment much as our eyes scan the terrestrial world and, in so doing, they provide the basis for recognition. Because molecules have a specific shape that can recognize other shapes, they are the ultimate pattern recognizers. Although research is needed to see how far their recognition of shapes can go, it would not be surprising to find that this molecular recognition translates up to the distributed neural networks that underlie the perception of biological motion and recognition.

Navigational Grids and Place Cells

When everything else has gone from my brain—the President's name, the state capitals, the neighborhood where I lived, then at length the faces of my friends, and finally the faces of my family... what will be left, I believe, is topology, the dreaming memory of land as it lies this way and that.

—ANNIE DILLARD

One example of how structural information is enfolded within neural networks comes from experiments showing how laboratory rats acquire new information and reorganize their entorhinal cortices each time they run a new maze.[16] In 1948, Edward Tolman proposed that rats in his laboratory constructed "cognitive maps" in their brains that allowed them to learn and remember the twists and turns of mazes.[17] In the 1970s, researchers expanded Tolman's work by locating "place" cells in the rat's hippocampus that fired in response to particular places. Then, in the 1980s, researchers discovered cells that projected into the entorhinal cortex that specified the direction a rat was facing. From this base, Edward Moser and his colleagues found cells that fired in grid patterns that matched the rat's position in space, and Moser's graduate student, Francesca Sargolini, and her collaborators isolated conjunctive cells, a class of grid cells that integrate place, speed, and direction.[18] The rat's movements reorganize their neural networks to replicate the maze they are running; that configuration is reorganized again when the rats run a new maze. Rosamund Langston and her colleagues at Norway's Kavli Institute showed that even before such informed feedback occurs, head-direction cells were already in place in two-and-a-half-week-old rat pups before they had any experience outside the nest.[19] A companion study by Tom Wills at University College, London, found that the directional, locational, and rhythmic organization of neural firing was present in rat pups' initial exploration outside the nest.[20] UCLA Neuropsychologist Hugh Blair, who studies this type of memory in rats, speculates that grid cell fields can not only help us navigate in space, but may also be the mechanism through which we perceive and remember other configurations such as faces.

The human capacity to recognize the dynamic structural patterns produced and displayed by the things around us is reciprocal to the patterned similarities we ourselves produce with our motor movements. We also include these patterns in our amendable neural networks. For example, we recognize the meaning of a facial expression we see in others because we make the same expression ourselves, and we know how we feel when we do so. As biologist Richard Lewontin wisely noted, "Evolutionary process ensures that we have become the embodiments of many aspects of our environment whose existence is necessary for our survival."[21] Indeed, we humans, as philosopher Mary Midgely indicated, are not "purely mental creatures trying on various instantiations."[22] We are structured to resonate to the structures of our world.

To recap, our brains are physically organized along dynamic neural networks that may be tuned by shape-changing molecules in our synapses to respond to the world's dynamic structural information. Because we coevolved with and adapted to that world, our neural networks enable us to reflect and respond to the patterns that the world displays and our senses evolved to detect. These networks form and reform in response to feedback from our sensory and motor experiences of seeing and acting on that structural information. The gist of this is that our perceptions of the physical world carve out receptive pathways that create the interconnected neural structures in our brain. Each new perception amends these patterned channels and in doing so increases their range of responsiveness. Georgetown neuropsychologist Karl Pribram notes that "we perceive a physical universe not much different in basic organization from the brain. This is comforting since the brain is part of the physical universe as well as an organ of perception."[23]

Walking in Other People's Moccasins

I am because we are.

—DESMOND TUTU

Research pioneered by Italian neurologist Giacomo Rizzolatti at the University of Parma uncovered a substrate of neurons that form networks that respond directly to the movement patterns we see.[24] The research community calls them mirror neurons because they mirror the structural patterns that humans (and monkeys) produce when they move. What is most fascinating about mirror neuron networks is not only that they activate when we see other people move, but they activate the same neural patterns when we make those same movements ourselves.[25] This means that when Tracie Dean saw the tense, fearful movements that Wiley and the girl were making, she intuited what each of them was feeling because she would move the same way if she were tense and afraid. Her mirror neurons echoed this feeling. The fact that mirror neurons respond to the same structural information both outside and inside us shows that such information, while specifying unique events, has universal properties.

It seems reasonable to assume that the movement patterns Gunnar Johansson isolated using a point light paradigm in the 1970s are virtually the same ones found mirrored in our brains by Giacomo Rizzolatti and his colleagues in the 1990s using brain scans. Both found that each purposeful movement produces its own signature pattern, and consequently, each activity triggers its own pattern of brain activation. Because many movement patterns overlap with other movement patterns, they constitute a combinatorial system much like our alphabet. All sorts of movement patterns and their variations can be produced using various combinations of the same basic forms. This is the case regardless of whether that pattern was exhibited by another person's movements, came from our own experience of making that movement, or from our mirror neuron network's response to both our own and the other person's movement.

This adds another dimension to the adage that you can know how another person feels by walking a mile in his moccasins. We do so by walking the same mile in our own mirror neurons. In fact, Rizzolatti states that "accord is inherent in the neural organization of both people," lending credence to the universality of these spatial patterns.[26]

Vittorrio Gallese and his collaborators, who were colleagues of Rizzolatti's, agree. They believe that our capacity to understand others is intuitive and requires only the "penetration" of visual information "into the experiential (first person) motor knowledge of the observer."[27] Gallese's visual penetration is what we call recognition. In other words, when we see someone move, we experience the same response as when we make that movement ourselves.

Christian Keyers of the University Medical Center Groningen in the Netherlands expanded this view to include our emotions. Keyers reports that when we see someone express an emotion, we have no need to think about, analyze, or build theories about how they feel, "because your mirror neurons just know it."[28] According to Keyers, mirror neurons respond on a direct, subliminal level to both movement patterns and the meaning those patterns display. Since all of us are members of the same highly interdependent social species, have the same bilateral structure that produces very similar movement patterns, and have similarly structured perceptual systems, it is not surprising that there is considerable overlap in what we all see and know.

Tracie Dean's ability to comprehend the emotional content of the movements that Wiley and the little girl made as they walked through the store was aided and abetted by the direct, unmediated connection we humans have between our eyes and the emotional center in areas of our brain called the amygdala.[29] The amygdala's primary role, along with the insula and thalamus, is to review what our eyes see and, when necessary, to instantly alert us to its emotional content, especially if that content spells danger. Even if we are not consciously aware of the information we detect, our amygdala, informed by our eyes, "understands" that information and sends warning signals to those parts of our body (such as our gut, which has more neurons and bodily connections than our spine[30]) that alert us that something is wrong. Those neural connections mediate our emotions and evaluate what we see.

The direct neural connections between our eyes and our amygdala parse the meaning of what is going on in the world by evaluating the dynamic structural information that specifies those circumstances. In Tracie's situation, this structural information was body movements. Tracie's eye-amygdala connection, in league with her mirror neuron networks, responded to the little girl's fearful movements because her own movements would be virtually the same in the same circumstances. In fact, we all have the same fundamental emotions and can recognize our own feelings in others. Since newborns also come equipped with the ability to understand and respond to others' emotions and to show their own emotions through their facial expressions and body movements, it's a good bet that our species comes hardwired to comprehend others' feelings using this type of structural information.

Experiencing Empathy

*The greatest gift of human beings is that we have
the power of empathy. We can all sense the same
mysterious connection to each other.*

—MERYL STREEP

In 1907, philosopher Theodore Lipps at the University of Bonn anticipated that we have mirror neuron networks in our brains when he proposed that empathy was generated by our "inner imitation" of another person.[31] He noted, "When I observe a circus performer on a hanging wire, I feel I am inside him."[32] If you have seen such a performance, perhaps you experienced some of the performer's fear and exhilaration in yourself. Empathy is the quintessential example of mirror neurons in action. Because Lipps could feel the sensory-motor feedback from his own muscles and joints, his neural networks were alerted to the spatial configurations that his own body would assume and thus how he would act and feel on the high wire. Lipps recognized the same patterns in the actions of the performer he was watching.

In 1999, psychologists Tanya Chartrand (now at Duke University) and John Barge (now at Yale University) coined the phrase "the chameleon effect" to describe our imitative empathetic responses. They found that without conscious awareness, empathetic people mimicked the postures, mannerisms, and facial expressions of others more than nonempathetic individuals.[33] In fact, researcher Laurie Carr and her colleagues found that deliberately imitating other people's facial expressions increased their own mirror neuron activation when compared to simply observing those expressions.[34] From infancy on, we spontaneously imitate what others do as long as they are doing things within our capabilities and interests.[35]

If you watch two people who are talking with each other or who are walking arm in arm, you may actually see their originally unique bodily postures and facial expressions start to converge and resemble each other. Although each person typically starts out with the facial expressions and body postures that they brought to the encounter, as their conversation progresses, the expression on both their faces and the configuration of their bodies end up mirroring each other. When one looks concerned or excited, the other tends to looks the same.[36] People who are walking side by side also adjust their strides and end up strolling in synchrony.[37]

Our interconnected neural networks support our capacity for empathy by receiving and distributing patterns of structural information. Mirror neurons in our cerebral cortices network with our motor and sensory systems through our limbic system, which, via our insula, modulates our visceral and emotional reactions.[38] Our limbic system modulates our emotions and our memories. For example, when we watch a movie showing someone in pain, our own gut often wrenches at the sight. Psychologist Paul Ekman (who retired from the University of California, San Francisco in 2004) showed that our facial muscles are inextricably connected to such emotional responses, and even if we are not experiencing much feeling, when we make certain facial expressions, our muscle action feeds back into our emotional system and we end up feeling the emotion that matches the facial configuration we deliberately produced.[39]

Although as a social species we are particularly attuned to respond to facial expressions and body movements, as we saw with the radar screen layouts in chapter 1, if we do not succumb to our theories, we are also tuned to respond to the structural configurations that every one of Earth's structures and systems displays. Chapter 4 shows that when we ignore or dismiss the value of these natural forms and instead impose our own theories on the world, we court catastrophe.

4

Restructuring Reality

*Whilst this planet has gone cycling on according
to the fixed laws of gravity, from so simple a beginning, endless forms most beautiful and most wonderful have been, and are being evolved.*
—CHARLES DARWIN

ON AUGUST 29, 2005, Hurricane Katrina hit the Gulf Coast. The devastation was, and still is, incalculable. Many people died without water, food, or medical attention. Thousands of homes and businesses were destroyed, and much of the infrastructure of the city and its services were submerged. When the calm returned, there was nothing but emptiness where homes had been, and dead bodies were floating in the floodwaters. The final death count, estimated by the National Hurrican Center at 1,833, will never actually be known. But while the hurricane was blamed, it was only a catalyst. It was not the primary cause of the flooding. When Katrina hit New Orleans, it was a Category 2 storm, not strong enough to do such serious damage. Even so, the levees were breached. If Hurricane Katrina was not the culprit, what or who killed all those people and destroyed so much of the city?

Clouded Vision

*The Corps of Engineers can make the Mississippi
River go anywhere the Corps directs it to go.*
—DIRECTOR, CORPS OF ENGINEERS

The answer to the question of who killed the people of New Orleans has a long history. It begins 200 years ago, when the Army Corps of Engineers closed its eyes to the complex system that constitutes the Mississippi Delta's natural topography, cranked up the theory-making processes in its collective mind, and created a misconceived strategy to stop the Mississippi river from overflowing its banks during the spring rains. The end result of the Corps' thought processes was the decision to replace the Delta's natural structures—its meandering waters and branching tributaries—with straitjacket-like, no-outlet levees. The Corps proceeded to cast that theory in miles of concrete whose total length rivaled the Great Wall of China.

A no-outlet levee is just what its name implies: a pair of continuous barricades without weep holes through which water can exit. In the case of New Orleans, it restricts the river's flow to preordained channels and shuts off the yearly distribution of water, sediments, and nutrients critical to maintaining the Delta ecosystem. Like plaque built up in our arteries, the blocked levees deprived the Delta of its life blood, promoted an alarming buildup of fertilizer in the locked-in waters, and paved the way for one disaster after another. Each year, this foolhardy design fast-tracked 365,000 tons of fertilizer-infused sediment over the continental shelf into the Gulf of Mexico, where it produced dead zones the size of Rhode Island.[1] Instead of accumulating the sediment that the river used to deliver each spring and that replenished the levels of the Delta land, the Delta lost 2,500 square miles of territory.[2] Its marshes and islands slowly disappeared. Without these natural storm barriers, the already flawed levees, coupled with the action of the pent-up water between its walls, broke under Katrina's Category 2 storm surges.[3]

The Corps actually knew how the physics of the Delta ecosystem worked. Their spokesperson, James Eads, a civilian engineer on the Federal Government's Mississippi River Commission, stated that

> every atom of water is controlled by laws as fixed and certain as those which direct the majestic march of the heavenly spheres. Every phenomenon and apparent eccentricity of the river—its scouring and depositing action, its carving banks, the formation of the bars at its mouth, the effect of waves and tides of the sea upon its currents and deposits—is controlled

by laws as immutable as the Creator, and the engineer needs only to be insured that he does not ignore the existence of any of these laws to feel positively certain of the results he aims at.[4]

Yet, the Corps' theory that no-outlet levees would work deliberately flouted these laws and dismissed the natural structures those laws mandated. In short, the Corps believed they could outsmart fluid dynamics. The result was they eliminated the river's normal meandering structure and capped off its tributaries' ability to restore the fragile resources that sustained the Delta. Despite Captain Eads' statement, the Corps ignored the fact that confining the meanders of a river the size of the Mississippi would lead to retaliation. Confined waters turn meanders into whirling vortices that will eventually scour the ground under the concrete and bring the levees down.

By 1879, the Corps had built miles of no-outlet levees. Three years later, during the flood of 1882, the levees broke in 284 places and water flooded a seventy-mile swath of the Delta. In 1885, in spite of the destruction their no-outlet levees had wrought, the Corps again publicly announced that they were "distinctly committed to closing all outlets"—and that they "opposed the fallacy known as the 'Outlet System.'"[5] The problem with the Corps' policy is that the physical laws that govern rivers do not answer to government agencies or their theories. To deal with the floods, the Corps simply built higher and higher levees. By the 1920s, the levees had risen sixfold but still provided no guarantee of safety.

When 1927 brought an even greater flood, the levees had constricted water flow so severely that, when they collapsed, the pent-up waters broke free and destroyed the entire valley. In response, Congress passed the Flood Control Act of 1928, which ordered all sorts of mitigation: spillways, dams, higher levees, and dikes. By the time the Corps had installed these "improvements," their water-control system was housing and handling 25% more water than it had before the 1927 flood. By 1937, the Mississippi was encased in miles of levees that were longer and higher than China's Great Wall. As all this was occurring, the Delta was dying; it was starved for the sediment and nutrients that the cut-off tributaries no longer delivered. Its plant life shriveled, and its land sank lower and lower.

A river like the Mississippi typically does several related things. It flows in meanders, using the least energy possible, along the shortest, steepest route to the sea.[6] It switches its meandering course every so often to one that is more efficient, and it generates tributaries, which distribute sediment and nutrients across its flood plain that extend on either side, forming a delta. During the rainy season, rivers overflow and bring nutrients and sediments to the land along their banks.

Rivers do not operate according to theories. They operate according to the laws of fluid dynamics.[7] Before the Army Corps of Engineers intervened in the flow of the Mississippi, it meandered and branched from Minnesota to the Gulf of Mexico, and its tributaries spread over the entire Delta. But in the first half of the twentieth century, it became clear that the river was threatening to change course. If this unexpected change occurred, it would leave New Orleans high and dry, without a sea route to the Gulf. Congress ordered the Corps to stop Big Muddy in its tracks.

Controlling Nature: Eliminating Tributaries and Meanders

The river used to meander all over this flood plain.
People would move their tepees, and that was that.
—H. KASSNER, DIRECTOR, ARMY CORPS OF
ENGINEERS PUBLIC RELATIONS

In 1940, one of the Mississippi River's main tributaries, the Atchafalaya, offered a much steeper, more attractive route to the sea. Geologist Harold Fisk at Louisiana State University alerted the Army Corps that this inviting possibility might cause the Mississippi to switch course and merge with its former tributary.[8] This possibility was not unexpected. Over the centuries, all major rivers—the Yellow, Mekong, Po, Indus, Volga, Tigris, and Euphrates—have changed their courses by as much as four hundred miles. The Mississippi is no exception. The meander pattern not only weaves a river through the landscape, it guides it into new territories. In the Delta, this is known as Delta lobe switching, and it can encompass miles of territory. The Mississippi's main channel three thousand years ago is now Bayou Teche. Before the birth of Christ, this channel switched to the east. A thousand years later, it rerouted south. As the 1950s approached, the Mississippi's natural course was ripe to shift again, and the Atchafalaya was ready to incorporate it.[9] (I owe a debt to John McPhee for the facts—but not the analysis—that follows.)

If the Mississippi were allowed to merge with the Atchafalaya, it would relocate two hundred miles away. Baton Rouge would end up underwater and New Orleans would be left high and dry. Without this access, New Orleans, and the area's concentration of economic power—the "American Ruhr" of petrochemical, gas, and oil interests located along the banks of the Mississippi in and around New Orleans—would lose their access to the sea. The Army Corps of Engineers set out to prevent what Washington, DC saw as a looming economic disaster. It immediately defaulted to theories of control and conquer. They decided to prevent the coming debacle by replacing a critical natural meander 100 miles up the Delta from New Orleans (at the strategic confluence of the Mississippi, the Red River, and the Atchafalaya) with a two-hundred-thousand-ton, straight-walled concrete behemoth they called the Old River Control Structure. They bet against nature that they could make the Mississippi stay where it was.

The Corps made a film touting this project that declared that our economy depended on our winning the battle with a powerful adversary, Mother Nature. They were actually pitting themselves against the laws of physics. The meander form uses the least energy to flow the farthest because it piggybacks on the alternation of kinetic and potential energy that the river produces as it weaves back and forth. The Corps' plan to fight Mother Nature involved replacing this energy-conserving, natural meander with a straight, artificial wall that would bottle up the water's flow energy and create an enormous buildup of pressure. This Old River Control Structure would do more than disrupt the river's natural flow pattern. It would also invite disaster. Removing the meander and constricting the river's waters would cause turbulence that would create vortices. As the Corps' own Captain Eads pointed out, those vortices could eventually scour the earth out from under the wall and bring the whole structure down. Ignoring this possibility, the Corps began construction.

When an unrealistic straight-wall design was pitted against the natural fluid dynamics of a meandering waterway, the advantage was with the water. But the Corps was not about to capitulate. Brigadier General Thomas Sands reiterated the message of their public relations film by declaring, "Man against nature. That's what life is all about…Old River is a true representation of a confrontation with nature."[10] There were other points of view within the Corps. Leroy Dugas, who became flow manager at the Old River Control Station, remarked, when he was told of the project, "They were going to try to control the flow. I thought they had lost their marbles."[11] Dugas was not, however, in charge of design.

The Old River barricade went online in 1963. Ten years later, after the normally meandering river had banged itself back and forth against the sides of its straitjacket walls, it reasserted itself. In 1973, echoing the disaster of 1882, the Old River Control Structure vibrated into multiple pieces. The built-up turbulence had created spiral eddies that excavated the earth supporting the structure from under its walls. Eventually the water's action produced a hole the size of a football stadium. In April, a fisherman told Dugas that an eddy at the south end of the guide wall had become a whirlpool. He claimed the guide wall had moved, and Dugas told him he was seeing things. But when Dugas went to investigate, he agreed. When the Corps drilled holes into the structure and lowered a TV camera down into the hole, "they saw fish."[12]

After the Old River Control Structure failed, the Corps added three more spillways to the south. This enabled them to dump half the Mississippi's flow, a million cubic feet per second, and divert a flood from New Orleans and its environs. But when it came to installing the levees surrounding New Orleans proper, the Corps continued to install straight levees. They apparently did not learn from the problems at the Old River Control Structure. They discounted the vortices and turbulence that their designs produced, and continued to build no-outlet levees that eventually ringed the city.

During Katrina, these levees self-destructed. They were not only buffeted by the storm surge from the outside, but also by the trapped vortices from within. Because there were also flaws in their construction, the levees around New Orleans were a disaster waiting to happen. In contrast, the levees along the Mississippi had deeper footings and by and large followed the river's meandering contours; although some were overtopped, none of these were breached. But the story does not end here.

The Whole Is More Than the Sum of Its Parts

Actuality is through and through togetherness.
—ALFRED NORTH WHITEHEAD

In complex systems such as river deltas, the whole is more than the sum of its parts. The Mississippi Delta is a single ecosystem and every component of its river's branching structure—the spring rains and nutrient-rich sediment that feeds its plants—influences every other component. The Corps' no-outlet theory led to actions that partitioned the Mississippi Delta into parts. They then proceeded as if these parts—which were only separate in their minds—were unconnected to the whole area in which they were embedded. When they built a levee to protect one community or commercial enterprise, they gave little thought to that levee's relationship to what could happen to other communities or levees that were part of the same, larger ecosystem. This way of doing business may have prevented water from flooding a particular area at a particular time, but because it squeezed all that local water into less space, it simply moved the problem downstream, increasing flooding in another area.

For example, when the Corps built the Mississippi River–Gulf Outlet Canal (MRGO, known locally as Hurricane Alley), they neglected to consider its relationship to other levees built along its companion, the Intracoastal Waterway, and to the ecosystem around it. The Corps had long ago dredged and installed two yoked

shipping routes to the Gulf of Mexico—the Intracoastal Waterway
and the MRGO—that branched off from its longer companion.
MRGO was slashed into the coastal marshes by removing more soil
than was excavated for the Panama Canal. What started out as a
650-foot-wide channel morphed into a 2,500-foot-wide liquid highway that sucked saltwater into adjacent freshwater marshes, destroying thousands of acres of critical wetlands.[13]

But that was not the only problem that the construction of the
MRGO caused. This project broke another natural law—every
action has an equal and opposite reaction. If you restrict natural
water flow into a progressively narrower channel, the extra water you
concentrate will translate downstream. The T formed by the two
Gulf routes to the sea created a funnel six miles long that singlehand-
edly accelerated, enlarged, and channeled storm surges that rolled
across Lake Borgne, east of New Orleans, directly into the city. On
the morning that Katrina made landfall, the surge of water building
on Lake Borgne was eighteen feet high.

Ivar Van Heerden, deputy director of the Louisiana State
University Hurricane Center, wryly commented, "The federal
powers that be had inadvertently designed an excellent storm surge
delivery system—nothing less—to bring this mass of water with an
enormous load of potential energy directly into New Orleans."[14]
When the Corps decided to ignore the structural information that
specified the Delta topography, they disrupted the Mississippi
River's entire flow and caused "catastrophic structural failure" of
the levees designed to prevent the flooding of New Orleans.[15]

The latest news from the Mississippi Delta is that not only is it
sinking further below sea level as we speak, but it is also slipping like
a melting glacier into the Gulf. The American Geophysical Union
reports that the bedrock lying under the Gulf Coast is fracturing,
inch by inch, year by year, under the enormous weight of the sediment the no-outlet levees ended up channeling to and depositing
in the Gulf.[16] As the bedrock breaks away, Louisiana follows suit.[17]
Meanwhile, massive floods upriver are now occurring yearly. The latest proposed solution? Build bigger levees.[18]

Restoring a Meander

Let us give Nature a chance, she still knows her
business better than we do.

—MONTAIGNE

Between 1936 and 1937, the Army Corps of Engineers also straight-ened Cook Slough near the mouth of the Stillaguamish River, north of Seattle. They disconnected and abandoned the river's North Meander Slough, and the native salmon disappeared. When natu-ral meanders are removed from streams and rivers, the water's flow speed increases, log barriers that create the dams that shelter baby fish wash away, and fish populations plummet. But again, the Corps never connected the dots of this complex river system.

In 2004, the Snohomish County, Washington Public Works Surface Water Management Division worked with local volunteers and initiated the North Meander Restoration Project. They recon-nected the cut-off meander and provided an off-channel rearing and refuge habitat so that the tiny salmon fry could develop into adults, and the salmon populations, particularly those of the spring Chinook, could increase. Over three thousand feet of abandoned channel meander was reconnected to the Stillaguamish. Seventy thousand cubic yards of sediment buildup were excavated from the once cut-off meander. Seven hundred logs were put in place, recre-ating the floating and fixed jams that once provided refuge for the baby fish.

The Surface Water Management Division's 2009 *Project Effectiveness Program Report* states "fifteen different fish species and various larval, juvenile and adult life stages" have returned. "Juvenile Chinook are observed using the North Meander at densities that are comparable to other watershed studies for similar habitat types.... In addition to Chinook salmon, we caught Coho salmon (yearling and fry), steelhead, chum, cutthroat, and pink salmon within the North Meander channel."[19]

Of course, if the Corps had not straightened the river in the first place, Snohomish County would have saved a lot of money, time, and effort. If they had tracked the river's complex flow system, they would have seen that the meanders created the dams and pools necessary for the fish to prosper. In the same way, if the Corps had left the meanders in the Mississippi, maintained more of the Delta's natural ecosystem, and protected the barrier islands, New Orleans would not have ended up almost completely submerged in 2005, with so many people dead.

Structural Pattern Generators and Natural Structures

In matters of visual form we sense that nature plays favorites. Among her darlings are spirals, meanders, branching patterns and 120-degree joints. Those patterns occur again and again. Nature acts like a theatrical producer who brings the same players each night in different costumes for different roles.

—PETER STEVENS

The physical layout of a structure is, in effect, a pattern generator that both organizes such structures and provides the structural information that specifies them. That pattern is generative because it provides the basis for variations that maintain its core organization while tweaking it to conform to specific circumstances. For example, all trees are organized by the branching configuration. Oak trees are organized by a species-specific variation of that tree configuration, and the oak tree in your yard is a location-specific variation of the oak configuration. In this way one can see that what philosophers separate into "universals" and "particulars" are simply variations of the same configuration. These configurations act as reusable blueprints for the development and subsequent operations of all real-world phenomena. Because each basic configuration gives rise to an infinite number of variations, each particular entity adopts the variation that best suits its operations while simultaneously retaining and manifesting its unique identity.[20]

Branching

If mass is the measure of gravitation and energy is the measure of movement, information...is the measure of the organization of the material object.

—OLIVIER COSTA DE BEAUREGARD

Branching is one of Earth's most successful organizational structures. It provides the spatial layout that allows many disparate complex structures and systems such as trees, river deltas, and vascular systems to ply their trades. Trees, for example, branch both above and below ground because that geometry uses the least energy to acquire and distribute the nutrients and fluids that they need to grow and maintain themselves. A tree's above-ground branches create the scaffold that supports the leaf canopy necessary to conduct photosynthesis—a process that, via the chlorophyll in a tree's leaves, converts the sun's radiant energy into chemical energy, and thus, into tree food. Tree roots branch below ground, and as water evaporates from the leaves above, the tree becomes a passive pump that sucks in water and nutrients from the soil, and distributes them throughout its entire structure. But in order to survive assaults from winds and droughts, as each tree grows larger it must continually remodel itself in order to maintain its "dynamical similitude"—its state of harmony with the laws of space.

To accommodate gravity's invisible but persuasive forces of compression, tension, and shear, trees tailor their branching configuration to one that mirrors the diagram of the forces that create the equilibrium of space itself.[21] A tree's gravity-guided development is a graphic display of the potential energy locked into its jointed support system like the struts of a suspension bridge.[22] When that tree accesses nutrients and grows larger, it temporarily breaks this symmetry but then reorganizes itself by producing new branches in such a way that reinstates its balance on a larger scale, within the constraints of the branching pattern. Ultimately the laws of physics cap how large a tree can be; if at some point its proportions and properties cannot adapt and remodel sufficiently to accommodate its increased size, it will self-destruct.[23]

Branching provides the most efficient spatial layout for all other systems that require similar distribution services: lymph networks, pulmonary and kidney channels, and neural architecture, as well as economic and social systems such as markets that distribute goods and friendship circles that distribute information. In each case, the branching pattern does double duty as the structural information that reveals the identity and properties of the various phenomena it organizes.

Spirals

Each of my oars produces a pair of vortices, those spiral waves that drill into the surface, and smaller swirls burble out behind the boat.... My small liquid spirals spin the same shape as the deep gyre of water that circles the bay ... the same as the circular storms that roll over us from Siberia ... the same as the counter-clockwork current that spans the North Pacific Ocean.

—CHARLES WOHLFORTH

Spirals provide a second organizational blueprint for phenomena on all scales and in all places, from the double helix of DNA, to the snail's shell, to the ocean's whirlpools, and some galaxies in the sky. Spirals come into existence when the rates of growth of two adjacent surfaces are unequal. The slower growing surface is on the inside, and the faster growing surface curls around it. DNA forms its spiraling double helix because the edge bonds of the two columns of sugar and phosphate are of unequal length, and the longer one twists around the shorter. Similar to the way a tree branches in response to its own internal interactions and its local environmental input, there is no prior plan or central authority that causes the helical structure to emerge. The edge bonds of DNA simply follow the laws of fluid dynamics in league with the mandate to fit the most genetic material in the smallest amount of space.

Just as branching supports distribution systems, spirals support their own particular functions. They can, for example, operate as pressure pumps. Consider the heart of the zebra fish embryo. This tiny creature's blood starts to flow early in its development, and the pattern of that flow is instrumental in the formation of its minuscule heart. Vortices, the whirling dervishes of the spiral family (the same pattern that brought down Old River Control Structure), are produced by the fluid dynamics of the embryo's own blood pressure. As blood spurts from the fish's partially undeveloped atrium to its ventricle, it whirls itself into these persuasive patterns. These spiraling forms create a gravity-driven physical stress called shear that guides the fish's epithelial cells the way a sculptor molds clay.[24] These cells control the development of the embryo's heart, and their spiraling, shear-determined shape dictates the heart's final configuration and ultimate function.

Organisms that need help propelling themselves also recruit spiral vortices to give them an extra push.[25] For example, the moon jellyfish (*Aurelia aurita*) does not meet the stringent requirements of fluid dynamics, as its bell-shaped top is broader and flatter than those of its svelte, thimble-shaped, jet-propelled relatives. Its stolid form resists efficient forward motion. To make up for the extra drag that its shape incurs, the moon jellyfish recruits the vortex's power. This sea creature propels itself forward by using its muscles to squeeze water from its bell-shaped top in the form of a vortex. It also recoups energy from a second vortex that naturally forms when it relaxes its muscles and water rushes back into its bell. The collision of these two vortices produces enough power to compensate for the drag created by the moon jellyfish's broader shape.

We humans co-opt spirals to design things for ourselves. Bio-mechanist Frank Fish at Westchester University and his colleagues, Laurens Howle at Duke University, and Mark Murray and David Milosovik at the United States Naval Academy, researched how to duplicate the spiraling abilities of the humpback whale in order to build a small, agile submarine. The fifty-foot-long humpback manages to turn in tight, ten-foot circles.[26] These giants blow a hollow column of bubbles as they circle. They then swim in spirals up this vertical cylinder, dining on the shrimp and small fish that they have trapped within.

Professor Fish discovered that the whale's ability to swim in tight spirals was a function of the scalloped structure of their flippers. Lift (comparable to how an airplane wing rises) turned out to be 8% more with scalloped flippers than with smooth ones. Drag, the counterbalancing force that slows down anything gliding through water, turned out to be 32% less with scalloped flippers than with smooth ones. Fluid flowing off a smooth flipper would shunt a boat or whale off course, like a car taking a turn at too high a speed. But a more scalloped geometry keeps them within a tight circle. Professor Fish has parlayed the structure of the humpback whale flippers into constructing wind turbines that turn at lower wind speeds than competing models, yet use less energy to obtain the same output. This "biomimicry" design has hydroelectric applications and can also be used to turn energy-efficient ceiling fans, propellers, and mixing devices.

Spirals also structure air to provide the lift under airplane wings and the support for birds' migratory formations. They help propel the square boxfish swiftly through the water (which helps explain the low gas mileage of the boxy Honda Element).[27] On the other hand, vortices in combination with other factors emerge from turbulence, the wildly irregular motion of air and water currents that we see in liquids boiling on the stove, roiling ocean waters, and in streams spilling around rocks. A familiar case is the tornado. When factors such as heat, moisture, and electricity amplify to a certain point, they combine and create the initial conditions that trigger turbulent air to organize into vortices. A tornado co-opts cumulonimbus clouds to form its whirling air columns, and aided by downdrafts, pulls these columns to the ground. Temperature gradients—warm, humid air near the ground, and colder air above—are mixed and spun by shearing winds that change direction, speed, and height and pick up dust particles to produce a tornado's highly visible and dangerous vortex.[28]

Meanders

Meandering leads to perfection.
—LAO TZU

A third generator pattern, the meander, occurs when two surfaces vary periodically and thus weave back and forth, like a snake alternately tightening and relaxing its muscles on each side, or like a river alternating kinetic and potential energy as it oscillates its way to the sea.[29] Meanders not only organize water flow; they also lay down the weaving striations of the rock we see exposed in roadside cuts. They wend their way efficiently up mountain roads as well as through cosmic space. At the California Institute of Technology Jet Propulsion Laboratory (JPL), Martin Lo and his team were trying to reduce the energy expenditure of the spacecraft Genesis, which they planned to send aloft to sample the solar wind.[30] They needed to find an optimum, least-energy-use path through the cosmos. The problem was the gravitational tug-of-war formed by the sun, Moon, and Earth. The scientists on the project calculated the best route by taking advantage of energy-efficient tubular pathways that they dubbed the "interplanetary superhighway." This superhighway is a meander that, in weaving its way through space, avoids these gravitational territorial disputes while being energy efficient.

Soon after this research was published, Charles Jaffe, a chemist at West Virginia University in Morgantown, noticed that the space route plotted for Genesis bore an uncanny resemblance to the path taken by some interesting atomic-level items called ionized Rydberg electrons when they travel around protons. On both the cosmological and atomic levels, apparently, when moving things need to expend the least energy, the meander is the most efficient route. Jaffe is now collaborating with JPL staff using statistical chemistry techniques to plot the path of asteroids through space.

Six-Sided Symmetry

Complex objects, whether living or not, are produced
by evolutionary processes in which two kinds of fac-
tors are involved: the constraints that, at every level
specify the rules of the game and define what is pos-
sible within those systems; and the historical circum-
stances that determine the actual course of events and
control the actual interactions between systems.

—FRANÇOIS JACOB

The spatial organization of earthly items is neither random nor arbitrary. It is inevitable, which is why their physical structures provide such accurate information. The molecules in ice crystals, for example, transform into snowflakes by following their own built-in penchant for six-sided symmetry. These crystals develop into snowflakes according to the constraints of space as they travel from the molecular level of cloud formations, to the terrestrial level of your lapel. On its journey down, a snowflake comes into being through the temperature, humidity, and the atmospheric dust it encounters. By embodying these atmospheric influences, a snowflake that starts out as homogenous specks of ice ends up a wonder of intricately ordered sixfold symmetry. Within the constraints of this spatial pattern, these various environmental inputs combine to make each snowflake different. Disturbances that ruffle the air as a developing snowflake descends carry each one along a slightly different path that includes unique dust particles and wind gusts. Each snowflake is, in effect, a record of all the obstacles and constraints that it encounters on its journey, molded by its molecular mandate for six-sided symmetry.

This mandate, as well as those for branching and meanders, comes from nature's demand for efficient function: using the least energy to do the most work to obtain the maximum results. The quintessential example of this efficient structural formation is the beehive. Bees not only communicate with one another about the location of food by doing a spatial waggle-dance of figure eights, they also adopt the most efficient structural arrangement for both their living quarters and their storage facilities—the six-sided symmetry of hexagonal cells. Hexagons offer the strongest structure, for the least material and energy used, that provides the most space for the honey they produce. These amazing structures emerge from the interaction of the bees' ability to produce wax, their pheromone communication system that informs each one to do what her neighbor is doing, and nature's passion for energy efficiency.

In sum, each of these four generator patterns abets the fittest, least energetic, and most probable solutions for particular real-world items and circumstances. Meanders would not suit a tree; while branches can take a spiral path up the trunk, their shape is needed to distribute nutrients from the largest limb to the tiniest twig. Nature may sometimes appear inscrutable or overwhelming to our conscious minds, with their parts-oriented perspective and simple representations, but it is quite organized and understandable from the spatial and temporal perspective of the structural information that our senses evolved to parse. Chapter 5 documents this structural information by reviewing Earth's geometry, and the geometric patterns that both animals and people use to communicate with one another.

5

Reality's Geometry

Wave patterns on the ocean differ from the waves written in the sand and buried in the rock only by the tempo of their changes. What appears permanent, bedrock itself, seems so only because of the short span of our lives and our attention.

—CHARLES WOHLFORTH

AT 5:36 P.M. on March 27, 1964, a 9.2 moment magnitude earthquake erupted fifty-six miles west of Valdez, Alaska, and seventy-five miles east of Anchorage at a depth of sixteen miles. "Immediately following the quake, long-period seismic waves traveled around the earth for several weeks. Basically the whole earth vibrated (rang) like a church bell."[1] The earthquake lasted four minutes. In that time it liquefied the land along the coast, pulled huge swaths of territory out to sea, and triggered tsunamis that remade the coastline. It was the largest earthquake ever recorded in the Northern Hemisphere and the second largest in history. Centuries of the Pacific Plate's northwestward motion, compressing and warping the earth's crust along the southern coast of Alaska, finally snapped back in a sudden southeastward movement. Along the quake zone, the Pacific Plate slid an average of twenty-nine feet under the North American Plate and was accompanied by vertical displacement over an area of about 323,000 square miles, ranging from about thirty-eight feet of uplift to about 7.5 feet of subsidence that covered 177,700 square miles."[2] Prince William Sound, Kodiak Island and its island group, the Chugach Mountains, and most of the Kenai Peninsula were involved.

The open-ocean tsunamis that followed produced waves up to 220 feet at Valdez Inlet. Landslides both on land and underwater triggered local tsunamis throughout Prince William Sound. These smaller waves wiped out whole communities and stripped the tree cover from the land as high as 110 feet above the water. The indigenous village of Chenaga was washed away, and the town of Valdez was abandoned and rebuilt on top of solid rock a few miles to the west. In these ways, the earthquake and its subsequent tsunamis wiped out whatever changes we humans had made and restored the land to its natural forms. As Charles Wohlforth wrote:

> The sea's mysterious intelligence remembered the beach's shape from before the earthquake.... through a complex, many-step process, gradually refocused back into the same patterns, until each grain had been placed accurately in the geometry that had existed before.[3]

Even as the coastline shifts its position and our property lines dissolve in the actions of the sea, reality reasserts itself. At every level creatures detect the inevitable geometry of this universal structural language, and by reading the meaning inherent in earth's structures all living beings are able to self-organize, self-sustain, and interact with both the inanimate world and one other. In the same sense, our reciprocally structured perceptual systems and their associated neural systems are organized to access and relay that information. It is as if on every level, starting with single-celled organisms such as bacteria, a geometric language of phenomena tells nature's tales.

Bacteria's Quorum Sensing

A gene is presumably to be regarded as a question to which the answer is provided by its neighborhood.
—GREGORY BATESON

Single-celled organisms such as bacteria chat with one another by releasing molecular chemical messages called auto-inducers that also present themselves in geometric patterns.[4] For example, Bonnie

Bassler at Princeton University showed that one of the primary goals of the common seagoing bacteria, *Vibrio harveyi*, is to inform their cohorts that they are in the neighborhood and ready to form a quorum that will support group action. Using chemically induced signals, these typically separate creatures communicate with one another and begin to congregate. When they reach sufficient numbers, they form a decision-making quorum and behave in tandem. These tiny creatures act as a goal-directed community, much like an ant colony that uses chemical pheromones to communicate among themselves to build their nest.[5] Rather than responding to chemical odors like ants, however, *Vibrio harveyi* bacteria turn on regulator genes that guide their reciprocally tuned actions. These genes remain dormant as long as a bacterium lives the single life, but they turn on when an aggregate reaches the critical density. At that point, their mass acts like a switch that triggers single bacteria to produce enzymes, which then emit photons of beautiful blue light like a Christmas tree! Bacteria can also communicate among their various species because their geometric signaling system is multilingual—their molecules are the words of their shared language. Our immune cells use a similar, geometrically patterned chemical language as they create protein patterns that inform one another what is happening in our bodies.

Immune Cells Communicate Using Structural Configurations

The novelty is that we reveal a potential communication, involving the neurotransmitter serotonin, between immune cells that is normally only found between neurons.

—GERARD AHERN

Our immune system is a prime example of a complex system whose components—B and T cell lymphocytes, antibodies, and macrophages—patrol the body and form self- organized cooperative alliances to attack invading predators such as unfriendly bacteria. This system "can be viewed as a chemical signaling-processing network in which the recognition of an invader by one cell triggers a cascade of signals among cells that put into play a complex response."[6] Each cell has receptor molecules on its surface that receive information. Whether a receptor binds to a molecule "depends on whether their physical shapes match sufficiently."[7] Just as we communicate our feelings and intentions to others using the configurations produced by our body movements and facial expressions, our immune cells communicate with one another using a lexicon of protein patterns.

This marvel of cellular signaling not only reveals the reciprocity between our cells, but also demonstrates the interactive operations of our body. Since most of us are not sick, we might conclude that our bodies are typically free of malevolent organisms. Not so. Our bodies are continually under siege by destructive invaders. Until the 1990s, we knew little about how this undercover warfare was conducted. However, given the rapidity of our immune cells' ability to dispatch alien invaders, and the fact that it often takes many cells to accomplish this feat, several scientists proposed that these cells not only "talk" with one another, but that they must also listen to the messages of other body tissues that are in trouble.

In 1995, Abraham Kupfer of the National Jewish Medical and Research Center in Denver stunned the immunological community at the Keystone Symposia by presenting a video of three-dimensional images of actual immune cell interactions.[8] He showed that when immune cells run into diseased cells, they put out the word to their colleagues that they need backup to help eradicate these dangerous invaders. By using protein patterns that their membranes manufacture, immune cells that read the same pattern language signal one another, get the message, and show up to help stamp out the problem.

Just as our perceptual system is structured to perceive configurations that distinguish our friends from our foes so that we can welcome the one and avoid the other, our immune cells have the capacity to instantly recognize aliens so that they can marshal forces to eradicate them in a timely fashion. To keep up with changing conditions, immune pattern production is dynamic, which allows its protein arrangements to continuously transform, signaling success or failure, as the guerilla warfare against alien invaders progresses. Since Kupfer's pioneering work, so many studies have been done on cellular communication that the professional journal, *Science*, has a special online archive of this work (Science Signaling, the Signal Transduction Knowledge Environment, at http://stke.sciencemag.org/).

Volatile Compounds Send Structured Aromatic Messages

More than 7000 flavor volatiles have been identified and catalogued from food and beverages...a small subset [from each plant] generates a "flavor fingerprint" that helps animals and humans recognize appropriate foods and avoid poor and dangerous food choices.

—F. A. GOFF AND H. J. KLEE

Perhaps the most fascinating and little-known use of structural information occurs between plants that use mutually understood, spatially deployed patterns of smell.[9] These aromatic configurations become airborne as volatile compounds and modulate such real-world interactions as pollination, defense, and nutrition. For example, when deer graze on sagebrush, the damaged plants emit a particular smell that is detected by neighboring wild tobacco plants. The tobacco immediately girds up its defenses by emitting an odor that repels deer. This is more than a two-way conversation between the sagebrush and the tobacco. It is a three-way relationship among the sagebrush, the tobacco, and the deer. The tobacco eavesdrops on the sagebrush's encounter with the deer and uses that information to protect itself by emitting a foul smell. In addition, the release and volatility of these foliar compounds interact with other factors such as temperature, moisture, wind direction, and light. This locates the deer, plant behavior, and patterned odors in an even larger, dynamic, and more complex ecosystem.[10]

Human beings also parse the information in volatile compounds, many of which are critical to our health. The scents that vegetables emit "provide important information about the nutritional make-up of foods."[11] In the tomato, for example, each volatile is linked to an essential nutrient.[12] Our preference for a particular wine also relies on the complex of volatiles that results from the interaction of the type of grape, its environment, and its cultivation technique that the French call the wine's *terroir*.[13]

Animal–Environment Reciprocities

*Let it be borne in mind how infinitely close fitting
are the mutual relations of all organic beings to
each other and to their physical conditions of life.*

—CHARLES DARWIN

Frogs

All creatures seek out structural opportunities that match their needs, and complex systems, such as ecosystems with their subsystems of niches, provide those matches. For example, Borneo tree-hole frogs fashion mating calls by choosing a hole to inhabit and then calibrating their call to the size of that hole. They raise and lower their call's pitch until they produce a frequency that resonates with the size of the cavity they have chosen.[14] The tree-hole frog also chooses cavities that contain puddles of water because the liquid enhances the sound level of their calls.

In a controlled experiment, David Ingle at Harvard University did an elegant study with a little green frog.[15] Ingle placed a barrier between this frog and its food. The barrier was perforated by several variously shaped openings, which the frog could see from a sitting position. When the frog jumped up to reach the food, however, it did not choose the opening that matched its squat, seated little body; instead, it used the one that matched the shape of its body in flight (which resembled a flat green pancake). While seated, the frog was able to calculate the parameters of the opening that would reciprocate the shape of its airborne body—a remarkable feat.

Crows

David Attenborough filmed an amusing example of a complex system on a road way in Australia that involved the automatic sequencing of traffic lights, the reciprocal and purposeful behavior of crows to those lights, moving cars, crosswalks, and nuts.[16] Crows have a long history of cracking nuts by dropping them on hard surfaces such as rocks. A group of crows in Sydney perceived that a far more reliable affordance for cracking nuts was specified by the configurations produced by roads and cars. The crows began to drop their nuts in the areas of the road where cars would run over them and crack them open. Although this was a surefire method of cracking nuts, it was also dangerous, because the crows had to dart in and out of oncoming traffic to retrieve their nuts. So they adjusted their strategy and turned to an even better affordance: roads with traffic lights and crosswalks, where the cars stopped periodically when the light turned red. The crows then began to drop their nuts in the crosswalks of these roads when the light was green and the cars were moving. As soon as the light turned red and the cars stopped, the crows would waddle across the crosswalk with the rest of the pedestrians and retrieve their nutmeats from the shells the cars had cracked open.

The Hawk–Goose Configuration

Ethologist Konrad Lorenz, who was followed about by a gaggle of geese that had imprinted on him at birth and concluded he was their mother, did a seminal study on the effect of such structural information on fear responses in goslings. He designed a two-dimensional cardboard cutout that simulated two birds. When this cutout was sailed overhead in one direction, it resembled the configuration and cast the shadow of a goose, but when it was was sailed overhead in the other direction, it appeared to be a hawk. The goslings cowered when the "hawk" shadow configuration was flown above their nest and ignored the shadow configuration that was cast by the "goose." This simple geometric configuration elicited the same response from the goslings as a real hawk, showing that it was the informative configuration that carried the critical information that specified hawk to these babies.[17]

Ethologists Niko Tinbergen and D. J. Kuenen used geometric configurations to study the gaping response in thrush nestlings.[18] Baby thrushes open their mouths to beg for food (gape) as soon as they spot their parents. Tinbergen and Keunen presented the nestlings with the choice of two sizes of cardboard circles to simulate their parent's heads. The baby birds gaped for food to the larger circle in preference to the smaller one. But when the circle was attached to a body shape, Tinbergen and Keunen found that the nestlings would gape to the smaller size circle as long as it exhibited a particular proportion to the body. It was not the size of the head per se, but the ratio of the head size to the body size, that constituted this informative pattern. Since parents probably come in a range of sizes and proportions, such a response to the ratio would cover the entire range, while absolute size would not. Recall that it is people's unique proportions that sum to the movement patterns that specify their identity and actions, not their size or shape. Nature seems to choose information dimensions that are reusable and serviceable in many situations.

Mating, Foraging, and Escaping

Different bird species also use all sorts of amazing movement configurations to attract mates and conduct their courtship rituals: albatross dance and fence, ravens look away and raise their bills, gulls head-flag, and male greylag geese raise their heads and wings and approach a female after driving off competing males. Most amazing are the birds that imitate each other's movements as if they had been trained for a chorus line. To see two upright waterfowl running on the top of the water in sync with one another as the water sprays up from their rapidly paddling feet puts Valentine chocolates to shame.[19,20]

Animals also use structural layouts to increase their efficiency. Deer forage in meander patterns to cover the most territory using the least energy (the same reason why rivers meander in their run to the sea). Rabbits flee predators by using a faster, meandering route that gives them wiggle room from easy capture because their weaving course makes their exact location less predictable. Stickleback fish meander together like tango dancers to facilitate mating. Configured information is so compelling that birds will change their instinctual migration patterns rather than change the information they use to migrate.

Indigo Bunting Migration

Steven Emlen, professor of Behavioral Ecology at Cornell, raised fledgling indigo buntings inside a planetarium where the ceiling simulated the complex system of stars and planets that are visible across the sky.[21–23] He rotated that ceiling to change where the stars were located. When he released the fledglings into the real world, they navigated according to the rotated planetarium, not the actual sky, indicating that the celestial configuration under which they were raised, not a built-in instinct, orchestrated their migration patterns. Buntings are not born with the night sky etched into their brains. Rather, they are born with the ability to read the geometric language that patterns the sky above them. As we saw in chapter 3, many years ago Edward Tolman described such abilities in rats and called them "cognitive maps."[24] For birds, the map in the world that matches the map in the brain may be organized by magnetic fields. Recent research shows that migratory songbirds can read the geometry of electromagnetic patterns and migrate along Earth's electromagnetic fields.[25]

Professor Henrick Mouritsen at the University of Oldenberg and his colleagues showed that there is a visual pathway between the eye and brain that allows migratory birds to actually see the configurations of the earth's magnetic field.[26,27] Previous research isolated photoreceptor molecules in the bird's retina called cryptochromes that provide information about these birds' orientation in space relative to the magnetic field.[28–30] Cryptochromes are linked to night vision, which may explain how birds can fly around the clock. These same molecules have been found in humans as well. There is as yet no evidence that we can sense patterns in magnetic fields, but it would be fascinating to find that humans can perceive such information in electromagnetic spectra beyond the wavelengths of visible light. One indication that this may be possible is that there are magnetic bones containing iron oxide in our sinuses.[31]

Human–Environment Affordances

An affordance, according to perceptual psychologist J. J. Gibson, who first pointed them out, is an "opportunity for action" for a particular creature (such as the layout of a level surface to sit or walk upon, or the configuration of a bush to hide behind).[32] Like an economy that provides the structure within which we can trade real goods (such as wheat and pork bellies), but that has no physical heft, an affordance is not an abstract category that exists in our heads. Rather, it is the reciprocal fit between your invariant structure and the invariant structure of an item in your environment, and is specified by structural information. As such, an affordance is not a physical entity such as a tree; it is the information that reveals all the useful properties of that tree that support various actions. For example, a tree's branches afford climbing to escape predators or to reach fruit; its canopy affords shade to shelter under on a hot day. A low wall with a flat top can afford a tired jogger more support and a better place to sit than a picket fence. When a jogger perceives the flat-topped wall, she does not see it as an example of the general conceptual category we call walls. Rather, she perceives the layout of its structure and proportions as matching her own posterior parts and affording a resting place.

Affordances specify the reciprocal relationship between invariant structures—one belonging to the environment, the other to a person or animal—that fit together like a hand in a glove or a jigsaw piece in the larger puzzle. When you look at an object such as a chair, for example, you do not necessarily perceive its features—the spokes of a Windsor chair or the metal frame of an Eames chair—unless you are a furniture dealer. Typically you only perceive the affordance of sitting down that it offers. When you enter a room that contains various chairs, you are likely to head for the one whose structure best matches your own. That match *means* comfort and a chance to get off your feet. Thus, "to detect affordances is to detect meaning."[33] As Scott Kelso, director of the Center for Complex Systems, points out, "What could be more meaningful to an organism than the information that specifies the coordinative relations among its parts or between itself and its environment."[34]

An affordance can even tell you something that seems intangible, such as how much energy you need to perform a task. In a fascinating pair of experiments, ecological psychologist Bill Warren at Brown University showed that by simply looking at the black-and-white photographs of sets of stairs, we can perceive how difficult each set would be for us to climb.[35] Warren showed people photographs that varied the height of stair risers—the vertical part of each stair that supports the horizontal tread on which we place our feet as we climb. Varying the stair risers in turn varies the staircase's steepness and thus its degree of difficulty to climb. The results of Warren's experiment were that participants with different leg lengths chose stairs with different riser heights. The steepness of stairs may be a physical fact to someone with a tape measure, but the participants in Warren's experiment perceived steepness as a structural relationship between their own leg length and the steepness of a particular set of stairs. The longer their leg length, the higher the riser they chose, and thus the steeper the stairs. To corroborate these results, Warren built actual stairs that matched the dimensions of the pictured stairs. The same participants actually climbed all these sets of stairs while Warren tested how many calories each one burned while climbing each set. The stairs that required the least energy to climb turned out to have the same riser height as the photographed stairs that each participant had originally chosen as the easiest for them to climb. Each person was able to perceive the invariant structure of the set of stairs that best matched their own invariant structure and that afforded them the least energy expenditure to climb. One might consider this study to be about the geometrics of energy use.

Perceiving and Representing Structural Information

*Our cognitive and perceptual categories, given to us
prior to individual experience, are adapted to the
environment for the same reason as the horse's hoof is
suited to the plains, and the fin of the fish is adapted
to the water before the fish hatched from its egg.*

—KONRAD LORENZ

From infancy on we are primed to know much of the world with which we coevolved without having to think about it.[36,37] What experience does for us is to expand our sensory reach. This capacity does not necessarily give us more to think about, but it does lead to an increased ability to know what is going on without thinking about it. That may be why a great deal of our behavior occurs successfully on autopilot. The assumption that we need "higher mental processes" to organize our perceptions of the world comes in part from our unfounded assumption that the terrestrial world in which we live is made of a multitude of separate objects that we must mentally reassemble and insert back into the context from which we abstracted them.

It only adds to our confusion when various disciplines that rely on this atomistic perspective claim special access to reality. For example, there are particle physicists who claim that ultimate reality exists only on the atomic level or below. Since we live on the terrestrial level, you can test these claims. Try sitting down on an atom or eating a quark. Practically speaking, we evolved to live in, and are structured to know, the terrestrial level of reality in which we live. We do not live on an atomic level that requires a cyclotron to bring its constituents to our attention.

Most neuroscience texts fail to make their parts perspective clear. Even though they may state that the brain is a complex system, their actual studies, and the results they report, come from studying parts of the brain and trying to locate where particular functions occur. Although we do have different areas of the brain devoted to vision, motor, and other functions, all these areas operate in tandem, exhibit enormous plasticity, and respond to the same structural information. In this sense, where something happens in the brain may be irrelevant to what we know of that something in the world.[38] If one part of our brain is temporarily out of commission, another part can often take over its role. Studies that are undertaken using a parts perspective do not typically report findings based on people's responses to the world itself, but rather to "stimuli" that researchers create to stand in for the parts of the world they have abstracted from their context to investigate (e.g., rows of dots, visual illusions, rapidly presented pictures, questionnaires, or nonsense syllables).

Experiments that probe or scan parts of the brain and record static snapshots of where our blood flows or our neurons activate can tell us how we respond to these stimuli, but not how we respond to the real world. Such studies cannot tell us whether such responses occur when our body, including our brain, operates as the complex whole system it is, a system that is operating in a complex world. This parts-based input-output model treats the brain as if it is a machine and has led to endless attempts to show that it is like a computer. Although we can program computers to learn, they still need us to program them and make necessary changes in those programs. This process is orderly and linear and can be predicted. In contrast, our brain is a complex system that operates nonlinearly, and that is why, in distinction to computers, we have "aha!" experiences where something totally new and unexpected emerges from our brain's complex operations.

It is not that laboratory research yields no information. It is more that the information it does yield sometimes has the feel of self-fulfilling prophecy. If you start out believing that the world can be separated into parts, or that real items and stimuli created to represent those items are somehow equivalent, then the experiments you design will investigate things from that view. But on a terrestrial level, nothing is made of separate parts, everything is interconnected with everything else, and ignoring that fact involves constructing an impoverished universe in one's head. Without our necessarily realizing it, our reliance on linear forms of mathematics and Euclidean geometry to represent and model the world forms another barrier to our realization that we can know the world directly. Since the

1970s, however, there has been an alternative nonlinear mathematics: fractal geometry, which does a far more credible job of simulating the world's structures more realistically.[39] Fractal geometry does not try to make its forms conform to a preconceived model or category. As Mandelbrot's protégé, Nassim Taleb, testily pointed out, to build models, you have to fudge your assumptions and manufacture phony premises.[40] Instead, fractal geometry uses algorithms and computer graphics programs to coax the complex structures of the world—its trees, mountains, river systems, and coastlines, as well as our human-made inventions (such as stock markets and their fluctuations)—to emerge in geometric form onto a screen.

Benoit Mandelbrot's Fractal Geometry

For me the most important instrument of thought is the eye. It sees similarities before a formula has been written to identify them. We will recognize fractal patterns intuitively long before we specify them logically and mathematically.

—BENOIT MANDELBROT

Benoit Mandelbrot's fractal geometry emerged directly from his perceptions of the natural world, not from a set of axioms, as is more typical in mathematics. He was fond of pointing out that clouds are not spheres and mountains are not cones, and that these "smoothed over" representations completely abandon the actual roughness, irregularities, and complexities that are characteristic of these items in the real world (just as our minds categorize complex, unique items as members of general categories in which unique peculiarities have been eliminated). In a memorial obituary for Mandelbrot in *Science*, Otto Pietgen wrote that Mandelbrot's seminal book, *The Fractal Geometry of Nature*, "opened our eyes to patterns in nature on all scales and across diverse disciplines…finance, medicine, chemistry, physics, earth science, cosmology, computer science, astronomy, many of the engineering disciplines, and of course, mathematics."[41] In a sense, Mandelbrot's fractal geometry is to conventional

Euclidean geometry what the direct perception of the structural configurations that specify real-world items is to our limited pictorial representations of those items. While our senses calibrate a phenomenon's parameters, and relay that information directly to our right hemisphere and other associated body locations, we produce fractal images by iterating (repeating) an algorithm in a computer program over and over until the properties of worldly items such as trees or mountain ranges emerge onto our computer screen. Fractal images depict the world much more realistically than Euclidean geometry because they follow the roughness of its parameters instead of eliminating them (as we eliminate many of an entity's properties when we categorize it).

For example, consider the problem of measuring a coastline to make decisions about defending the country's shores or shipping its goods. Traditional measurements of physical phenomena typically use whole numbers, which reduce the complexities of those things to fit the limitations of our numbering system. Fractals, as their name implies, use fractions that lie between the whole numbers 1 and 2 to measure uneven structures such as trees, mountains, or coastlines. Fractal measurements (called *fractal dimensions*) can record, for example, the many ins and outs of a particular coastline while whole numbers cannot. When fractal dimensions are used, we get a much more accurate measurement of the coastline in question. Thus the coast of England has a fractal dimension of 1.26, while the much more serrated coast of Norway is considerably longer and has the higher fractal dimension of 1.52, giving it many more affordances for mooring boats or running contraband.

Possibly the most useful characteristic of fractals in helping us know the world is their ability to depict self-similarity. Self-similarity reduces our perceptual load because it is the repetition of the same structural layout on all scales from big to small, which limits what we need to learn to one pattern with multiple sizes. For example, if you break off the tip of a branch on your Christmas tree and compare that small section, with its tiny branching layout, to the whole tree, with its much larger branching layout, you will see that the structure of the branch tip is approximately the same as the structure of the whole tree (or any other part of the tree), from the smallest twigs on top to the largest limbs at the base.

Unexpectedly, self-similarity is also a property of much larger systems. For example, the same self-similarity that we see on all scales within a particular tree (i.e., the relationship of any of its branches to its whole structure) also characterizes the relationship of individual trees to the larger forest system of which they are a part. When James H. Brown, Brian J. Enquist, and Geoffrey B. West at the Santa Fe Institute studied trees and the forests that they constituted, they found that self-similarity minimizes energy use in both individual trees and in whole forests.[42]

The within-tree efficiency of self-similarity repeats itself in the distribution of single trees within a whole forest. Individual trees with the same mass (the sum of their branches and leaves) are scattered throughout a mature forest in such a way that the distance between each tree is proportional to the diameter of its trunk. This proportional relationship echoes the proportional relationships of the branches of each individual tree to that tree as a whole. The result is that all the trees in a forest are distributed in one large fractal pattern that follows the same self-similar scaling, as each tree's branches follow in relation to the whole tree that they constitute.[43] This arrangement minimizes energy use, maximizes growth, and provides structural information about trees and forest systems on all levels of inquiry. All this information is displayed in one basic energy-efficient, gravity-driven, fractal branching pattern that simply varies in size on different scales. Within this structural information system, each tree species adopts its own variation of the branching pattern with its own fractal dimension that allows us to distinguish one tree species from a simple variation, rather than having to recognize an entirely new structural layout.

Self-similarity can be seen in structures throughout our planet: from the immensity of the cracking faults in the earth's crust to the hairline cracks in a glazed cup; from the devastation pattern of a huge earthquake to that of an avalanche in a child's sand pile; from the whirling dervish of the sky-to-earth tornado to the swirling water exiting a bathtub drain; or to the neighbor boy's face that peers out of the portrait of his great-great-grandfather—fractal patterns such as the meander, the spiral, and branching combine and permute, nest and fold, repeat and reconfigure in self-similar fractal hierarchies that reveal the identity and functions of all the structures we see. The same patterns are repeated over and over in telescoping sizes as they structure phenomena on different scales, down to the minute branching dendrites of our neurons, which look like delicate twigs, and the double helixes of our DNA, which resemble miniature pairs of tornadoes. In league with space, evolution has endlessly and continuously provoked diversity from existing forms. The narrowest rivulet expands to become a stream and then a river, all with the same form of organization—the meander.

Our Fractal Brain

The existence of these patterns (fractals) challenges us to study forms that Euclid leaves aside as being formless, to investigate the morphology of the amorphous. Mathematicians have disdained this challenge, however, and have increasingly chosen to flee from nature by deriving theories unrelated to anything that we can see and hear.

—BENOIT MANDELBROT

We perceive the dynamic configurations that specify the structures, systems, and processes around us, and we organize that knowledge in an open system of fractal neural networks. Those networks are capable of switching instantly from one pathway to another in response to the changing world around us. One way to consider this state of affairs was laid out in a research project by Danielle Bassett and her colleagues at the National Institute of Mental Health. They demonstrated that the neuron assemblies in our brain operate in the same, self-similar fractal patterns as the larger world and its phenomena.[44]

Building on the "small world, neural-network-simulations" of Steven Strogatz at Cornell and Duncan Watts at New York University,[45] Bassett had people lie under a "small world" network of sensors while she measured the magnetic field produced by the electrical discharges of neurons at 275 points on their scalps. She then monitored her participants' neuron activity and recorded their responses as they tapped their fingers when they were presented with a square geometric shape. The perception of the squares generated six types of brain waves that differed in frequency (how fast they oscillated), but all frequencies displayed the same self-similar fractal branching pattern. Bassett proposes that such synchronized (patterned) dynamic brain activity is the brain's typical response to perceptual information, even a simple square. Walter Freeman, a neurophysiologist at the University of California at Berkeley, has speculated that the self-similar structure of our brainwaves supports "split-second" switches among related neural networks that act as an information distribution system.[46] Because each of the frequency channels that Bassett isolated can both transmit information and switch back and forth among themselves, their interactions are self-organizing. There is no need for a cognitive control center to direct their activities. Rather, they control each other's activities as they receive directly perceived information. The important implication of Bassett's work is that both the structure and functions of our brain, as well as the information that we perceive from the world, follow the same physical laws. Those same laws guide the development and operations of all the phenomena on our planet, including ourselves.

Fractals, and the generator patterns discussed in chapter 4, constitute geometric languages that, with limited combinatorial alphabets, can describe an infinite number of things on many scales. Fractals use the language of nonlinear mathematical geometry to model real-world entities. Generator patterns provide the nonlinear language of gravity, dynamic relationships, and energy flow that French physiologist Étienne-Jules Marey called "the language of phenomena." The patterns that constitute this universal language are the same ones that produce the structures that constitute our world. The generator patterns that structure the earth's phenomena and fractal patterns we produce on computers that reflect those phenomena are both examples of the type of information to which our perceptual systems are structured to respond.[47-53]

In chapter 6, I recount case studies of various experts who use structural information to understand and solve the problems they confront at work, and show how their expertise depends on such use.

6

Experts' Experts

To understand phenomena, one must have a method-
ology that is transparent to it, not one that replaces it.
—SHIRYU MORITA

ON FEBRUARY 3, 2002, the New England Patriots defeated the
14-point-favorite St. Louis Rams 20 to 17 in one of the biggest upsets
in Super Bowl history. The Patriots had never won a Super Bowl before
and their circumstances were precarious at best: Dick Rehbein, their
quarterbacks coach, had died of a heart attack earlier that year; Terry
Glenn, their leading receiver, was benched; and their starting quarterback, Drew Bledsoe, was out due to a hit by Jets linebacker Mo Lewis
that sheared off a blood vessel. Bledsoe's replacement was Tom Brady, a
sixth-round draft pick in his second season with not much of a record.

What no one knew was that Tom Brady was a perceptual expert.
His ability to track the continually transforming structural layout of
the game in play without stopping to think about it was superb. With
a scant minute and a half left in a tied game, Brady opened his final
plays with three completions to running back J. R. Redmond. The ball
was now on the Patriots' 41-yard line, and with thirty-three seconds
left, Brady completed a 23-yard pass to wide receiver Troy Brown and
followed it up with a 6-yard pass to tight end Jeremy Wiggins. This
put the Patriots' kicker Adam Vinatieri in position to make the winning 48-yard field goal.

If Brady had tried to pull off this last-second win by considering
all the important variables for each pass, he'd still be on the 41-yard
line sifting through alternatives. Since it was impossible to think

about that many things in the limited time available, Brady's expertise had to rest on his extraordinary ability to use structural information, to perceive the interactions of all the components of the game's complex system, while still seeing that game as a single, continually transforming event, not an assemblage of separate parts.

Yet on October 14, 2012, despite Brady's unbelievable skills and the fact that he threw a career high of fifty-eight passes for 395 yards, Seattle Seahawks receiver Sidney Rice hauled in a 46-yard touchdown pass from rookie quarterback Russell Wilson (who threw for 293 yards, his own career high) to give the Seahawks a stunning 24 to 23 victory over the Patriots in the final minute. I saw this game. The Patriots played well and Brady was extraordinary as usual, but the Seahawks had an over-the-top team drive that was palpable, and it drove them home. Regardless of the skill of both teams' individual quarterbacks, a football team is a complex system that requires all its components to be working together, and on this day, the Seahawks were the better organized team.

But the world is still a random affair. During the playoffs, on Sunday, January 13, 2013, the Seahawks were three touchdowns behind the Atlanta Falcons, and despite a heroic sequence in the last minutes of the game that evened up the score, Atlanta got the ball, scored with eight seconds left in the game, and won by 2 points. The Seahawks played a better game because they were better attuned to one another, yet they lost. While the ability to parse the structural information that reflects the game is critical, random influences such as timing or weather can still be the deciding factor. Nonetheless, perceiving structural information is the more important factor because it gives the players the ability to adapt to changing situations.

"Repetitions Without Repetition"

A baseball swing is a very finely tuned instrument.
It is repetition, and more repetition, then a little
more after that.
—REGGIE JACKSON

One reason that the direct perception of movement patterns is critical to elite sports is that every movement is unique—and this, because of the overwhelming amount of data, eliminates the possibility of relying on mental representations for each one. Thus, while a player's goal remains constant—getting a ball in the basket or the hole—each movement an athlete makes to accomplish that goal is always somewhat different. Russian physiologist Nicholai Bernstein rightly calls this "repetitions without repetition."[1] In the simplest sense, muscle fatigue from a previous movement, even if minimal, prevents a player from repeating the exact same movement. Even more to the point, expert players constantly play different teams, in different settings, amidst unpredictable weather conditions and unexpected injuries. They necessarily respond to an ever-changing environment that mandates adapting their movements to the particular situation at hand.

When Earl Woods was training his son Tiger, for example, he "encouraged working the ball…hitting the ball deliberately from right to left or left to right, high low, under the wind, using a variety of skills to cause the ball to arrive at a single target by different methods and directions."[2] Earl pointed out that variable environmental factors such as "wind, lie, grass thickness, and target all affect the shot and influence club selection"[3] As athletes practice many different moves in various situations, they educate their perceptual systems to attend to more and more articulated structural information that in turn serves to reorganize and expand their neural response networks. If the wind kicks up and moves a baseball a bit to the left of its original course, an expert batter's neurons can immediately guide him to change his arm movements to adjust his undercut.

We all need to adjust our movements constantly to navigate our environment. The surfaces we walk on can be slippery or uneven, or there may be obstacles in our way that require spontaneous, flexible, and adaptive bodily adjustments—the more flexible and the more spontaneous, the more expert the response. Bernstein tells of a pole vaulter whose pole broke midflight. Rather than crash down four meters, he switched into a somersault and landed unharmed on his feet.[4] The pole vaulter's perception of the ground four meters below immediately reorganized his "vaulting neural assembly" to include the somersault as an alternate way down and an adaptive way to break his fall. Adaptive behavior involves the continuous coordination of our perceptual, motor, and nervous systems with our environment. No one component of this complex response system can claim credit.[5] However, such rapid responses leave no time for reflection and attest to the primacy of direct perception over mental representation or mediation.

Minimally Essential Information

Surface simplicity reflects deep complexity.
—SCOTT KELSO

Structural configurations that specify the continuous, overall actions of a football game, including those interactions that can often reveal a player's intentions, are the most efficient source of information that is available to the players. These visual patterns of play integrate the contributions of all the game's components into a coherent whole. Sports psychologist Bruce Abernathy at Australia's University of Queensland calls such configurations "minimally essential information." He reports that it is this type of visual instruction that guides both tennis and squash players to predict where their opponent's ball will land, and what their next move should be. Players make these predictions by observing the configurations produced by the relative motions of their opponent's core area, their waist and hips, as they prepare to hit the ball.[6-8] Core movements contain the seeds of a player's final swing.

Studies of minimally essential information have also been done with juggling, a sport in which both the juggler's body and the balls he or she is using are in constant, simultaneous motion. The paths that their balls trace through space and time produce continually transforming structural configurations.[9] Researchers have tracked the relationship between the pattern of the jugglers' eye movements and the configurations traced by their balls' trajectories and have shown that both trajectories become tighter, more organized, and more efficient as the juggler's expertise increases.[10] Expert jugglers focus on the core area that emerges from the interactions of the balls' interleaved movement patterns, while less able folks scramble around, distracted by and trying to coordinate each ball as a separate component. Because experts focus on structural layouts, rather than on separate parts, they are better at distinguishing relevant and irrelevant information and making faster, more informed decisions.[11]

Expert judges for athletic events operate in a similar fashion. They focus on the center of the layout of play because that area reveals the most information about the quality of the play.[12] In contrast, novice judges focus on various locations. The extra eye movements that novices make in their attempt to track separate components lowers their information-gathering efficiency.

The figure eight that oscillates around our belly button at each stride cycle is another example of minimally essential information. It is the natural outcome of the counterclockwise spirals that our legs produce when we walk.[13] When the right leg goes forward, the sitz bones in the pelvic girdle go out, the hip bones go in, the femur goes out, the tibia goes in, the heels go out, and the forefoot goes in; as the left leg moves to the rear, the sequence is reversed. At the same time, the arms are swinging, and the upper torso, including its occluded back and sides, torques. All our body parts interact with one another and synchronize their movements while simultaneously revealing our identity in the signature figure-eight configuration we produce. In other words, our body's underlying structural organization becomes explicit in the dynamic structural configurations it produces when we move.[14]

Experts' Experts Rely on Structural Information

Few people have the imagination for reality.
—GOETHE

Experts like Tom Brady are born with the same perceptual capacities as the rest of us. The difference between experts and the rest of us is that once we exit childhood, our curiosity and passion about the world shrinks, and we tend to abandon these characteristics in favor of our own thoughts and beliefs. A common sign of this choice is when our tennis coach warns us against thinking before we hit the ball, but we still default to our mental processes, and are then baffled as we watch the ball whiz by. Aside from having considerably more experience and training in their fields, which provides them with more opportunities for perceptual learning, experts keep their immediate perceptions at the ready and thus detect far more information than the rest of us. They lose themselves in the task at hand and sideline their mental interpretations. For example, Nobel Prize–winning geneticist Barbara McClintock, who looked into her microscope and saw genes jump and transform their structural arrangements, explained her strategy:

> I am not there. The self-conscious I simply disappears.... When I look at a cell, I get down in that cell and look around.... I find that only a relatively few people get the point... they haven't yet recognized the meaning of organization.[15]

McClintock's point is well taken. As I have noted, an entity's organization or structure produces the information that tells us what it is and what it does. Each profession has produced experts' experts—people who seem to be have born to see into the heart of matters that baffle others. For example, Darwin, an amateur naturalist, saw the sweep of evolving species by observing differences between separated groups of Galápagos finches. His explanation of evolution came from his noticing and understanding the spatial, temporal, and structural parameters of evolving life. Bach created intricate polyphonies that make our neurons sing by interleaving the structural and temporal layouts of harmonics using the same old scale everyone else relied on. Picasso unraveled the structural invariants of the structure of matter and painted occluded structural dimensions that physics explained years later. Cézanne saw through the world's endless surface details to the underlying structural arrangements that made those details possible—the veritable "lifelines" that Chinese landscape painters use to reveal the structure of reality. All these experts looked closely at our world and saw reality etched in space and time in a way that most people had not understood before. They did so by relying on visual and auditory information that was specific to their areas of expertise: morphological structure for Darwin, harmonic structure for Bach, invariant properties that remained constant over different views of the same phenomenon for Picasso, and physical structure itself for Cézanne. The same dynamic configurations inform experts today.

Diagnosing Injuries: Reading the Dynamics of Deviation

> *As in a martial art, the body takes the print*
> *Of some deep principle of torque and* chi
> *And in the stress of tournament*
> *Exacts an excellence of purity*
> *Compelling both contender and antagonist*
> *To trace the ancient pattern of a dance*
> *Whose subtle leverage and twist*
> *Wrung from the flesh of apes, the human stance.*

—FREDERICK TURNER

The human body evolved to have an upright stance that produced a newly minted set of body movements that distinguish us from our primate relatives. Since evolution is a tinkerer, not a planner, it creates change from whatever is at hand—and that often leaves problems along the way. Some suspect that the upright, bipedal human stance and stride never quite adapted to the range of motions we nonetheless attempt. The result is that the stresses and strains we impose on our spine and extremities, combined with the ubiquity of cars and ski slopes, make us particularly vulnerable to injury. When we suffer injuries, the configurations that our normal movements produce remodel to accommodate the trauma, often in ways that are disabling but that are also visible.

Cures for such unwanted changes are the provenance of physical therapy, a professional practice that, when done right, bases its work on observing a patient's patterns of movement. Internal muscle and joint traumas typically limit our normal range of motion, and these changes are visible in our restricted movement patterns. Injuries

transform the normal configurations of our movements using a positive feedback loop to insert the limitations they impose back into
the complex system of muscles, joints, and nerves that produce those
actions. The result is that such feedback reorganizes our once normal
movement configurations to include and reflect these limitations.
An expert physical therapist can diagnose a patient's problems and
decide on the proper protocols to fix those problems by viewing the
configurations that her patient's impaired movements produce. For
example, clinical doctoral candidate Mikki Townshend, PT, OSC,
a board-certified physical therapist and pain expert at New Motion
Physical Therapy on Bainbridge Island, Washington, focuses on the
whole body as a complex system in order to make a diagnosis of what
others might consider to be a local trauma. Her methods are not
as widely used as might be hoped. Orthopedic texts and less-skilled
practitioners often focus on the injury site as if it were an isolated
island unattached to the whole, a strategy that invites associated
problems down the line. Townshend points out that "it is not possible to separate the action of muscles from that of nerves. From a
neurological point of view, the body is one dynamic system. That
is one reason why, when someone loses a limb, the pain one would
normally feel in that limb is 'referred' and is felt somewhere else in
the body. Any time one component of a system is injured, the whole
system is affected and remediation is limited if it does not take those
relationships into account."[16]

Townshend describes the information she uses to diagnose people and restore them to effective functioning:

> I begin looking at injured people before they realize that
> I am watching them so that their movements reflect the full
> impact of their trauma. I peer out of windows and watch the
> way they get out of their cars, how they walk into our build-
> ing, and how they open doors. I observe them leaving the
> elevator and I follow behind them on the way to a treatment
> room, never taking my eyes off them. I look at every move
> that they make from every angle. In the exam room, I watch
> them sit on a chair or lie down on the exam table while they

tell me exactly what movements they can and cannot perform and their level of discomfort. By the time my observations are complete, I have a fairly good idea of what is wrong and what I can do about it. As I work with patients, I constantly reexamine their movements to see what improvements have been made.[17]

Townshend adds that in graduate school her professor would come into class each day mimicking the problems of a different injury, expecting the class to identify it and diagnose what to do using only the structural information displayed by her movements.

Our movements rely on sensory receptors in our joints, muscles, and tissues to inform us where we are in space. These receptors respond to gravity's tension, compression, and shear, which put pressure on the tissues in which these receptors are embedded. The tissue deformations that result create mechanical energy, which is converted to electrical impulses that carry structural information to the motor neurons in the spinal cord, and then on to muscle fibers to match our final movements to the situation at hand. These normal signals change when injuries disrupt the shape of these tissue deformations and our movements become compromised. In other words, changes in tissue deformation caused by injury become visible as abnormal movement patterns and indicate treatment possibilities.

As Townshend emphasizes, "Injuries reveal themselves in the variation that they produce in bodily movements."[18] For example, a common problem that brings people to a physical therapist is tennis elbow. On the one hand, the problem may actually be a simple, local case of an inflamed tendon that can be treated with ultrasound. But if there is no improvement, the problem may be rooted in the long-term effects of pain itself, which can take on a life of its own and sensitize the entire system. It may also be traceable to a nerve root in the neck that can affect the elbow area. In other words, even though the pain may be localized in the elbow, it can involve the dynamic interaction of several other areas of the body that must be taken into account to alleviate the pain.

Curing Pain in the Brain: How the Brain Restructures Reality

Thought viruses are powerful enough to drive your pain, are more likely to sustain your pain if you don't know how pain works and can increase your pain enough to take you right over the edge.

—DAVID BUTLER AND LORIMER MOSELEY

Until now, we have discussed mental processes and their products as a parallel system to our perceptual systems, which represent and sometimes misrepresent reality. When we are injured, our mental processes can actually alter the physical reality of the brain to match their own illusions. Because many parts of our body such as our hands are etched into their own slot in our brain, when we sustain an injury, the neural networks associated with that area may become oversensitized and take off on their own. Mikki Townshend points out that this problem is not trivial because a pain that accompanies a trauma can affect our ability to heal. She explains that when the pain we experience feeds back into our nervous system, it changes the physical layout of the brain's regions that match the injured area of our body. For example, pain can produce a fear of moving, especially if we have suffered pain from such an injury before. As a result, we rationalize staying still because the pain we experience when we move not only triggers physical pain itself, but also our unsubstantiated theory that moving will make our condition worse. That theory can have unexpected consequences; it reorganizes the normal neural maps of these motor areas that govern parts of our bodies so as to distort our perception of reality and hamper our healing.[19]

By switching from acting on information directly from our perceptual/motor processes to relying on our mental processes, our brains create a condition where we become so oversensitized that the pain we experience is no longer coming from the physical site of the injury; instead, it has taken over the related area of our brain and has assumed a mentally driven life of its own.[20] In fact, simply thinking about moving will actually trigger pain. In effect, pain acts like an antigen that triggers an immune reaction in the brain, which in turn starts a central sensitizing process. When this happens, our thoughts and theories about pain take over and override reality.[21]

Anxiety can further exacerbate our pain because "catastrophizing" the situation recruits brain areas that respond to fear, thereby removing us further from the reality of our actual sensory input.[22] Once our mental operations create a parallel phantom system made up of our theories and fears, that system operates like any complex system; small local inputs create large global effects, and our pain becomes chronic and out of our control. If we do not inject real-world experience into this phantom system and cut the positive feedback loops that sustain it, illusory pain perception can permanently replace our accurate perceptions.[23] There have been cases in which trauma that affected one hand resulted in loss of ability to tell the left hand from the right.

To thwart these hostile mental takeovers, one clever pain expert has developed a set of perceptual exercises to co-opt the brain's responsive mirror neurons.[24,25] Recall that mirror neurons combine in networks that activate to the configurations such as body movements that we perceive. According to pain expert Lorimer Moseley at the University of South Australia, our hands (which have their own area of the brain) can be seduced, when they are injured, into participating in these networks in a very special way. The trick is to use a mirror neuron network to recruit our accurate perceptions of our uninjured hand to fix our distorted perceptions of the injured one. In this way we can replace the phantom system we have created in our heads and cure the now-chronic brain pain that originated in that injured hand. The goal is to overcome what amounts to an "out of focus" or smudged image of the injured hand, which currently occupies that area of our brain normally devoted to our hands. The injured hand appears to be much larger than it actually is and there is an accompanying enlargement of the neural layout of that hand in our motor area.[26] In addition, phantom pain disrupts the normal connections between our sensory and motor systems.[27]

The first step in treating this type of trauma is called left/right discrimination (implicit motor imagery) training.[28] The way it works is that computer images of a hand pop into view, and the patient's task is to identify them as left or right hands. Successful performance is calculated by response speed. The faster the patient can do this, the more the perceptual-motor system begins to normalize and respond to real situations instead of the phantom one in the brain. In the second step, the patient recruits the help of her mirror neuron network by using a mirror box. The patient puts the uninjured hand in front of a mirror and keeps her injured hand out of sight in the box. (Remember that mirrors present us with reversed images of what we are looking at.) Next, the patient moves the fingers of the uninjured hand. Because both hands and eyes are wired to the opposite hemisphere in the brain, as the patient perceives these reversed-image movements in the mirror, her brain responds as if they are actually occurring in the injured, hidden hand.

Viewing the reverse image of the uninjured hand triggers a mirror neuron response that recruits all the muscle, nerve, and vascular input in the injured hand without requiring any physical involvement of that hand.[29] Like Einstein's information at a distance that had no physical connection, the injured hand does nothing, yet its functional parts receive messages from the brain telling it that it is just like its mate, the good hand, and is really all right after all! Physiologically, these exercises bring our experience of the injured hand back into focus (from its smudged, enlarged brain image) and normalize its function. The neurons for that hand in the brain (or what pain researchers call the *neuro-tag*) can be likened to a tune that the brain plays. Instead of playing the melody out of tune, the mirror therapy retunes the brain image of the hand and shifts it back to its normal size and location. Neurologist V.S. Ramachandran has done similar experiments with phantom limbs using both vision and touch and a "virtual reality mirror" device. He showed that "there is considerable latent plasticity even in the adult human brain.... And there is a great deal of interaction between vision and touch."[30]

In the end, the relationship between perception and action is restored and the perceptual-motor pathways in the brain are normalized. Brain pain stops. Going through just the observation part of the program produced a 96% reduction in developing chronic pain in extrasensitive people who would normally have developed that condition without the training. Recruiting the structural information of hand movements allows us to distinguish between real pain and brain pain.

Diagnosing Cancer: Pathology and Structural Information

The best pathologists have an eye.

—BRENT WOOD, MD, PHD

In the spring of 1999, a family physician told one of his patients that a large, soft lump just under the skin on her left thigh was a lipoma— a harmless fat tumor. After the lump was removed and found to be a 3-centimeter-long lymph node, it was sent to the hospital's pathology lab for analysis. That act started a cascade of diagnostic errors that ended up clearly separating an extraordinary pathologist from the rest of the field. To make a long story short, after much bickering and no definitive answers by a number of the hospital's in-house staff members, the patient had the section slides of her tumor sent to an expert's expert, Brent Wood, MD, PhD, board-certified hematologist, who was then at the University of Washington (and is now head of the hematopathology laboratory at the Cancer Care Alliance in Seattle).

Pathologists train to distinguish the structural pattern variations that distinguish diseases from one another and normal cells from diseased ones. Although section slides may appear to depict static structures, the configurations they display nonetheless include and reveal the dynamic history of the disease's progression up to that point. Dr. Wood, an expert in the diagnosis of blood and lymph cancers, needed only a quick look at this patient's slides. He immediately knew that she had an aggressive form of diffuse large B cell lymphoma. Even though the original laboratory personnel could not make a definitive diagnosis, they nevertheless took exception to Dr. Wood's diagnosis. To settle the issue, Dr. Wood sent the slides to

Dr. Elaine Jaffe, the lymphoma maven at the National Institutes of Health, who agreed with Dr. Wood.

Errors are not unusual in pathology. This patient has had three subsequent lymph node tumor removals, each one at different hospitals, and the same type of pathology disputes and errors were repeated each time. Each time, the tumor samples had to be sent to Dr. Wood for an accurate diagnosis. Reading slides, similar to reading X-rays, MRIs, CAT scans, and PET scans, is the ability to read structural information. Many practitioners fail to do this because their view of the slides is blurred by their mind's eye, which overrides what they directly perceive with verbal, written, and pictorial material obtained from books and lectures rather than from the actual slides themselves.

Pathologists like Brent Wood first look at slices of a tumor under a microscope at low magnification so that they can view the structural layout of the whole specimen at once. Next, they increase the magnification to get a detailed comparison between the architectural features of the possibly abnormal sample—in this case, a lymph node and its specific rogue cells—to the architecture of a normal node with its normal cells. This process, often involving several slides, is similar to the way a physical therapist compares the movements that emerge from injured areas to movements that are normal; both experts look for deviations from patterns. All lymphomas have structural pattern similarities. Each particular one is a variation on the basic structural layout that characterizes lymphoma (just like whirlpools and tornados are variations of the spiral configuration that organizes turbulent events).

Even though all tumors exhibit abnormal growth, variations in their proteins reveal the unique properties of each variety and dictate the protocols that can best combat their proliferation. But proteins are typically not visible, and in order to tell one variety from another, Dr. Wood stains the slides and applies antibodies to the cell's receptors that bind to antigens both inside and on the surface of the cell. This technique highlights the proteins and brings forth the cell's unique variation of the basic lymphoma configuration. The structural layout of the antibody distribution reveals the cell's type (B or T) and whether it is normal or abnormal.

Once Dr. Wood identifies these abnormal areas, he increases the magnification to reveal the intracell patterns. These patterns have a coarser kind of chromatin than those of normal areas (a mix of the cell's DNA and its organizing proteins). At this point, he says, "I look and immediately say yes, it is B cell lymphoma, or no, it is not lymphoma, or it's another type entirely." The diagnosis is typically made in an instant. He explains that "it is the direct perception of the lymphoma pattern at hand that tells the story of a particular cancer."[31] A considerable body of research tells us that top experts do not waffle, but typically make immediate, accurate decisions. They have no need to consider alternatives, because the structural information on which they are basing their conclusion comes directly from the actual structure of the tumor, not a theory of the tumor that can be disputed because people hold different opinions. The tumor is what it is. It is not open to interpretation except when viewers are unsure of the configuration they see.

Dr. Wood also notes, "By simply observing, I can see that these structures show they have been stimulated. Chronic stimulation is due to inflammation, which gives rise to errors or problems that often develop into cancer. Perceiving a state of stimulation is more an intuitive than an analytic process."[32] It is easier to look at such abnormal structural patterns to know what they are rather than to attempt to describe those patterns using words.

Condensing the Structure of Reality: The Japanese Garden

*Learn about a pine tree from a pine tree,
learn about a bamboo stalk from a bamboo stalk.*

—BASHO

Doug Tanaka is an award-winning Japanese landscape designer and master pruner. He taught pruning at the University of Washington, gave demonstrations at the Northwest Flower and Garden Show, set the rocks at the Japanese garden in the University of Washington's arboretum and at the Bloedel Reserve on Bainbridge Island, and created the pruning workshops at Kubota Gardens in Seattle. He started gardening with his father when he was nine years old and, aside from a stint at the University of California at Santa Barbara (where he obtained a degree in the philosophy of religion and had a gardening route), he is still pruning the trees he planted forty years ago.

Almost all Japanese landscapers start out as apprentices who receive no instruction. They are supposed to watch carefully and "steal their master's secrets." Those secrets concern how the world and everything in it is structured over time and space as it applies primarily to pine trees. Tanaka points out that if you walk along a coastline strewn with rocks, you will notice that the larger boulders and smaller stones are dispersed in regular patterns, depending on the properties of the material from which they were made, the centrifugal action of the waves that deposited them on the beach, and the coming and going of the tides that may shift them about. If you spend enough time strolling down the beach and looking around, you will find the location of certain rocks and stones is predictable. Japanese garden designers borrow and distill this type of universal landscape pattern in their work, as in the case of Ryōan-ji, a dry gravel Zen garden at a temple in Kyoto, Japan.[33]

Japanese gardens condense the structure and dynamics of reality. As a result, a twenty-five-by-forty-foot garden appears to be the same as a much larger natural landscape, only on a smaller scale. Designers choose the pines, small maples, azaleas, and miniature conifers in these gardens because these trees and shrubs take well to judicious pruning without looking scalped or compromising their structure. It is possible to prune certain species of trees such as pines this way and not destroy their character, because their structure repeats itself as it grows in scale-free self-similar patterns, as we saw in chapter 5. If you prune a tree according to its self-similar structure, you can scale down its size while retaining its natural form, because that form is the same on all scales. The result is that a twenty-year-old Japanese garden can appear like a natural landscape that has been in place for thousands of years. When Doug Tanaka prunes, he taps into the scale-free, self-similarity of the Earth's complex structure. This allows him to duplicate the largest structures on the smallest scale, while keeping all the same fundamental relationships intact.

To build these relationships, Japanese gardens are designed and installed in situ. In contrast, Western landscape designers typically use computer design programs and tend to tailor their designs to fit the feature-driven, conceptual resources that those programs provide. Computer-generated landscapes typically rearrange the site's natural topology to match a prior concept or style, such as a garden outside an English cottage or in the tropics. The result is a landscape that resembles an image in a book but often has little to do with the natural world or the surrounding terrain.

You cannot design an authentic Japanese garden by combining separate features on a computer. You must start with the complexity of the site at hand—the existing topology, light, rainfall, soil type, available rocks and plants—and work within the few degrees of freedom that these constraints allow. A Japanese garden cannot have a preconceived mental plan because it emerges from the characteristics and constraints of the site and the materials available at that time. If, for example, the site topography calls for a stream, the result should look as if the Ice Age had just departed and left a scour in the land with boulders and smaller rocks strewn along its path. The boulders simply punctuate and emphasize the lifelines that were already there in the land. Every step of the design enlarges on the organic whole by consistently interrelating everything within its borders and with the larger "borrowed" landscape of distant mountains and larger trees that can be seen outside its boundaries. If you are inside a house looking out on such a garden, you feel as if you are looking at the virtually infinite expanse of the countryside, because the structure of the garden reflects the same structure as that of the more expansive real world.

Everything in a Japanese garden contributes to the whole. Each tree is chosen not only because of its harmony with the garden as a whole, but also because of its internal harmony within itself, which in physics is called its dynamical similitude. Dynamical similitude is the tree's physical organization that produces its intrinsic structural balance. Expert Japanese gardens give one a feeling of serenity because they are of a piece; nothing is extraneous and everything works together following the laws of our complex universe.

Reading the Seascape: Sea Gypsies Survive a Tsunami

It is not what is inside the head that is important. It is what the head is inside of.

—WILLIAM MACE

At almost 7:59 a.m. on December 26, 2004, the floor of the Indian Ocean shattered. As magma beneath the Earth's crust expanded upward, the Indian tectonic plate slipped beneath the Eurasian Plate and triggered a 9.3 megathrust earthquake. If a satellite had tracked that event from beginning to end, it would have recorded the following sights: Approximately twelve hundred kilometers of the Sunda Trench ruptured, causing areas of the sea floor to rise by as much as eight meters. Hundreds of kilometers of seawater were displaced, creating a massive subsurface wave that ran unchecked toward the coastlines of Sumatra, Sri Lanka, Thailand, and Indonesia. When that tsunami made landfall, it topped a hundred feet, surged up to three miles inland, and swept away most everything in its path.

But most important, before the wave hit the shore, the long arm of the seismic system to which it belonged etched two unexpected and compelling visual signals into the seascape. First, it pulled the tide out far beyond the horizon, leaving the fish behind flopping about on the bare sand. Second, it simultaneously sent spiraling whirlpools to the surface of the Bay of Bengal. These two unusual visual signs should have put an attentive viewer on alert. Whirlpools are the signature patterns of turbulence—the chaotic motion of unruly waters that breach levees, sink ships, and at the very least signal that danger could be imminent. The tide presented an added threat. When such an enormous amount of water travels so far out, it accumulates enough potential energy to flood interior lands on its return. Both these visual signs signaled the danger at hand, and as if on a schedule, a killer tsunami made landfall.

Most people on the beach and the bay ignored, overlooked, or misunderstood the meaning of the tide and the visual messages of the whirlpools. In the end, 230,000 people perished. Yet one small indigenous group, the Moken Sea Gypsies, who live on their boats in the Andaman Sea, survived intact. As soon as they saw the tide recede and the whirlpools surface, and heard the cicadas fall silent, the Sea Gypsies ran to higher ground with the elephants. They even convinced a handful of tourists to come with them to the hills, and those tourists survived as well. The Moken on boats on the bay headed out to sea with the dolphins. Minutes later, the tsunami struck. The tourists and locals who ignored the receding waters and the rising whirlpools were swept away. Fishing folk who remained on their boats were catapulted into the water and dragged under as the wave came through.

Although the Moken have neither formal instruction nor personal experience with tsunamis, "they read nature's signals," says Jacques Ivanoff, an anthropologist with the Research Institute on Contemporary Southeast Asia who has lived with them for many years.[34] During an interview, one Moken elder told *60 Minutes* reporter Mike Wallace that they knew that danger was afoot because the water "was swirling like a whirlpool as if it was boiling up from the bottom of the sea."[35] They knew immediately that whirlpools on the surface meant turbulence below—and that turbulence meant danger. The tide and whirlpools were not isolated visual signs. They were the leading edge of the seismic event that started deep within the Earth's crust that lies beneath the ocean floor, sped beneath the water's surface, and culminated in a tsunami on the shore. The presence of these signs predicted that the wave was coming. The Sea Gypsies' expertise at reading these dynamic structural signals saved their lives.

The whirlpool's signature configuration, the spiral, is a common danger signal. Spirals orchestrate the twisting of tornados and the spin of hurricanes. If you absentmindedly stash your wedding ring on the bathtub rim and it tumbles in, the spiral action of the exiting waters will suck it down the drain. It was not coincidental that the Moken were aware that whirlpools indicate danger. But when these geometric forms surfaced, and the Sea Gypsies nearby headed out to sea, the local Burmese squid-gatherers in adjacent boats stayed put and continued to carry out their plan to catch as much squid as possible to sell in the market. Their preoccupation with acquiring squid edited their visual reach and they failed to register the whirlpools' warning. One Moken elder remarked that the squid-gatherers "saw nothing, they looked at nothing. They did not know how to look ... suddenly everything rose up, their boats were thrown up in the air."[36] None of the squid- gatherers survived. The plan in their mind distracted them from the information in front of their eyes.

After the tsunami, many people turned to theories to explain the Sea Gypsies' survival. Some attributed the Moken's decisions to a legend handed down in their culture about "the great wave that eats people." They do have such a tale, and it certainly could have put them on alert. But how could the legend alone have guided the Moken's flight? This story told only of a great wave. It did not tell about the whirlpools that signaled its coming. Present-day Moken had never seen a tsunami before and this one hit the coast after they had already fled. We know this because Thai movie star Aun had been photographing in the area and coincidentally documented the Moken running into the hills before the first wave struck.

Indeed, if the Moken legend had included descriptions of these informative signals, that narrative would be common to other people in the area because this is Krakatoa country. When Krakatoa erupted on August 27, 1883, it created an immense set of waves that hit the same shores, produced similar destruction, and garnered worldwide attention. Krakatoa's waves not only decimated these very same coastal villages, but were also so powerful that they spread across the oceans to ripple up the Thames in England and surface in the waters off New York City.[37] Few people now living near areas ravaged by both the recent devastation and by Krakatoa—the Sundra Strait, the Indian Ocean, the Andaman Sea, and the Bay of Bengal—are unaware of that earlier, historic incident. If a legend had guided the Sea Gypsies' flight, the rest of the local population would have fled as well, instead of remaining behind to drown.

Translating Structure Into Words

Nature is a language.... But it is not a language
taken to pieces and dead in a dictionary. I wish to
learn this language... that I may learn to read the
book that is written in that tongue.
—RALPH WALDO EMERSON

Our ability to parse the structures of the world is quite separate from the words we use to describe those structures. For one thing, words are not equipped to describe the complexity of every worldly entity. Writers who attempt to describe even a tiny leaf of thyme, with its more than fifty chemical components—each with their own name and description—have an uphill battle to be accurate, comprehensive, and understood. They have the impossible task of translating their own and other's experience of complex structures, systems, and events into words. Words typically refer to categories, not to unique events; they have multiple meanings, are subjectively chosen, and are tied to our faulty memories. Words easily distort, reframe, or replace what actually is the case without anyone becoming the wiser.

But there are people who have the gift of holding fast to their direct experiences and choosing words with such sensitivity that they actually reflect the real world. Journalist Charles Wohlforth is one of those people. In his books *The Whale and the Supercomputer* and *The Fate of Nature,* he manages to put together descriptions that are transparent to reality. Poets do this by shaking words loose from their conventional moorings, cloaking them in metaphors, and directing them to our emotions, which have built-in physiological reality detectors. But Wohlforth does double duty. He combines a poetic voice with scientifically accurate descriptions of what is happening on the ground. His concern revolves around the effects of commercial activities on his home turf of Alaska and the Arctic, and, radiating from there, on the entire world. Through his own vision and his ability to accept and thus understand the vision of Alaska's indigenous people, he gives the very structure of physical place a voice. After the 1964 Good Friday earthquake, Wohlforth wrote:

> The earth's crust had pivoted like a seesaw on a line running along the western edge of the sound; east of the line the land rose, but to the west it sank.... Raised or sunken the sea's mysterious intelligence remembered the beach's shape from before the earthquake...until each grain had been placed accurately in the geometry that had existed before.[38]

In a minimum of words, Wohlforth lets us know that, regardless of human interventions, the physical laws that produce the structures of our planet always have the last say and that the coast of Prince William Sound had, in an instant, not only discarded any boundaries that we had imposed, but also had returned to the state that physical laws required it to have. While the very earth had been heaved up and seemed to wash away in the receding tsunami, the invariant structure of the land—its lifelines, in the Chinese usage of the term—had been restored. The results of this restoration could be perceived. But just as experts' experts rely on structural information, people who are locked into their minds also rely on mental processes and categories. With chapter 7, which discusses the nature of theories themselves, this book will turn to what happens in the real world with its multicomponent complex systems when we humans ignore the structural information that specifies those systems and default to theories and other mental fallout as the sole guide for our decisions.

PART TWO

Manufactured Information and the Biased Brain

7

Mind Over Matter

THEORIES AS MENTAL FALL-OUT

*If the Confederacy fails, there should be written on
its tombstone, "Died of a Theory."*
—JEFFERSON DAVIS

IN THE 1860S, British surgeon Charles Moore became increasingly
frustrated as his breast cancer patients relapsed. To isolate the cause
of their tumors' return, Moore meticulously recorded "the anatomy
of each relapse, denoting the area of the original tumor, the precise
margin of the surgery, and the site of the recurrence by drawing tiny
black dots on a diagram of the breast."[1] He found that the disease
typically recurred around the margins of the original surgery. He
concluded, "Mammary cancer requires the extirpation of the entire
organ."[2] In the 1880s, surgeons at Dr. Richard von Volkmann's clinic
at Halle, Germany, removed the pectoralis minor muscle under
patients' breasts in a more aggressive attempt to stem breast cancer.[3]
Yet these cancers also returned.

Building on Moore's and von Volkmann's findings, New York
surgeon William Stewart Halstead developed a theory during the
1890s that even more extensive surgery would be better. Halstead's
theory led him to excavate deeper into the chest cavity in a procedure that became known as a "radical mastectomy." In his extraordinary book, *The Emperor of All Maladies,* cancer physician and

researcher at Columbia University School of Medicine, Siddhartha Mukherjee, notes:

> A macabre marathon was in progress. Halstead and his disciples would rather evacuate the entire contents of the body than be faced with cancer recurrences.... One surgeon evacuated three ribs and other parts of the rib cage and amputated a shoulder and a collarbone from a woman with breast cancer."[4]

Despite these radical procedures and the profound disfigurement of these patients, the cancer returned. Halstead's theory that "more is better" was impossible to achieve because it failed to include a critical component of the cancer's ever changing complex system: it metastasizes, and once it does, it often travels beyond the benefits of the surgeon's knife. Like many theories, Halstead's was based on a single component: Since cancer grows from the margins of the tumor, enlarging the margins will cure the cancer. His theory assumed that cancer was a local condition. Indeed, this assumption seemed reasonable when it was caught before it metastasized, and cancer could be stopped, at least for a while, with a local procedure. However, the data Halstead collected pointed to the fact that cancers often went beyond a local area, no matter how radical the surgery.

Halstead, his students, and followers "remained unfazed. Rather than address the real question raised by the data—Did radical mastectomy really extend lives?—they clutched at their theories even more adamantly."[5] Cancer operations became more and more radical and the notion of curing cancer was left to the future. Trapped in the limits of Halstead's theory, surgeons criticized less aggressive procedures as inadequate. They not only missed the point that cancer could metastasize, but they also could not know that future research would show that cancer, rather than being a unitary local disease, is a complex system involving genetics, mutations, transposition, hormones, proteins, and a host of other factors that are constantly evolving and transforming.

The conclusion that follows from the fact that cancer is a multi-component, dynamic, complex system is that its cure likewise will require a complex system approach. As cancer researcher Philip Sharp at MIT has pointed out, "The hero scientist who defeats cancer will likely never exist."[6] Cancer is too complex for people such as Halstead and their unitary theories to deliver on their predictions. Yet cancer research is often limited to such isolated researchers and their graduate students. To counter the celebration of such isolated practitioners and the limits such a system puts on the progress of cancer research, Stand Up To Cancer, a nonprofit organization created by entertainment figures such as *Spider-Man* producer Laura Ziskin, talk show host Katie Couric, and former Paramount CEO Sherry Lansing have funded a more realistic way of doing cancer research if the goal is to cure the disease. They recognize that cancer is a complex system that needs a complex system approach, so they have funded "a team based, cross-disciplinary approach to cancer research [that] is upending tradition and delivering results faster."[7]

For example, one team of twenty-eight researchers is attacking the problem of one of the worst of the breed, pancreatic cancer. After surgeon Jeffrey Drebin of the University of Pennsylvania takes out someone's tumor, it is flash-frozen to preserve its integrity. A cell sample is shipped to the Salk Institute's Gene Expression Laboratory, where cancer biologist Geoffrey Wahl and his colleagues analyze the cells involved in repairing tissue. Another specimen of the tumor is sent to chemistry and integrative genomics professor Joshua Rabinowitz at Princeton who looks at its amino acids, sugars and many metabolites. At the same time, their teammates at the Translational Genomics Research Institute and Johns Hopkins analyze the tumor's genome sequence. In a two-year period, the team developed a drug that looks promising in treating pancreatic cancer and has entered clinical trials—results and time periods unheard of in isolated laboratories led by a single star researcher.[8]

Where Do Theories Come From?

The truth of a theory is in your mind, not your eyes

—ALBERT EINSTEIN

Theories are supposed to be about the world, but they do not originate in the world. We construct them in our minds. Although we typically use information that we perceive from the world in our constructions, we filter and sometimes distort that information to fit our preconceptions and beliefs. One way we do this arises out of the way our left hemisphere deals with the information at its disposal. Our right hemisphere specializes in the spatial or structural information that specifies the structures and systems that exist in the world. In contrast, the left hemisphere specializes in constructing representations, making interpretations, and—depending upon the strength of a person's built-in biases—out-and-out confabulations. Neuroscientist Michael Gazzaniga has a compelling explanation for how this comes about. He explains that our brain is made up of various independent modules that process information from multiple sources and that those various sources vie for space in our conscious awareness.[9]

Gazzaniga views the left hemisphere as the gatekeeper that determines which information is retained and projected into our consciousness and which gets tossed out. He calls this gatekeeper "the interpreter."[10] From this view, our conscious awareness is orchestrated by our left hemisphere. Its quest is to explain the complex world that we access largely subliminally using only the bits and pieces that manage to pop into our conscious awareness. Gazzaniga believes that "this is a post hoc rationalization process."[11] One problem that we rarely consider is that our subjective awareness is not based on our direct experience. It takes many milliseconds for the information we sense directly and comprehend subliminally to be relayed to our left-hemisphere interpreter and converted into the symbol systems that our conscious awareness relies on.[12] In other words, our conscious awareness relies on memory traces because the original experience that triggered this process has already occurred.

In the 1980s, researcher Benjamin Libet at the University of California, San Francisco's physiology department recorded the neural substrate for this effect. He showed that

> a freely voluntary act was found to be preceded, by about 550 ms [milliseconds], by the readiness potential....But subjects reported becoming aware of the wish or intention to act only about 200 ms before the act. This meant that the brain was initiating the volitional process unconsciously, at least 350 ms before the person was aware of wanting to act.[13]

One example that Libet gives of this effect occurs as follows:

> You are driving along in your car at thirty miles an hour on a city street. Suddenly, a young boy steps into the street in front of your car, chasing a ball. You slam your foot on the brake pedal....Were you consciously aware of the event before stepping on the brake? Or was it an unconscious action that you became aware of after you hit the brakes?[14]

Libet asserts that this action is unconscious. Given the 550 milliseconds needed to become consciously aware of an event, he claims that you are able to slam on your brakes 150 milliseconds or less after the boy enters the street. This suggests that your response is not a simple reflex response but is rooted in your perceptual acumen, because you have to recognize the presence of the boy and make a decision not to hit him.[15] In an experimental study, French neurophysiologist Marc Jeannerod at the Claude Bernard University Lyon 1 showed that when subjects reached for a target that the experimenter shifted after they started to reach for it, the subjects shifted their movement toward the target midstream in order to reach it. What is most interesting is that the subjects were not aware of making that midstream shift.[16] Later work by Chun Siong Soon at the Max Planck Institute for Human Cognitive and Brain Sciences and his colleagues showed that

> two specific regions in the frontal and parietal cortex of the human brain had considerable information that predicted

the outcome of a motor decision the subject had not yet consciously made.... Thus a network of high-level control areas can begin to shape an upcoming decision long before it enters awareness.[17]

In sum, *the interpreter is a complex, after-the-fact system that combines multiple information inputs to construct post hoc theories about the situations we have already encountered and now interpret rather than take as given.* Some of the modules that contribute to those theories come from our more realistic, right-hemisphere processes such as our ability to recognize thousands of different faces or to navigate space without colliding with lampposts. Other modules, however, consist of our prior beliefs that have little to do with the evidence at hand and tend to distort our interpretations to match our preconceptions, biases, needs, and expectations. In addition, the world is constantly changing and by the time we interpret what we have already seen, it has become old news. Gazzaniga goes so far as to conclude that while our right hemisphere detects and accepts the world as it is, our left hemisphere is "the last device in the information chain in our brain that reconstructs the brain's events and in doing so makes telling errors of perception, memory and judgment."[18]

This description of the different functions of each of our hemispheres is certainly true and serves to illustrate the key points that are made in this book, but it may not be complete. Although the linguistic and spatial functions are hemisphere specific, it is unclear whether there is more mixing and matching of information between the hemispheres than we currently are aware of. It seems reasonable to assume, however, that regardless of which hemisphere is on call, before we have amassed a host of adult beliefs and biases, our ability to gather and combine information originates in the curiosity that is characteristic of most children. As babies, we pick things up, turn them over in our hands, and stare intently at every facet. We put things in our mouths to get another point of view, all the while trying to discover their secrets. We are tiny explorers delving into everything around us in our need to know what things are and how they work. When we learn to talk, one of the words we say most is "why."

Our knowledge-gathering strategies are critical to our survival, so it is no surprise that they are central to our lives. Even though there are many situations that as children we are unable to investigate because they are beyond our ability, we still feel called upon to explain them either to ourselves or to others. In these cases, we take the various things we do know and assemble them into what seems to be a credible answer, even though it may be wrong. Years ago, Art Linkletter had a very funny TV show called *Kids Say the Darndest Things* that capitalized on this tendency. Linkletter would ask a child a question:

ART: When will you reach maturity?
CHILD: Never.
ART: Why not?
CHILD: Too far away.
ART: What makes you think it's too far away?
CHILD: Well, isn't it an island in the South Pacific?[19]

A child who does not know the answer may present his own theory of the situation for verification. One three-year-old boy asked his balding father: "Dad, did your hair slip?"[20] Sometimes children present a fully developed theory of their own. One little girl announced that "when it gets dark, God turns out the lights so he can sleep."[21]

Even though our early attempts to explain why men lose their hair or why it turns dark at night are innocent and often amusing, we nevertheless start at a very young age to explain situations of which we actually have no knowledge by confabulating. It is also likely that we are not conscious that we are doing so. Recall that Gordon Allport's experiment in chapter 1 showed that the bulk of his participants mentally switched a knife from a white man's hand to a black man's. When they were questioned later, it turned out that they believed black men are more violent than white men, and that belief overrode and replaced what their eyes saw in their conscious awareness.[22] Neurologist V. S. Ramachandran at the University of California, San Diego suggests that prior false beliefs can repress conflicting information. He attributes this state of affairs to the differences between our two hemispheres, and proposes that the left hemisphere creates belief systems and models about the world and interprets new experiences in light of such prior mental models.[23]

Theories and the Brain

You come to nature with all your theories and she knocks them all flat.

—PIERRE-AUGUSTE RENOIR

Ramachandran suggests that when we are confronted with experiences that conflict with our prior beliefs, our left-hemisphere processes either deny or repress the new information. If that doesn't work, we use those processes to confabulate a new explanation that matches our preconceptions. However, Ramachandran also suggests that when our left-hemisphere processes go too far, "our right hemisphere strategy is to play devil's advocate to force a revision of the entire model."[24] Someone whose brain is impaired may not make this "reality check." One example is Ramachandran's patient, Mrs. Dodd, a woman confined to a wheelchair due to a stroke, who patently denies that her arm is paralyzed, even though she is unable to move it. Even though she cannot hold a glass with that hand and spills water all over herself, Mrs. Dodd makes up all sorts of explanations that deny her paralysis. Ramachandran writes that "there is literally no limit to how far she will wander along the delusional path."[25]

But people with intact brains often have similar left-hemisphere responses if their pet theories are challenged. This has been shown repeatedly when people who believe in evolution debate those who believe in creationism, or when people who think that global warming is here to stay debate those who question its existence. Gazzaniga argues that "if you feed the interpreter incorrect data, you can hijack it."[26] The problem is that we often feed ourselves false "data" that originate in our own heads and we ignore evidence from the world that would prove us wrong. Because our interpreter, just like Mrs. Dodd's, does not distinguish between the facts of a matter and our opinions or desires, it often defaults to confabulating a theory that meets those desires.[27]

Hijacking the Interpreter

Our minds have their own agendas.

—ROBERT BURTON

The biologist and philosopher Jean Rostand once remarked that *theories come and go, the frog remains*. Rostand died in 1977, but since then theories and other mental constructions have been proliferating as the number of frogs has been declining. Because we have too often ignored the world as it actually is, and acted on what we theorized it to be, we have created an alarming disjunction between the outcomes of our choices and the surety of our own continued survival. It is not the case that we cannot see and understand reality. We evolved to do so, or else we would be extinct. Our recognition of the structural information that specifies danger, for example, is neither learned nor arbitrary. In fact, eight-month-old babies with the ability to crawl, but no prior experience with precipices, refuse to cross over a safe but simulated visual cliff, even though their mothers are urging them to join them on the other side.[28]

Although some of us conjure up dire circumstances in our minds, or succumb to propaganda and scare ourselves silly, we usually have to actually see the information that specifies a situation to detect if it is dangerous or not. But with the interpreter this is not always the case. In February 2002, when Mohamed El Baradei, director general of the International Atomic Energy Agency, and Hans Blix, chief UN weapons inspector, scoured three hundred sites in Iraq, not one weapon of mass destruction was found.[29,30] Yet President George W. Bush and Vice President Dick Cheney stuck to the theory that these nonexistent weapons existed and used it as the basis for their decision to invade Iraq.

They may have had their reasons for acting on this misconceived theory, according to George Tenet, head of the CIA at that time, or else Cheney would not have kept asking the CIA to find evidence that supported their invasion plan.[31] But it is less clear why Congress backed their strategies and provided the funds to fight an unprovoked war. It is even less clear why so many investigative journalists cheered on this action without evidence, or why many of the rest of us allowed our collective fear button to be pushed with tales of terrorism that, as we saw with the Boston Marathon incident, are often very difficult to predict. Weapons of mass destruction were never found to back up any if these decisions. Indeed, once we had invaded Iraq and it became clear that our government's basis for this action was untrue, the administration's public relations machine switched their reasons to the despotic behavior of Saddam Hussein. In fact, the promotion of terrorism seems to be centered more in Pakistan, our purported ally, which sheltered Osama bin Laden, the leader of the terrorist group al-Qaeda.

When we do not have accurate information, our interpreter easily comes to conclusions on the basis of what we believe, not what is actually the case. A classic experiment that demonstrates this effect was done by psychologists Christopher Strenta and Robert Kleck of Dartmouth College.[32] They recruited participants, put a nasty-looking simulated scar on their faces, arranged for each one to have a private conversation with a confederate of the experimenter, and asked the recruits to report if they noticed any signs that this other person reacted to their disfigurement. Just before the experiment was to begin, the experimenters told their participants that they needed to apply moisturizer to the scar to keep it from cracking. Instead, they removed the scar without the participants' knowledge. Thus, they engaged in these discussions still believing that they had a scar on their face.

The experimenters videotaped the talks between the participants and their confederate. When the participants were asked how their discussion partner reacted to them, most reported that they were treated very badly. To check on those attributions, the experimenters showed each participant a video of their discussion and asked them to point out incidents where the other person had reactions to the scar. The participants pointed out instances of the other person looking away instead of looking at them because they did not want to see the scar. Because the participants thought they had a scar, they misread other people's reactions and made up a theory of why these nonexistent reactions were occurring. Their theory of the situation may have come from their own feelings about people with scars or perhaps their interpretation of how people in general respond to those with disfigurements.

Even more peculiar is the fact that most of us act on the interpreter's take on things despite the fact that it is often wrong. One example: Michael Gazzaniga and his colleagues performed an experiment using a probability-guessing paradigm that looked at whether our right and left hemispheres analyze the world differently.[33] They flashed lights in a random sequence. Each light was flashed 80% of the time above a line and 20% of the time below that line. The participants' task was to estimate where the next flash would occur. Gazzaniga found children under four, animals, and the realist right hemispheres of patients whose hemispheres were split "maximize" by guessing that the light will flash "above the line" all the time, thus reaping rewards 80% of the time. In contrast, the left hemisphere of his split-brain patients made "frequency matches." In other words, the left hemisphere does not use the information that is actually available to get the most correct answers (maximizing their successes). Instead, it gets caught up in figuring out a strategy to explain what is going on. The left hemisphere's analytic ability tends to figure out that the experimenters' strategy is an 80/20 split, and as a result, it assumes the light will flash above the line 80% of the time and below the line 20% of the time. Unfortunately, since the sequence of light flashes is random, there is no way to predict where the light will flash each time, only that it will flash above the line 80% of the time. The result is that frequency matchers who have figured out the experimenters' strategy are right, at most, 67% of the time, while the right hemisphere "maximizers" are right 80% of the time. Gazzaniga concludes that the left hemisphere does not accept the idea that the world is random and, instead, "is driven to infer a cause for the frequencies of the flashes and create a theory to explain them."[34] The bottom line is the interpreter constructs theories "about the structure of the world even in the face of evidence that no pattern exists."[35]

According to linguist and cognitive scientist George Lakoff at the University of California, Berkeley, these patterns are frames that structure how we see the world and therefore understand reality.[36] The interpreter not only makes subjective judgments about what current information is acceptable or not, but also uses a prior mental framework to make these judgments. Under these conditions it is very difficult for people to think outside their frames, or to give up the idea that they are right, and they typically reject conflicting information. One explanation for this bias comes from the work of psychologist Jonathan Haidt, now at New York University's Stern School of Business. Haidt argues that most of us are locked into what he calls a particular moral system, and as a result, when we construct our theories of the world, we do not seek the truth. Instead, we rarely listen to people with views that differ from ours, and we devote ourselves to promoting the point of view consistent with our moral system.[37] The media and our dominant political parties oblige our interpreters by dividing the airwaves into conservative and progressive news stations that slant their reporting to match their own and their audiences' frames.

The side effect of living according to frames and the theories they promote is that our views become entrenched, and we then interpret "news" stories that come along to reinforce these views. We feel compelled to draw lines in the sand that separate us from others who have conflicting beliefs, which leaves no room for learning something new and, as a result, changing our position. This standoff situation makes cooperating to get things done very difficult. Evidence for this state of affairs is especially clear in the reactions that people with different frames have to the problem of global warming. On one side of the divide, led by the oil and coal industries, are people who want to continue to maintain our fossil fuel–based economy at all costs and who declare that global warming is unproven at best and a hoax at worst. On the other side are people who believe what the scientific community argues—that global warming is increasing due to emissions from human fossil-fuel use. They champion replacing fossil fuels with alternative energy solutions. The fact that the news media gives both these groups equal airtime in an attempt to be fair, without taking into account the credibility of the evidence supporting each view, leaves the public without the critical information they need to understand this issue.

When real life looms large enough, however, we often develop new frames. After the horrific Newtown, Connecticut massacre of

20 five- and six-year-olds and their teachers by Adam Lanza with an assault rifle that used multi-bullet magazines, many new groups of people organized to fight the gun lobby and take such weapons off the street. Unfortunately, the gun lobby blocked any regulatory legislation, even universal background checks and a ban on these types of magazines. This may be hard to fathom in the face of the evidence that many of the children who escaped the massacre did so while the gunman was reloading. It is, however, a testament to the power of theories that push our fear buttons, triggering either fantasies of unknown gunmen threatening one's family or primary election fights set up by a gun lobby with a great deal of money. For the rest of us, once situations like the Newtown shootings disappear from the evening news, we tend to default to the theories that support our frames.

One difficulty we have in thinking outside our frames and interpretations is that they are inextricably tied to the words we use to express them. Thus, changing our words gives us a way out of political paralysis. A study by psychologist Irina Feygina and her colleagues at New York University showed that by changing the language used, we can breach the divide between conservatives and progressives on a controversial topic such as global warming. These researchers hypothesized that the reason many conservatives did not believe in climate change was because they "had a tendency to justify and defend the societal status quo in the face of the threat posed by environmental problems."[38] In order to justify the status quo, conservatives deny threatening "environmental realities."[39] Feygina found that by changing the language used in a frame of environmental intervention from words that threatened the status quo to one that portrayed environmental protection as patriotic and supporting the status quo, conservatives could be brought on board.

Our frames are also inextricably tied to words that can lead us away from the truth.[40] In another interesting piece of research, experimenters found that people who have aphasia and "cannot understand words are better at picking up lies about emotions...suggesting that loss of language skills may be associated with a superior ability to detect the truth."[41] Nancy Etcoff at Harvard Medical School and her colleagues showed that aphasics use facial expressions as opposed to voices to judge whether people are lying or not. Aphasics, as well as the rest of us, perceive the structural information that reveals the meaning in facial expressions directly with their right-hemisphere processes and without their left-hemisphere interpreter intervening to compromise their judgments.[42]

Neurologist Oliver Sacks reports that in working closely with aphasics, he has found that

> one cannot lie to an aphasic. He cannot grasp your words, and so he cannot be deceived by them; but what he grasps with infallible precision, namely that expression.... That totally spontaneous, involuntary expressiveness which can never be simulated or faked, as words alone can.[43]

Sacks claims that many aphasics' understanding is so acute that it is difficult to believe that they suffer from this disability. To prove that they actually are aphasic, it is often necessary for a researcher to remove all extra-verbal cues to the point of using a voice synthesizer when speaking to depersonalize the situation completely.[44] This is even truer of blind aphasics, whose sensitivity to every vocal nuance, tone, modulation, and inflection makes it almost impossible to fool them.[45] The opposite is true of people who suffer from whole tonal agnosia, a condition in which they understand words perfectly, but are completely baffled by the nuances involved in communication.[46] Sacks notes that aphasia is a disorder of the temporal lobe in the left hemisphere, where language ability is located; by contrast, whole tonal agnosia is a disorder of the temporal lobe in the right hemisphere, where our perceptual skills are located.

To demonstrate his aphasic patients' skill in discerning exactly what is going on despite their inability to understand language, Sacks tells a story of how these patients became hysterical with laughter at a televised speech by President Reagan, while viewers with normal language skills had no idea what the aphasics were laughing at. Sacks noted in analyzing Reagan's speech that "so cunning was deceptive word-use combined with deceptive tone, that only the brain-damaged remained intact, undeceived."[47]

Two Widely Accepted Unsubstantiated Theories That Threaten Our Survival

How empty is theory in the presence of facts.
—MARK TWAIN

The world is not only complex; it is continuous. Yet we keep attempting to separate it into the discrete parts we "see" with our mind's eye. The French philosopher René Descartes even argued that contiguous entities, such as our minds and bodies, are nonetheless separate because they are vastly different kinds of entities. For Descartes, the body was a machine and the mind was pure thinking substance.[48] Descartes never adequately explained where the mind was located, or how it operated if it was separate from the body, but his theory's legacy can still be found in perceptual theories that rely on mental mediation instead of direct perception, and in two widely believed, related theories that, at our peril, we seem to take as fact. The first is the theory that *each of us is an individual that is separate from everyone else,* which confuses uniqueness and rights with separateness; and the second asserts that, as individuals, *we are also separate from the environment in which we live*, as if we were not completely dependent on its resources. Both these theories mentally abstract us from the complex systems within which we live our lives as participants and components, and to which we make unique contributions that are critical to the diversity and sustainability of those systems.

One interesting evolutionary argument against our status as individuals has been suggested by philosophers Michael Ghiselin, last at the University of California, Berkeley, and David Hull, last at Northwestern University.[49,50] Both Ghiselin and Hull argue that it is not each one of us that is an individual, but the entire human species. Their analysis goes something like this: Given that species are evolutionary units, the traits that make up the species must be passed down from one generation to the next, forming an interconnected lineage that cannot be cut into parts and maintain itself—for where would one make the cuts? Therefore it is the entire species that is the individual, and each person or organism is one of its parts. An organism belongs to a species only if it is causally connected to other organisms in that species by genetic or other hereditary processes. Thus, the organisms of a species must be part of the same lineage. Those parts make up the species.

In other words, species are evolutionary units or lineages that, at any particular time, contain all the genetic or other hereditary material that makes it what it is and that separates it from other species. If you take a complex system view, then a species is a multicomponent complex system that evolves over time through natural selection, and each organism is a part or a component of the that system. One reason why is that each organism only has a portion of the genetic material that makes up the whole species, while the rest of that material is distributed among the rest of that species' components. This of course is evolution's strategy for creating the diversity needed to maintain the system's complexity by mixing up the gene pool through propitious mating. To be a separate individual and remain human, one would have to have all the genes in the gene pool and all the characteristics that make epigenetic changes possible when developmental challenges occur. Since no one person has the full complement of the species' genes, and yet obtains their identity and function from being a part of the species, each one is a component of the species rather than an individual. As for our theories that we are above and thereby separate from our environment, in which we are necessarily inextricably embedded, those theories started long ago:

> Let us make mankind in our image…and let them have dominion over the fish of the sea, and over the fowl of the air, and over the cattle of the fields, and over all the earth and every creeping thing that creeps along the ground. (Gen. 1:26: King James Version)

One might ask if we could survive without our environment's resources and, if not, do we stand alone enough to be considered separate? On a practical level our separateness is even more suspect. Most of us are standing on a road someone else built, in shoes someone else made, with our eyes and ears open to and influenced by other people's opinions and actions. Indeed, as helpless infants, we need as many people and community resources as we can muster to help us develop. We wouldn't even be here without eons of genetic material that was donated to your mother's fertilized egg and that ended up as you. One might suppose that individuality is the sum of all these outside inputs if it were not for the fact that so many of us fail to act independently and can be so easily swayed by outside influences.

The notion that we are separate individuals has led to disastrous outcomes. Consider how this theoretical detachment misguides people who have directly perceived unprecedented flooding, crop-killing drought, enormous storms, and unsettling coastal erosion in their hometowns, and yet who continue to exercise what they consider to be their rights as individuals to drive SUVs that exacerbate those conditions. Whether we like it or not, we are individuals only very tenuously. Everything we do influences what happens to others and to the Earth. More accurately, we are components of many of the complex systems that constitute our world and within which we live our lives. Our survival depends on our interactions with all the other components in those systems. Again, this does not make us less important or less unique. In fact, it is just the opposite, because each complex system is created by, and dependent on, the many different interactions of its various, unique components. As such components, we privilege the information that triggers our interactions with other components and ultimately our survival.

Given the primacy of structural information for our survival, can we have theories about the world that we construct in our minds and still see the world as it is? English physicist David Bohm proposed an answer:

Can we be aware of the ever changing and flowing reality of the actual process of knowledge? Although this is a task we are not used to, if we can put the preconceptions in our minds aside and think from such awareness, we will not be led to mistake what originates in thought and what originates in reality that is independent of thought.[51]

In his seminal book, *Wholeness and the Implicate Order,* Bohm proposed that the world has an intrinsic order. This book adds that this order is manifest in the dynamic structural information that reveals the organization of Earth's complex, adaptive systems. Bohm also suggests that our minds are privy to this order and that it is a dimension in which both the physical world and our minds participate. In other words, the complex systems of our world and those of the neural networks in our brain reciprocate. Physicist Robert McLaughlin at Stanford University echoes this view: "Human behavior resembles nature because it is part of nature and ruled by the same laws as everything else."[52]

Let me be clear. This view in no way argues against the progress we have made using the scientific method, nor does it question the ability of our imaginative minds to produce great works of art, ask profound ethical questions, or invent the light bulb. But it does mean that those enterprises require ground rules.

How to Judge a Theory

In theory, there is no difference between practice and theory. In practice, there is.

—JAN VAN DE SNEPSCHEUT

Our job is to see that the theories we live by do not get out of hand or work against our well-being. Clearly, this has not always been the case. A credible theory such as Darwin's biology-based theory of natural selection, for example, was once reframed into the ideologically based theory of social Darwinism, which designated certain groups of people as "unfit." This reframing of Darwin spawned the dangerous theory of eugenics, which proposed we could breed people to approved specifications and cull others out.

Although the standard scientific method is currently the best way we have to test a theory, we still need to be vigilant to make sure that this method is not compromised. Problems arise when researchers change the rules of the game, and instead of using direct observations to test their theories, they replace perceivable evidence with models and mathematics that they have constructed to match the theories in their heads. While theories can gain some confirmation by observation, experiment, and peer scrutiny, they are less reliable when they are based on models that cannot replicate reality and are based on biased interpretations.[53] Theories are even less reliable if they piggyback on other theories or on expert opinions as opposed to direct experience, and we hit the bottom of the reliability barrel with theories that are rooted in ideologies, mask hidden agendas, stir up controversy, and get a great deal of press. The false theory that "climate warming is a liberal hoax" is one example. It came from the American Legislative Exchange Council, the legislative and public relations arm of the oil industry and their associated business interests.[54]

If we cannot count on experts to judge the validity of theories and if we have limited knowledge ourselves, how can we distinguish a good theory from a bad one? As a start, we can ask the following questions.

What evidence supports this theory?
Who created this theory? Are they credible?
Who benefits from this theory?
Who suffers if this theory is acted upon and does not work?
Who is providing the money to publicize and support this theory?
What uncertainties are inherent in this theory?
Does this theory simply confirm a belief that you already have?

In chapter 8, I scrutinize scientific theories that are typically assembled according to the rules of scientific evidence and, as such, help to advance our knowledge of the world.

8

Are Scientific Theories Different?

My theory of evolution is that Darwin was adopted.
—STEVEN WRIGHT

ON WEDNESDAY, JUNE 22, 1633, Galileo Galilei, considered by many to be the father of science, was publically tried, convicted of heinous crimes, and banished to the dungeons of the Holy Office of the Inquisition. The Inquisitor's court declared, "You Galileo.... vehemently suspected of heresy namely of having held and believed the doctrine which is false and contrary to the sacred, divine scripture that the sun is the center of the world and does not move from the East to the West and that the earth moves and is not the center of the world."[1] Further, "we order that the book *Dialogue* [*Concerning the Two Chief Systems of the World*] be prohibited by public edict."[2]

Galileo had confirmed Copernicus' heliocentric theory that the Earth revolved around the Sun using evidence that he saw through his telescope. On January 7, 1610, he saw three "stars" near Jupiter. For the next seven days he watched as these stars moved to new positions, disappeared, and reappeared. On the fifteenth, four stars reappeared west of Jupiter. Galileo wrote:

> Here we have a powerful and elegant argument....That the planets revolve around the sun in the Copernican system...not just one planet revolving round another while both make a circle around the sun, but our eyes show us four stars that wander around Jupiter, as does the moon around the earth, and these stars together with Jupiter describe a large circle round the sun in a period of twelve years.[3]

By contrast, the Church's conflicting geocentric theory that the Sun revolved around the Earth was distilled solely from scripture such as:

Tremble before him, all earth; yea the world stand firm, never to be moved. (1 Chron. 16:30: King James Version)

Nonetheless the Inquisition placed Galileo's *Dialogue* on its Index of banned books.

After considerable maneuvering by his influential friends, Galileo was eventually placed under house arrest for the rest of his life. A lively black market trade immediately began as priests and scholars bought up every copy of the *Dialogue* that they could find to prevent the Inquisitors from destroying them. People who owned a copy would not part with it. The book was not taken off the Index until almost two hundred years later in 1822.

Today, because everyone with a telescope can see Jupiter's moons, no one disputes Galileo's heliocentric theory of the universe. It may have started out as a theory, but in the intervening five hundred years, even with so many new scientific advances, no one has disproved it. Galileo's conviction of heresy is a prime example of how a false theory can trump perceivable evidence. In his seminal book, *A Brief History of Time,* physicist Stephen Hawking wrote, "Galileo, perhaps more than any other single person, was responsible for the birth of modern science.... For Galileo was one of the first to argue that man could hope to understand how the world works, and moreover, that we could do this by observing the real world."[4]

Scientific theories are very different from those that come from our unconfirmed opinions and beliefs. Scientists confirm their theories through systematic observation, experimentation, and peer review, and as we have seen with Galileo, their results can, on occasion, come close to gaining the status of accepted fact. But those theories that gain that status typically rest on a firm basis of observation and perceivable evidence. Galileo observed the ever-changing configurations of structural information that Jupiter's moons made as they revolved around Jupiter. But many scientific theories do not yield such irrefutable results; they are invented, go through periods of dominating their fields, and are replaced when a new or a better one comes along. Remember when B. F. Skinner's behaviorism dominated psychology before it was replaced by cognitive psychology? Now cognitive psychology is fraying around the edges of mental mediation and its focus on limited numbers of independent variables instead of on complex systems.

When new discoveries are made that account for existing data more precisely, and in turn falsify current theories, those theories are supposed to be replaced. Because new discoveries emerge every day and our knowledge is continually evolving, scientific theories are expected to remain open to new ideas and not get bogged down in any particular theory. Philosopher Karl Popper reminds us that there is no final proof for any theory. It can always be disproved by conflicting data or by another theory that fits the existing evidence better.[5] The key word here is *evidence.* When new evidence surfaces that challenges the claims of an existing theory, the whole investigative process is supposed to begin again. But, in reality, the acceptance of new evidence may be delayed as proponents of a prevailing theory try to preserve the territory they have fenced off with their particular frame. As physicist Max Planck pointed out, "A new scientific truth does not triumph by convincing its opponents and making them see the light, but rather because its opponents eventually die."[6] Or as one wag put it, science progresses one funeral at a time. When a flawed theory has a grip on the collective mind of a particular field, anyone who comes up with a conflicting theory is often mocked and marginalized.

Alfred Wegener and the Theory of Continental Drift

Nature uses only the longest threads to weave her patterns, so each small piece of the fabric reveals the organization of the entire tapestry.
—RICHARD FEYNMAN

A classic example of theoretical intransigence involved an early twentieth-century theory of how the Earth was formed. At that time, most geologists and geophysicists believed that the Earth started out in a molten state and was still solidifying. Their theory allowed for vertical movements that created mountains, but because they believed the Earth was still contracting, it did not allow for horizontal movement. When identical plants and fossils were found on different continents that were separated by an ocean, it seemed to indicate horizontal land movement, and so scientists invented land bridges that supposedly once spanned the ocean and had since sunk to the ocean floor.[7]

Then along came Alfred Wegener, who pitted an amazing amount of actual evidence against their prevailing theory. He proposed that there had once been one great continent called Pangaea that had split in two and then drifted apart to form Africa and South America.[8] The evidence for what he termed "continental drift" was compelling: The outlines of these two coastlines fit together as if they belonged to the same jigsaw puzzle; the bones of the same type of animals were found strewn along each coast; and the rock formations on each coast were virtually identical and lined up perfectly, even though there was an ocean between them. Further, Wegener showed that the prevailing theory that the earth was contracting could not be true because, in that case, mountain ranges would have risen up equally across the land like wrinkles on a drying plum as the skin rises from its drying pulp. Instead, mountain ranges are confined to narrow curvilinear belts. Wegener proposed that the substratum of the continents was a viscous fluid, and if land could move vertically within this medium (as the rising of mountains showed it did), it could also move horizontally (which the prevailing theory denied). Deposits of salt and sedimentary rock turned out to back Wegener's view.[9]

But because the accepted theory of the Earth had no place for the horizontal movement of land, Wegener's theory of "continental drift and its proponents were dismissed contemptuously as cranks."[10] Wegener's critics gained further support from geologist Harold Jeffrey's book, *The Earth*, which rightly argued that the Earth is far too strong to be deformed by the tidal forces that Wegener claimed caused the continents to drift apart. But Jeffrey's argument addressed only the mechanism behind continental drift. He failed to refute Wegener's much more important point: that a large land mass had split and its two parts had relocated, leaving an ocean between them. Jeffrey had simply ignored the overwhelming weight of Wegener's empirical evidence. As neuroscientist V. S. Ramachandran at the University of California San Diego noted, "one wonders what it would have taken to convince these people: two halves of the same dinosaur skeleton, each on a different side of the Atlantic?"[11]

Wegener and his direct perceptions of evidence performed an invaluable service to science. As geologist Anthony Hallam wrote, "he examined critically a model of the earth that was almost universally accepted. When he discovered weaknesses and inconsistencies, he was bold enough and independent enough to embrace a radical alternative.... Wegener possessed a sense for the significant that rarely erred."[12]

Given Wegener's ability to see through existing theories, and the fact that science purports to be based on empirical evidence, we must ask why opposition to his explanation was so vociferous and persistent. One answer comes from physicist Gunther Stent, who proposed that Wegener's theory was premature.[13] However, given that science proclaims to be based on empirical evidence, and that Wegener's evidence was clearly visible to anyone, a more accurate characterization is that he went against a prevailing theory that was wrong. Sadly, in many cases theories rather than evidence prevail.

Similarly, when Michael Polyani's theory of gas absorption was ridiculed and shelved for forty years, he explained that all new scientific assertions must be tested against prevailing opinion and considered invalid until that view is finally upended.[14] Thomas Kuhn calls such upending a paradigm shift.[15] These circumstances leave us wondering how scientific researchers choose the information they use to construct their theories if their choice is limited by a prior theory. This circular reasoning cannot be resolved as it stands. If, instead, we return to first principles—that science is based on empirical evidence—then any existing theory can be considered merely a theory to explain that evidence, not a scientific sacrament. Science, however, is as much a community as a discipline, and tends to hold beliefs as a whole body and to resist conversion.[16] Even though Wegener's direct perceptions of the evidence were correct, he was considered an outsider whose views could easily be dismissed.

Another classic example of theoretical intransigence involved Watson and Crick's central dogma: that DNA was set in stone. It flowed in one direction only and its information never escaped.

Barbara McClintock and Her Perception of Jumping Genes

The role of vision in her experimental work provides the key to her understanding. What for others is interpretation, or speculation, for her is a matter of trained and direct perception.... "Seeing," in fact, was at the center of her experience.... As she watched the corn plants grow, examined the patterns of their leaves and kernels, looked down the microscope at their chromosomal structure, she saw directly into that ordered world.

—EVELYN FOX KELLER

What, then, are we to make of the three decades of professional ostracism that Nobel Laureate and geneticist Barbara McClintock suffered when she presented evidence, based on her direct perceptions through her microscope, that genes were mobile?[17] Her finding conflicted with the prevailing theory that genetic information could only flow in one direction—from DNA to RNA to protein—and could not escape or be modified.[18] In contrast to Wegener, McClintock was an insider whose stellar reputation began with a 1931 paper (published with her student Harriet Creighton) that established the chromosomal bases of genetics.[19] Her reputation continued to grow as she modified a staining technique to make the processes of division and replication of maize chromosomes visible under a microscope, and demonstrated the link between physical and genetic crossover that revealed how chromosomes share information. She went on to perform experiments that linked a plant's chromosomes with its physical traits, and in the 1940s and 1950s, she discovered and fleshed out the process of transposition.[20–22] McClintock considered transposition "the release of a chromosomal element from its original position and its insertion into a new position to be a key to the complexity of genetic organization—an indicator of the subtlety with which cytoplasm, membranes, and DNA are integrated into a single structure," and she argued that the organism's overall organization is required for it to function.[23] McClintock saw genetics as a complex system in which its components' interactions created nonlinear changes in the larger system it helped create.

McClintock was different from many other scientists at that time in her ability to perceive and understand the structural information that was in front of her eyes. She had an unquestioned confidence in the value of that type of information, and in her ability to explain the genetic phenomena that such information revealed. Her methodology added perceptual acumen to elegant experiments. She studied organisms as complex systems by relating their components to one another on all levels of development, from their chromosomes to their leaves. In observing patterns of coloration on both the leaves and kernels of the maize plants, for instance, McClintock understood the plant's configurations of chromosomes as they appeared under the microscope. What she saw was that

> every chromosome...had a distinctive morphology, a length, shape, and structure of its own.... Certain morphological features varied considerably in different genetic stocks, suggesting the possibility of using these features as tags of particular genetic traits.[24]

McClintock's evidence of the distribution of color patches gave her the ability to discern the trajectory of genetic events that brought about each plant's development. Although she saw the plant as a single complex system, for her the keys to that system were in the smallest details. Those details revealed the plant's more complex process of regulation and control. McClintock counseled that "you let the material tell you where to go, and it tells you at every step what the next step has to be because you're integrating with an overall brand new pattern."[25] Her focus on, and ability to perceive, the many layers of complexity inherent in and available from structural information was extraordinary. She could walk down a row of maize plants and, by looking at nothing more than the leaves of a plant, she was able to describe its chromosomal structure.

In 1951, however, at a professional symposium at Cold Spring Harbor, New York, McClintock presented evidence that genes not only jump around, but also make new connections. This was a radical departure from what her colleagues believed—that information was locked into a preordained sequence and never changed. Perhaps even more damning in the larger scientific world, McClintock's direct perceptual methodology defied the widespread assumption that our senses and the data they access are suspect. Without any real understanding of her work, some of her colleagues not only thought she was wrong, but they went so far as to call her mad and broadcast their opinions to this effect, thus marginalizing both her and her work. The important point that they missed was that McClintock was describing genetic motility as a dynamic complex system that changed over time and space.

In the fall of 1961, however, François Jacob and Jacques Monod published a paper, "Genetic Regulatory Mechanisms in the Synthesis of Proteins," that tweaked the central dogma. Their theory claimed that protein synthesis was not regulated by the structural gene itself (the gene that codes for protein) but by two other genes—an operator gene located next to the structural gene, and a regulator gene at another location on the chromosome.[26] Even though this work was related to McClintock's 1950 and 1953 papers on gene motility, Jacob and Monod failed to reference her work at that time.[27,28] In 1965, Jacob and Monod received a Nobel Prize for the work reported in their 1961 paper. McClintock continued to fade from public view and worked in obscurity.

From these facts, it would seem that McClintock and her work were sacrificed to what we now know is at best an incomplete theory and the assumption that work on the molecular level is superior to work on the complex-systems level. The backstory may be that, at that time, genetics was influenced by an influx of physicists (such as Max Delbruck, who had fled Germany during World War II) who promoted reductionism and mechanism in biology. These researchers investigated phenomena in their simplest forms, and they believed the complexity of whole organisms muddied the waters. Biology rapidly descended into a science of molecular mechanics whose practitioners believed that there was no need to deal with the complexity of terrestrial-level organisms because molecular findings applied universally. In that light, Jacques Monod reportedly remarked that what is true for *E. coli* is true for the elephant.[29] But as it eventually turned out, what was true for *E. coli* was not only not true for the elephant, it was not even true for *E. coli*.[30]

The key point that the reigning reductionists seemed to overlook was that there is no maize plant on the molecular level. Its organization is what brought it into its terrestrial existence. By restricting their research to the molecular level, reductionist researchers never saw the self-organizing processes of the actual maize plant. Instead, they went in the other direction and reduced the maize plant to its chemistry. McClintock concluded that the molecular geneticists who dominated the field were not yet able to grasp the importance of complex organization, and as a result, she curtailed her publishing after 1953. She attributed her colleagues' attitudes to her work to "tacit assumptions"—a belief in theories and models that impose unconscious boundaries between what is thinkable and what is not. Evidence that conflicts with their assumptions is unacceptable, and their preference for making everything numerical blocks their ability to see things as they are in themselves. McClintock's enterprise was very different. In considering the whole plant as a complex system, she realized that its structure and function could not be explained by the operations of its separate molecular components because new properties emerge that their precursors do not possess. Those properties are a function of the organization of the maize plant, not of its separate parts.

By the 1980s the larger world had recognized McClintock's extraordinary research. Among many other awards, she received the first MacArthur Genius award in 1981 when she was 79, and the 1983

Nobel Prize for work on "mobile genetic elements." By that time, Jacob and Monod had apologized for failing to give her credit.[31] Despite these prizes and recognition, and MIT historian and philosopher of science Evelyn Fox Keller's superb biography of McClintock, *A Feeling for the Organism*, those who believed in the central dogma that reduced complexity to simplicity still managed to mount challenges to McClintock's work. In a 1980 paper published in *Nature*, molecular geneticists Leslie Orgel and Francis Crick claimed that a portion of DNA, including transposons (motile genetic elements), was "junk" that served little useful purpose. They argued that "the spread of selfish DNA sequences within the genome can be compared to the spread of a not-too-harmful parasite within its host." In other words, they argued that transposons had no value.[32] However, they were the key to McClintock's work on genetic motility. They were in effect dismissing the value of her research.

Today McClintock's work has another vocal and influential advocate. In her 2012 presidential address to the American Association for the Advancement of Science, geneticist Nina Federoff pointed out that Orgel and Crick assumed that there is DNA that can increase its real estate within the genome, yet responds to no influences and therefore has no effect on an organism's phenotype.[33] In contrast, Federoff argues that transposases (the enzymes on the tips of transposons that trigger their actions) are far from excess baggage; it is their ability to shuffle and relocate sections of DNA that drives variation. "Simply put," she said, "transposases drive genome evolution."[34] Indeed, since molecular geneticists did not look at how molecules combined to form higher order organizations, they had no way to account for how these organisms evolved.

McClintock's life and work clearly show the value of looking before and after you theorize. They also illustrate the sad situation scientists often face when they bring eyes that have seen new evidence to the table. Her work is testimony to the importance of human perception and of structural information in understanding how the complex systems of our world work.

This is also true of scientific methodologies. Today mathematical modeling and computer simulations have by and large replaced the keen eyes of a Darwin or a Galileo, or even those of an Alexander Fleming, who accidently discovered that common bread mold could be used to produce penicillin. Just as flawed theories can prevail despite conflicting evidence, scientific methodologies can do the same. If a methodology is backed with the mathematics that is currently "in style," it is considered to be more "robust"—a theory that has no basis in fact, as history has made clear with theories based on numerology. While mathematics can be extremely helpful when used as an adjunct to observation, the elevation of math models, along with other methods that reduce complex systems to their parts, marginalizes research such as Wegener's and McClintock's, which originates in direct observation.[35]

How Science Can Progress by Extending Our Eyes

A time will come when man should be able to stretch out his eyes.... They should see planets like our earth.

—CHRISTOPHER WREN, 1657

Today we have many ways of extending the reach of our eyes to gather scientific evidence that is not typically available to our unaided perceptual systems. Medical imaging from X-rays to PET scans to fMRI makes the inner workings of our bodies and brains more accessible. But the information that reveals the real-time operations and structural configurations of earth's large, complex systems comes from the 120 satellites we have positioned from a few hundred miles to 250,000 miles up into the atmosphere. By connecting those images using computer programs that preserve their original form, "we see the world as one big system rolling around the sun."[36] We can even perceive systems that are normally invisible to us because satellites can record their operations by using the ultraviolet or infrared parts of the electromagnetic spectrum that our eyes cannot see, or by bouncing radar off surfaces to tell tales of what lies below. We can now perceive the same type of structural configuration that our eyes see in body movements writ large in the fluid-dynamic patterns of ocean currents as they flow beneath the surface waters from pole to pole; in how the prevailing winds circumnavigate the globe, distributing clouds and rainfall; in how spiraling storm systems rise up and buffet miles of coastline; and how global warming affects biomass production as deserts encroach where once there was cropland.

In an extraordinary segment of PBS' *NOVA*, "Earth from Space," we can see (through the lens of satellite Terra) the Bodele Depression deep in the Sahara Desert, which houses an ancient lakebed with 24,000 square miles of dried plankton that has changed to phosphate-filled diatoms. The phosphates are caught up by the prevailing winds that blow dust storms west across Africa. At the coast, dust- and phosphate-laden air rises far up into the atmosphere and crosses the Atlantic Ocean to the coast of South America and the Amazon Basin. Here, five thousand miles from where it started, the phosphate dust dissolves into raindrops and falls to fertilize the plants in the rainforest. Thousands of tons of phosphates make this journey each year, enriching the forest soil. As the phosphates are taken up by each tree's roots, you can watch their tops grow in real time. Where there was one leaf today, tomorrow there are three, and the forest becomes increasingly green. From the forest floor, the phosphates also leach into the Amazon River, where they travel downstream to where the river meets the sea. When they are released into the sea, they cause a great plankton bloom that attracts and feeds fish from miles around and sends the phosphates on a new journey around the world.[37]

Another way we extend our eyes is with geographic information science, which involves a combination of GSI (the Global Positioning System), satellite remote sensing, and computer cartography. Douglas Richardson of the Association of American Geographers and his colleagues have shown that this system can "integrate highly accurate geographic location and time with virtually any observation...such as health, environmental, genomic, social or demographic data for interactive spatial analysis."[38] This technology allows us to see and track complex systems such as "pandemic flu viruses or evolving genetic strains of tuberculosis.... With real-time interactive

GPS/GSI functionality now increasingly embedded in cell phones and low cost navigation and other mobile devices, individual citizens also are contributing to the flow of health-related geospatial data."[39] Just as satellites can cover the physical world from the sky, research scientists aided by citizen scientists can cover it from the ground. By tracking fifteen million cell phone users, for example, Amy Wesolowski, a PhD student in engineering and public policy at Carnegie Mellon University, and her colleagues have monitored the spread of malaria in Kenya, and volunteers from Japan to California with GPS-enabled real-time air-quality monitoring systems are assessing exposures to air pollution and radiation at spatial resolution levels and data densities not previously feasible.[40,41]

Theories and Complexity

The immediate role of cognition is to control behavior.... The point of that control is to deal with environmental complexity.

—PETER GODFREY-SMITH

We evolved in a world of complex systems and our lives are lived within them. I have argued that our species has survived because our perceptual systems are tuned to detect the structural information that reveals the properties of these systems. Similarly, philosopher Peter Godfrey-Smith at the City University of New York claims that the evolution of human cognition is a response to the complex systems that constitute our environment.[42] But what happens if we find ourselves in situations where many of our environment's typical and necessary components have been eliminated or obscured, or the complex systems that are critical to our lives are simplified or destabilized?

On a physical level, research shows that when we perceive repetitive, monotonous, seemingly perceptually simple environments where structural information is too subtle to attract our attention, we often suffer from some degree of sensory deprivation. For example, when we drive through the desert, we are usually moving too fast and sitting too far away from its subtle structures and systems to discern them. From inside a car, the desert can appear to be nothing more than miles of beige expanse. Under such limited stimulation, we are far more likely to tune out, default to our own thoughts, and become less aware of our surroundings. The result of this lack of awareness is that we can end up in automobile accidents, many of them fatal.[43] Transportation engineers find that one way of keeping people alert and preventing accidents is to add components to the environmental system that increase its level of complexity. They add unexpected details to roads such as curbs and "eye openers" such as groves of trees or other appealing scenery at irregular intervals; in France, they have also tried art shows (like our Burma-Shave signs of times past).[44]

Environmental research also shows that people typically prefer natural to artificial environments and one reason may be that natural environments are infinitely complex.[45] This may be because the components of a natural complex system have not only coevolved in constant interaction with each other to self-organize the system, but they continue to produce needed change as new challenges occur. In addition, many components are needed to create the diversity that supports complexity. This finding may seem inconsistent with our tuning out while driving on highways through natural desert country, but when people report preferring natural environments, they perceive themselves to be in those environments: hiking in the mountains, jogging along the seashore, or simply sitting and viewing the terrain. If you have never spent time in the desert, at first when you are driving through, it appears uniform. But if you stop, sit very still on a rock, and look around you, what at first may have seemed an impoverished, monochrome landscape will start to articulate before your eyes. What had seemed to be a barren wasteland will come alive. Insects of all sorts will appear out of cracks in the soil and scurry about. All of a sudden, a greenish-beige lizard will emerge from the background of what had first appeared to be nothing more than a grayish-green rock where he had been sunning himself all the time. Dry gray-green and bluish plants that had seemed at first to look alike begin to separate themselves by structure or subtleties of color—a four-wing saltbush here, a flat-top buckwheat there, and the smell and look of sage on the wind.

In contrast, an artificial environment that promotes perceptual deprivation is one that has been deliberately designed by outside planners according to a preconceived theory. Because such an environment is not self-organized by its components, it is less likely to meet the needs of those components. One theory of design that had this type of effect on artificial environments was the Bauhaus School of architecture, which was influenced by the theories of French architect Le Corbusier. His theory of design, rooted in the principles of rationality, orderliness, and Euclidean geometry, glorified the mechanistic aspects of the industrial age rather than the actual needs of human beings. In fact, Le Corbusier's impetus was to clean up the mess that he believed poor people had made of their traditional neighborhoods, which he believed could be accomplished by tearing down what he considered to be slums and imposing clean, pure technology and design. He did not consider the way that complex self-organizing, environmental, and social systems actually work.

Following Le Corbusier's theories, urban planners all over the world destroyed existing urban neighborhoods that, although they may have been shabby, nonetheless included a complex mix of houses, apartments, stores, public transportation, and spaces that supported a vibrant street life and brought neighbors together. They replaced these dynamic neighborhoods with repetitive, high-rise concrete boxes, cut off from shops and transportation and lacking places for neighbors to congregate.[46,47] The residents that were moved into these sterile buildings felt little connection to their new homes or neighbors, and instead, felt alienated. Le Corbusier's rational, mechanistic theory of architecture imposed an order from without that disrupted the complex system that had been these people's lives—their access to resources, transportation, and the social networks and habitual ways of life that had sustained them.[48]

If you have ever been in the desolate housing projects in the South Bronx in New York City (before the city demolished them to rid themselves of the high crime rate such projects produced), or the blocks of monotonous, gray concrete buildings on the outskirts of Paris that house poor immigrant workers, no explanation would be necessary. Although the building style repeats itself until you cannot tell one place from another, the factors that make for a workable living environment—straight lines of sight so that you can easily see where you are going; shared, defensible communal spaces that discourage antisocial or criminal behavior; or adjacent gardens that provide a respite from city concrete and asphalt—were not typically included. In addition, the inside of peoples' flats have little relationship to the outside environment. Needless to say, with so little visual interest or practical amenities, residents barely took note of their surroundings. With no eyes on the street, no sense of belonging to their neighborhood, and no one "to mind the store," the buildings and grounds were trashed and crime became endemic.

Some years ago, I became lost in a maze of such identical, prison-like structures when I was traveling south out of Paris by car. When I asked a young man on a motorcycle for directions to the road south, he laughed and said we'd never make it out on our own. This neighborhood was not complex (which is perceivable), but it was complicated (which is not). A *complex* environment is one that is organized so that its components and their contribution to the landscape are easily perceived. In contrast, a *complicated* environment is either a hodgepodge of unrelated items that are difficult to keep in mind, or a simplistic repetitive one, where the sameness of its many parts make it difficult to tell one part from another.

The young man kindly asked us to follow him, and he led us out of this monotone maze to the road south. I remarked at the time that it would be very difficult to find a criminal that was hiding in what was then known to be a huge, crime-ridden warren where there are few eyes on the street. According to architectural critic Jane Jacobs, such eyes on the street are a hallmark of a lively, safe neighborhood.[49] To combat such conditions, urban planners have developed the burgeoning field of crime prevention through environmental design, which promotes adding the variety and thus the complexity that supports a vibrant neighborhood.

Given that our perceptual systems respond to the structural information that reveals the properties of our world's complex systems, what happens when our culture provides us with theories that distract us and obscure that information? Theories, both those that are scientific and those that are based on our opinions and beliefs, are a far cry from the complex systems that constitute our world. Instead, they are abstract mental creations that merely represent and sometimes misrepresent those systems, because they have partitioned only a small part for scrutiny. In our attempt to streamline the world so it fits into the confines of our mental processes and their symbolic methods of communication, the theories we create fall far short of providing us with enough of the accurate and comprehensive information that we acquire through our perceptual systems. When a theory partitions the world, it can actually destroy the very system it is being used to understand. We have produced this outcome, for example, when we isolate vitamins from their multicomponent food sources and lose the beneficial synergy they have in their original state. Our scientific investigations leave us with the "binding problem"—how to put the world we have partitioned back together again. If all we have to understand the world is theories with limited subsets of components, we can easily adopt unworkable policies, such as those based on Le Corbusier's flawed theory that simplistic architectural solutions could clean up neighborhoods that are rife with poverty and crime.

If we want to understand what is happening around us, we need to realize that the world's natural unit of analysis is not the separate object or variable. It is the multi-component, complex system. When we adopt theories that reduce those systems to their components and then manipulate or eliminate those components, we destabilize and often destroy these systems. As we shall presently see in chapter 9, on the basis of unsubstantiated theories and reality-challenged mathematical models, a single component of our economy, the financial sector, and its fairly recently minted dominant component—the over-the-counter derivative—took over our normally far more complex economic system, operated in a black-box environment that obscured what was going on, and led to the 2008 global economic collapse.

Are Economic Theories Different?

*Dogs are bound by biology. Humans can soar on
the wings of conventionalized misrepresentation.*
—JULES HENRY

IN 1995, CORPORATE giants Procter & Gamble and Gibson
Greeting Cards claimed that Bankers Trust, one of the most reputable banks in the country, had knowingly sold them over \$120 million
of unregulated over-the-counter (OTC) derivatives that were not
worth the paper they were printed on.[1] Both companies alleged that
Bankers Trust had convinced them to buy these complicated investments, misrepresented their value, and, when they suffered losses,
pushed them to buy more by assuring them that they would recoup
their funds.[2] Derivatives have no real value in themselves. They are
merely bets on the price of what other things, such as commodities
or mortgage bonds, might be worth in the future. Since Bankers
Trust traders created those bets in their minds, they could structure
them any way they chose. They chose to use sophisticated algorithms
that were so complicated that they obscured their true risk.[3]

The derivative dance between Gibson Greeting Cards and
Bankers Trust began when Gibson borrowed \$50 million at an
interest rate of 9.33% from another bank and was looking for ways
to lower that rate.[4] Bankers Trust offered Gibson a derivative "swap"
that allowed the company to lower its interest by switching from a
fixed-rate to a variable one (similar to a homeowner switching from
a fixed- to a variable-rate mortgage).[5] From then on, Bankers Trust

created "a chain link series of no less than 29 swap transactions" that became increasingly complicated.[6] Law professor Frank Partnoy at the University of San Diego noted that "Gibson's swap smorgasbord included the most sophisticated derivatives anyone had invented and they all were hidden from regulators and shareholders.... One trade called a Wedding Band, was too complex to describe without a mathematician and a psychotherapist."[7] These trades exposed Gibson to huge losses, of which they were unaware—possibly because "Bankers Trust started lying to Gibson at the end of 1992 by systematically under-reporting actual losses."[8] While Bankers Trust earned $13 million from transaction-related fees on these trades, they nevertheless refused to reveal their proprietary valuation models to Gibson. Without any knowledge of how Bankers Trust's valuation model worked, Gibson had no way to evaluate the validity of the bases upon which Bankers Trust had created these investments.[9]

Bankers Trust acted in a similar fashion with Procter & Gamble. We know this because tapes of secret telephone conversations between Bankers Trust employees surfaced during the trial that revealed that they knew they were selling snake oil. During a call to discuss the Procter & Gamble account, the traders boasted that "they had set them up," and in another call they boasted they were "going to clean their clocks."[10] "They had devised a formula that played havoc with Procter & Gamble's interest costs—a brain twisting concoction and a testament to Bankers Trust's 'rocket scientists.'"[11] Both companies filed suits for fraud and won. In 1995, when their cases came to trial, RICO violations (under the Racketeer Influenced and Corrupt Organizations Act, most famously used to prosecute mobsters) were added to the charges.[12] Bankers Trust settled the fraud charges for hundreds of millions of dollars and pled guilty to three other felonies.

This 1995 case was the canary in the mine. It was the first time any of the downsides of the OTC derivatives market had surfaced publicly. At that point, few realized exactly where the ability to create an investment instrument in one's head from little more than spit and imagination—with no perceivable counterpart in the world that could be checked—would lead. In 1998, however, that downside became clearer as it brought down the neck-deep-in-derivatives $1.3 trillion hedge fund, Long-Term Capital Management (LTCM), which presaged the derivatives-riddled economic collapse of 2008.[13] While many chapters in this book are primarily about the perceivable structural information that we require to make wise decisions concerning complex systems, both this chapter and the one that follows also cover the other side of the same coin: What happens when such information is rendered unavailable or eliminated? These chapters are largely about the negative outcomes that occur when outside interests with their own agendas conspire to hide critical information behind closed doors and private transactions or actually destroy a complex system entirely by replacing its components with ones over which they have control. In these circumstances, no one can access the structural information they need to make informed decisions, and we become vulnerable to the type of catastrophes we now face.

One might ask if the case of Bankers Trust could be attributed to simple greed rather than the misuse of both a theory and its mathematical barnacles. While the climate at Bankers Trust most probably encouraged greed, it was not greed, but physics, that provided the sophisticated tools for creating derivatives that obscured their risk. It was not greed, but our ability to create things in our head that ignore reality and then proceed to loose them upon the world without considering the consequences. It was not greed, but a misconceived theory of human rationality and self-interest that insisted regulation and oversight were not necessary. In short, it is unlikely that Bankers Trust's baroque deals could have been assembled without the support of unrealistic economic theories, accompanied by more and more sophisticated and less understandable mathematical models.

All of these factors promoted first the mental and then the physical detachment of economics as a discipline from the real economy's complex system of trading investments, goods, and services. Perhaps even more damaging, this cabal of causes unbalanced the real economy's multicomponent complexity by orchestrating its domination by a single component, the financial sector. Since the financial sector dealt mostly within its own ranks, for its own profit, and at best interacted minimally with the larger economy's other components, it became a law unto itself. In the end, it even refused to make loans, which had been its function in the real economy. And since that sector controlled most of the world's currency, the rest of the economy went wanting. Complex systems such as economies are self-organized and self-sustained by the interactions of their many components, and can easily be destabilized when those interactions fail to support the larger system or are paralyzed by a powerful rogue component. It is not too difficult to understand how a footloose financial sector armed with untraceable, dangerous derivatives could be implicated in less than lawful activities and the recent collapse of our economy.

Economist Friedrich Hayek did, however, make an excellent argument for why some types of regulation do not work. He asserted that if you impose restrictions from the outside on a non-linear, self-organizing, complex system such as the economy, it can have unintended and often unwanted consequences.[14,15] For example, when the United States ratified Prohibition and eliminated legitimate liquor sales, the liquor business simply reorganized itself outside the law with the added components of smuggling, bathtub gin, gang wars, and private clubs, but the law did little to curb either liquor sales or drinking.

Hayek argued that in an economic system, only price, as determined by buyer and seller negotiations, can reflect the general will of that whole system. He further argued that even though the market ends up hurting some people and helping others, attempts to regulate that system to produce social justice (which he calls a mirage) are foolish because they will also have unpredictable and often unwanted consequences.[16,17] In short, Hayek was against any form of economic regulation because he believed that in a complex, self-organizing system, the information contained in that system is distributed widely among its participants and no one factor can successfully impose restrictions on the whole.[18] This seems to make sense until one examines the system he had in mind.

Consider what happens when many participant/components of such a complex market system want to rein in one component—the banks that hold their deposits—from a repeat of playing fast and loose with their money, and to do so, they try to get Glass-Steagall, a law that does just that, reinstated. One component of the system, the bankers and their lobbyists, descends on Washington, and with a sufficient number of campaign contributions manages to squash any serious regulation of the very activities with which they had lost these depositors' funds. Hayek rightly understands that a complex system cannot be regulated by a few outsiders and continue to function. But he fails to consider that, for the same reason, that same complex system cannot be rigged by a few insiders with privileged sources of information and connections and still remain a viable system. The critical factor of information being distributed among all of a system's components is all but eliminated in this situation (as it was in the derivatives market).

There is a difference between banning legal liquor sales and shielding the derivatives market so people don't know what is going on. Prohibition may have closed the legal bars, but it did not destroy that part of the hospitality economy; instead, it gave rise to illegal speakeasies and business continued almost as usual. With derivatives, the financial sector cannibalized many of the other components of the system, such as the housing market. No new components of the economy (even illegal ones) arose that the majority of people wanted. Instead, many parts of the economy that people did want, such as small-business loans, became unavailable, while the price of homes rose beyond people's means. Hayek was a brilliant thinker, but he was nonetheless caught in the net of unrealistic economic theories that, in effect, limited the components of the economic theory he supported to inside traders with privileged access to policymakers.

This chapter chronicles how, over centuries, people with such unrealistic economic theories and practices have colonized our collective mind and, as a result, have managed to structure our economy to match their theories while obscuring reality, in much the same way that derivatives were structured to obscure their inherent risk.

Replacing Reality: The Evolution of the Derivative

Derivatives are financial weapons of mass destruction.

—WARREN BUFFETT

Economic theories today that support the sale of OTC derivatives evolved from roots in the seventeenth century when Adam Smith, the father of economics, created his theory of how markets worked. By overlooking perceivable evidence that was available from actual markets, and piggybacking instead on Newtonian mechanics and sixteenth-century enlightenment philosophy, Smith declared that "markets operate like machines and the people who participate in those operations are totally rational and always act in their own self-interest."[19,20] He seemed unaware that real markets are complex systems that continually evolve and change, more like organisms than machines. He also ignored our history of irrational behavior—speculation spirals such as the Dutch tulip mania, South America's rubber craze, and a series of real estate bubbles that have been recorded as far back as the time of Tiberius in ancient Rome. Although it is outside the scope of this book, the field of behavioral economics, started by Herbert Simon at Carnegie Mellon, Daniel Kahneman at Princeton, and Amos Tversky at Stanford, describes our predilection for making irrational decisions.[21–23] British economist John Maynard Keynes' observation that the market can remain irrational longer than you can remain solvent seems appropriate here.

Smith's theory also held that, similar to the way a machine functions, the forces of supply and demand, production and consumption, naturally bring the market to a balanced state.[24] Then along came mathematical economist Léon Walras, who reframed Smith's notion of balance into a theory of equilibrium in an attempt to make economics more rigorous and predictable. Walras "believed that a differential calculus could be applied to economics to create a science of economic forces, analogous to the science of astronomical forces."[25] Like Smith before him, he did not look to existing markets for evidence to back his theory. Instead, Walras borrowed "the concept of equilibrium from physics and laid the mathematical foundations for the traditional economic theory found in textbooks and journals today."[26] The problem was that equilibrium mathematics mandated "a set of highly restrictive assumptions that have increasingly detached theoretical economics from the real world." [27] The physicists and mathematicians of his day such as Paul Matthieu Hermann Laurent and Henri Poincaré pointed out that "while it was laudable for economics to become more mathematical and rigorous, throwing out reality for the convenience of making equations solvable was not the way to go about it." [28] More recently, Warren Buffett's mentor, Benjamin Graham, counseled:

> The combination of precise formulas with highly imprecise assumptions can be used to establish, or rather to justify, practically any value one wished.... Calculus gives speculation the deceptive guise of investment.[29]

But economic theories rarely match reality; they have mostly to do with mathematics and physics, not markets. Indeed, "some critics argue that this borrowing equilibrium from physics was a crucial misstep that has lasting consequences for the field."[30] Author John Cassidy summed up the problem in his *New Yorker* article, "The Decline of Economics": "Economics has disappeared into an ivory tower world of highly idealized theory, untested by data, and packed with unrealistic assumptions."[31] Despite its detachment from reality, Walras' equilibrium theory was widely accepted by economists, and the belief that *mathematical models can model markets accurately* quickly gained ground.

Once the Smith/Walras theory of the market as a self-regulating equilibrium machine was generally accepted, it easily evolved into its even more unrealistic current version: *Since markets are machines, their regulation mechanisms are built in, thus eliminating the need for outside oversight or regulation.* To recap, by borrowing mechanistic theories and mathematics from physics that were minimally applicable to human endeavors, and using them to construct economic theories that justified removing most regulation and oversight, we ended up elevating the financial sector into its own feudal kingdom. Once it was on this lofty pedestal, a lack of transparency eliminated feedback about this sector's activities and further detached it from reality. Then, by arming its products with sophisticated algorithms and models, Wall Street abandoned the larger economy and retreated into mathematical forms that encouraged irrational exuberance, increasing risky behavior, and ultimately produced outcomes such as the Bankers Trust fraud, the LTCM collapse, the dot-com bubble, and ultimately the global economic collapse of both the financial and the real-goods economies. Author Barry Lynn made this clear:

> The science of economics…has become a form of madness.…Most terrifying of all is this consolidation of power, and the political actions it took to achieve it, appears to have impaired our ability to comprehend the dangers we face and to react in an organized and coherent manner.…We do have an alternative though. We can believe what we see with our own eyes.[32]

If we use our eyes, we can see that markets are not like machines. They are complex systems that deal in real goods and perform a host of other functions. From village markets to Silk Road caravans, from garage sales to cattle auctions, from the Chicago Mercantile Exchange commodities market to the Paris flower market, people have self-organized complex market operations that served both local and global needs. Farmers have traded the crops they have grown, kings and queens have sent ships around the world to procure spices, Spanish silver has bought Chinese silks and porcelains, and power rose and fell with those who controlled the salt trade. Anyone who has seen the jewel-like displays of fruits and vegetables at the Pike Place Market in Seattle, Washington, in the Mercado Libertad in Guadalajara, Mexico, or the Granville Island Public Market in Vancouver, British Columbia knows that markets are not simply commercial operations. Every pepper and peach is lovingly polished and placed in an array of aroma and color that attracts not only buyers who need sustenance, but also tourists who come because they are dazzled by the beauty and the variety. The secret is that real markets in real goods fill real human needs. In a Mexican village, bargaining for the best price is the rule. On the surface that may seem like a commercial strategy, but when I tried to buy a serape in the Saturday market in Oaxaca, Mexico for full price, the vendor was dismayed. He explained that bargaining was not just for price, it was a process that filled his day and gave him and his buyers the opportunity to match wits. Without bargaining for each item, he would sell all his goods before lunch and an empty afternoon would stretch before him. So I bargained him down 100 pesos ($6 at the time). It was a win-win outcome. A primary feature of the markets described above is that most of their components such as goods, price, and comparisons and the way they function are perceivable, which allows people to evaluate them.

Even derivatives originally had a practical and useful purpose. They were created to lower volatility in the price that real corn or soybeans might sell for at some later date in the commodities futures market. This strategy protected the farmer from the bottom falling out of the market when his crop matured, and gave the buyers of his still-growing crop a chance at buying that crop at a cheaper price than they might pay at its maturity. The original derivative was derived from the farmers' crops, but it was closely tied to that source and served a useful purpose—it distributed risk on real goods among all the parties involved and insured most of the people involved against large losses. When the corn and soybeans derivatives futures became current, they converted back into edible crops in completely transparent transactions. Derivatives were only one harvest away from the perceivable and palpable crops that grace the fields of Kansas and Nebraska. In fact, British economist John Maynard Keynes used to speculate in wheat futures and once, when he forgot to sell his stake before it came due, he awoke one morning to discover a large mound of wheat berries piled up on the ground outside his rooms at Cambridge University. His futures had become current.

In contrast, the derivatives that Bankers Trust sold were far more theoretical. They were based on bets that had very little relationship to anything tangible, but were instead derived from mental processes that translated real items into symbolic substitutes and then doubled down and created more derivatives from those substitutes. We used to call this sort of product snake oil. In his book *The Big Short,* author Michael Lewis likened Wall Street's flights of fancy with subprime mortgages to playing fantasy football with one critical difference. He pointed out, "When a fantasy football player drafts Peyton Manning to be on his team, he doesn't create a second Peyton Manning." With these financial bets, shadow bonds were created that involved "no actual home loans or home buyers, only the gains and losses from the side bet on the bonds were real." It was as if the original home mortgages that provided the only real base under this pyramid scheme "existed only so that their fate could be gambled upon."[33]

It is also unclear whether the mortgage bonds from which many derivatives were created were real because the mortgages themselves were worthless. Former *Businessweek* journalist Tracy Holland told *Frontline* that "the fact that a financially savvy company such as Procter and Gamble was hit with such losses was an early indication that there were potential problems with these instruments, that they were complicated, that their value changed quickly and that they were bought and sold in a market that was not closely monitored."[34] Consider whether this would have happened without a theory and its champions that insisted the market would regulate itself. In a complex system such as our economy, a theoretical component like a derivative that replaces a real component such as a mortgage or a bond that is based on real collateral such as a house can easily destabilize the system. As we saw when the derivatives debacle finally imploded, no one even knew who owed what to whom or even what a derivative was.[35]

Seeing the Structural Information
That Reveals the Market

If you're not at the tables, you can't win the game.
—TRADITIONAL GAMBLER'S ADAGE

Although many Wall Street investment bankers pleaded ignorance of what had been going on in the aftermath of the derivative debacle, there were many other people who did perceive the information that warned it was imminent. Instead of focusing on making wilder and more complicated trades, several hedge fund managers simply read the abnormal patterns that emerged from everyone else's daily market transactions. Complex market systems typically have a dynamic network structure that branches among its many components—producers, buyers, sellers, distributors, transporters—and their interactions with one another. One might doubt our ability to perceive and understand such a structure since it extends beyond our visual field. But in *The Big Short*, Michael Lewis reports that Dr. Michael Burry of Scion Capital and Greg Lippmann at Cornwall Capital did just that. They simply observed months of transaction data, and as a result they saw a pattern emerge indicating that the financial market's *normal, sustainable branching structure* had been replaced by an *unsustainable pattern of systemic deviations*. Again, this is not that different from a physical therapist discerning the parameters of an injury from the perceivable deviations in the patient's patterns of movement. Both are systemic deviations from normal configurations. To Burry and Lippmann, that deviant structure presaged the 2008 collapse, and they used this critical structural information to short the market and make billions. In the simplest terms, the market situation could also be likened to a multibranched tree, which, after being hit repeatedly by lightning, has lost all its limbs on one side and now deviates from its normal branching structure. As a result of the structural deviations due to its loss of branches, the tree loses its balance and crashes to the ground.

I realize that people without knowledge of how the market works do not feel able to replicate these market mavens' strategy and may find this example difficult to believe, especially when investments such as derivatives are considered so complex that few people actually understand them. But whether or not particular derivatives are too complicated to grasp is irrelevant, because it is the perception of the abnormal state of the market's *structure*, not its derivative *content*, that informed these investment professionals that the market was tanking. Perhaps the next step for Wall Street's mathematical wizards, known as "quants," is to design computer programs that can illustrate the market's structural transaction patterns as they emerge from daily trading. Such patterns might reflect the market far better than daily media reports of the ups and downs of separate stocks. In this way the market could become more transparent to those who are interested and allow them to make decisions based on current evidence, rather than be hostage to the policies that have obscured reality because they follow misconceived theories.

Part of the difficulty that people had in seeing the coming economic collapse might be attributable to the fact that the game was played behind closed doors. However, the problem of derivatives became a bit more public as a line was drawn in the investment market sand during the Clinton administration between Alan Greenspan, the chairman of the U.S. Federal Reserve who championed zero regulation, and Brooksley Born, head of the U.S. Commodity Futures Trading Commission (CFTC), the little-known government agency charged with regulating derivatives, who was concerned that Greenspan's policies were an invitation to disaster.

The Sad Saga of Brooksley Born and the American Taxpayer

Why did Mr. Greenspan...get it wrong?...They got trapped in an echo chamber of conventional wisdom...[and] fell victim to the same weakness that bedeviled the engineers of the Challenger space shuttle, the planners of the Vietnam and Iraq wars, and the airline pilots who have made tragic cockpit errors. They didn't adequately question their own assumptions.

—DAVID LEONHARDT

Brooksley Born was a Washington, DC attorney with a stellar reputation in international derivatives law. On August 26, 1996, she was appointed by President Clinton to be director of the CFTC. Because the derivatives market operated without any oversight or traceable records, few people (outside of finance insiders) knew that the agency or derivatives existed. The questionable investments that Bankers Trust had created in their minds and then sold to Procter & Gamble were one of the first signs that this market was running amok. But there were other signs of trouble. Wendy Gramm (Senator Phil Gramm's wife), who was director of the CFTC just before Born, had exempted the Enron Corporation from existing rules governing energy companies, and as soon as she left the CFTC, she joined Enron's board of directors. In other words, the derivatives market was not only a mostly mentally driven fantasy that had no oversight; it was rigged from the inside.[36]

Brooksley Born believed that the lack of transparency and regulation of the OTC derivatives market obscured the inroads that derivatives had made in the economy's complexity and therefore its sustanability, and that this situation was an open invitation not only for fraud, but for systemic economic collapse. She wanted to bring derivatives and the information about their structure and sales out into the open where "eyes on the street" could determine their value and their risks. In contrast, Greenspan believed that zero regulation and oversight were critical to a robust economy and that the derivatives market should continue to be shielded from people's eyes. He failed to realize that in blocking access to information about derivatives, he was undermining the market by allowing a single component, derivatives, to take over. Greenspan also dismissed the Bankers Trust incident as a case of misguided individual behavior, not systematic market vulnerability, and continued to promote a lack of transparency that protected the behind-closed-doors sales of OTC derivatives.

In 2008, when a crushed and bewildered Greenspan was called before an angry Congress to explain the failure of his policies, he admitted that he had not been running the Federal Reserve on real-world information, but on an ideology that regulation would hurt the economy and an assumption that the market itself would winnow out any illegal activities that might occur. He confessed, "I found a flaw in the model [that he perceived as the critical functioning structure] that defines the world, so to speak."[37] But Greenspan also hedged his bets by adding that you have to have an ideology in order to operate in the world. An ideology is an untested theory. It is not based on evidence or even on what has happened in the past. The notion that you can only operate from an ideology that originated in your own or someone else's head may be the largest error that Greenspan (and many others) made. Just the opposite is true. You have to know the complexities of the real world in order to operate successfully, and to do so, you have to have access to the structural information that can keep ideologies that warp your vision at bay. But despite the evidence of the Bankers Trust fraud, the government deferred to Greenspan's opposition to regulating derivatives based solely on his flawed belief that regulation would harm the economy.

As director of the CFTC, Brooksley Born tried to bring derivatives back into the realm of perceivable reality and open-exchange regulation. She circulated a memo announcing that her agency planned to do a study that looked at the risk that the lack of transparency in the OTC derivatives market posed to the economy. Immediately upon hearing about Born's project, Greenspan called a meeting of the President's "working group" on economic policy: Robert Rubin, then Secretary of the Treasury; Tim Geithner, Rubin's protégé; and Arthur Levitt, head of the Securities and Exchange Commission (SEC). Their agenda was to stop Born.[38] Although the Bankers Trust case proved Born's point that the derivatives market was highly susceptible to manipulation, the group voiced their concern that if a rumor that the derivatives market was to be regulated leaked, it would cast a cloud over the trillions of dollars of derivatives that were already in play and send that seemingly lucrative market into a nosedive, taking the economy down with it. "A letter signed by Rubin, Greenspan, and Levitt according to a story the *Washington Post* reported, asked Congress to immediately pass legislation imposing a moratorium on the derivatives study launched by Born."[39] In other words, several members of the President's Group on Financial Markets asked the Congress of the United States to prevent a study (not the implementation of a policy) that would simply provide information to the public from ever being carried out. Born, who was the member of the group in charge of derivatives, was not told of that meeting. Not only were derivatives traded behind closed doors, but the policies administering these trades were also made behind closed doors that shut out the person with the most expertise in that product.

Although very few members of Congress knew a derivative from an ice cream sandwich, and in spite of the Bankers Trust debacle and Born's singular expertise, Congress bought the working group's argument and silenced Born. In 1998, six weeks after the Congressional hearings that scuttled Born, LTCM, whose portfolio was packed with derivatives, collapsed. LTCM's investment strategies were predicated on secret, proprietary, mathematical models that they had created themselves and refused to disclose to their clients. It turned out, however, that when they created their model, they neglected to track the ever-changing actual market conditions, and as a result of this oversight, they picked out-of-date data and inapplicable algorithms with which to model the economy's complexities.

But LTCM's demise was only the tip of the iceberg in revealing that market operations were too removed from reality to be sustainable. Just as Born had warned, LTCM's derivatives investments were intertwined with those of all the major Wall Street banks, and its losses threatened to take down the entire financial system. Since LTCM, like most of the banking sector, operated from an atomistic perspective where each bank was seen as a separate entity, no one noticed that their interconnections had created a single, monstrous, mindless mechanism that would grind to a halt when one of its cogs failed. This behemoth system required continual greasing by new investments (like any Ponzi scheme) or the whole operation would stall. But that was not the whole of it:

> LTCM's precipitous collapse stoked fears of systemic risk—that is of a domino effect engulfing the entire global financial system—so much so that the New York Federal Reserve Bank coerced fourteen major Wall Street firms—which were LTCM's main creditors—to come to its rescue with a bailout package of $3.6 billion.... The true exposure came in the trillions of dollars in over-the-counter derivatives contracts woven into an intricate web that engulfed all the key players

on Wall Street.... The financial tsunami of 2008 and the bail-
out of AIG is largely a replay on a much larger scale of the
LTCM debacle."[40]

Despite Born's stellar reputation in the field of derivatives law,
her insistence on evidence, and the accuracy of her predictions of
fraud and economic collapse, Congress, deferring to Greenspan,
removed the CFTC's regulatory powers. Derivatives would remain
unregulated.

> Despite...the LTCM collapse, nobody at the top wanted to
> hear her warning.... A month after the LTCM bailout, Congress
> acceded to the request to ban any new regulations on over-
> the-counter derivatives for six months.... A year later it would
> be made permanent with the passages of the Commodities
> Futures Modernization Act (FSMA) in 2000.... The govern-
> ment was washing its hands of financial regulation. From here
> on out, the banks could do whatever they wanted. In less than
> a decade they would cannibalize themselves in an accelerated
> rush of high stakes gambling, destroying $14 trillion of the
> wealth of American families in one 7 quarter period between
> 2007 and one quarter period of 2009.[41]

All along, government economists insisted that "parties to these kinds
of contracts are largely sophisticated financial institutions that would
appear eminently capable of protecting themselves from fraud" and
that "existing banking and securities laws were sound."[42] Bankers
Trust and Long-Term Capital Management proved them wrong.

Born resigned and returned to practicing law. There were no
knowing eyes left on the street, and nothing was done to rein in Wall
Street trading. Seemingly supporting Greenspan's views, the stock
and real estate markets rose steadily into what turned out to be a
high-flying, mentally driven speculative bubble that had little real
collateral to back it up. It had been created by historically disproven
theories lodged in people's minds, such as *real estate prices will keep
going up*. That bubble began to burst in 2007, leaving unsalvageable

toxic mortgages all over the globe and foreclosure signs all over an extraordinary number of neighborhoods that told an unending tale of ordinary people who lost their homes and in many cases remain deeply in debt.

The SEC eventually sued the Wall Street investment firm Goldman Sachs.[43] In a dubious strategy involving unsecured investments, Goldman had bought thousands of virtually unsecured and thus unreliable subprime mortgages from unscrupulous lenders who were making "liar loans" to people who could not repay them. Goldman then pooled these questionable assets to create mortgage bonds. Next, they used their imaginations to slice these largely baseless bonds into separate layers called CDOs (collateralized debt obligations), which were like your third cousin twice removed in their relationship to the original, virtually worthless mortgages. Goldman claimed that slicing these bonds into layers and having the worst ones rated Ba1 would spread the risk and allow the bulk of the remaining layers to be rated AAA. These layers were nothing more than a slew of repackaged IOUs that gained paper value for one reason and one reason only: their newly minted ratings. Moody's bond-rating service had given the bonds that AAA rating without even knowing which mortgages a particular pool would buy. Moody's had, as *New York Times* writer Roger Lowenstein wrote, used "statistical models based on historical models of default. This assumed that the past remained relevant in an era in which the mortgage industry was morphing into a wildly speculative business."[44] In other words, the ratings were invented. They were not real and they were wrong. Nonetheless, Goldman sold these CDOs to clients as AAA-rated investments. If Moody's hadn't made this mathematical model–based error, Goldman would not have been able to palm these risky investments off on clients who had no knowledge of the state of the underlying loans. Many of the financial market's principal components—the securitized investment inventors, traders, raters, and SEC regulators—were creating a house of cards on paper that had no relationship to how the real world worked. At every turn, the information that people normally use to make investment decisions was nowhere in sight.

To add to the housing market's flight from reality, lenders seduced people who had minimal incomes and no collateral who were unable to make even the first payment into taking out liar loans. The lenders simply left their income off the applications. One Mexican strawberry farmer who made $14,000 a year and spoke no English was recruited and lured into borrowing $747,000 to buy a house.[45] Chris Flanagan, the subprime analyst at JP Morgan, pointed out that the banks were simply gaming the system.[46]

Goldman Sachs was aware of all this because they worked both sides of the aisle. They nudged the rating companies into making inflated ratings with one hand, and with the other they sought and bought toxic mortgages from unscrupulous loan companies to bundle into the bonds from which they derived derivatives. Without the investment banks seeking and aggressively buying these mortgages, the loan companies would never have made sure-to-fail loans that would have put them out of business.[47]

Fast-forward ten years to 2008 when derivatives were insuring derivatives based on derivatives. The world markets collapsed, just as Brooksley Born had predicted. When all the dust had settled, Born cut through all the hype and excuses. She laid out the real consequences of the theory of unregulated free markets and its behind-closed-doors, unregulated, OTC derivatives swaps and bets when she said, "These toxic assets made us lose our savings, our jobs, and our homes."[48]

The only member of the President's working group who came completely clean about what happened to Brooksley Born and to the American people was SEC head Arthur Levitt, who confessed on camera that he was pressured by the President's working group to turn against Born. He now admits she is one of the most competent, knowledgeable, and dedicated public servants he has ever known. On an episode of *Frontline* titled "The Warning," Levitt quietly stated, "I could have done much better. I could have made a difference."[49] The problem was that in the government power hierarchy, Levitt just wasn't a "contender." Born, a lady to the end, refused to say anything about any of the people who upended her government career and in the process brought our economy to a halt. She simply predicted, "There will be disasters attributed to this regulatory gap until we learn from experience."⁵⁰ The Dodd-Frank financial reform bill passed Congress in July 2010, making derivatives somewhat regulated, but not completely so. Investment banking's lobbyists are leaning hard on Congress to keep it that way. In 2013, unemployment is still very high and Main Street is still in freefall. Financial analyst Nicole Gelinas summed up the situation: "The only thing protecting the American economy from the vaporization of the financial industry was the printing presses of the U.S. Mint."⁵¹

Various experts commented on how this financial debacle came about. Simon Johnson, former chief economist for the International Monetary Fund, pointed out that the American banking industry had captured the public mind (including Congress) by using propaganda that convinced people that their way of life would disappear if the financial sector's activities were regulated in any way. But since wages have not gone up since the 1970s,⁵² that way of life for most people went south long ago with the theory of trickle-down economics. Author Barry Lynn, a senior fellow at the New America Foundation, explained how the financial sector did this by co-opting the simple, innocent word *market* and appending the word *free* to it as if it belonged to no one in particular, but served all equally. Lynn wrote:

> America's Lords in perhaps the single most brilliant act of linguistic legerdemain ever perpetrated in our nation, figured out how to transmute the scrim behind which they disguise their predations into the religion of the American people."⁵³

In other words, it was a mental operation. A relatively small number of people made money on the market's speculation spiral because they sold their holdings before it imploded. But many others lost their life savings. In 2013, the 2008 recession continues and is still more than worrisome. Measures to correct the Main Street economy appear less than workable and no one seems to be addressing the underlying problem that started the fiscal disaster in the first place—*by ignoring the reality the world displays, we continue acting on inapplicable theories, such as "The market regulates itself," "Mathematical models reflect reality," "Banks are too big to fail," and*

"People are rational." Together these theories captured our experts' collective minds and fostered the deregulation, lack of transparency, and detachment from reality that ended up inviting an economic catastrophe that fell most heavily on Main Street.

Even when economists are simply doing academic research and are not caught up in Wall Street's frenzies, their attempts to explain the complexities of economies can still founder on their flawed mathematical assumptions and end up fostering policies that do considerable harm. In 2010, Harvard economists, Carmen Reinhart and Kenneth Rogoff published a paper, "Growth in a Time of Debt," in which they claimed that sovereign economies would falter if their debt went over 90% of their GDP.[54] Even though these results came from only a single paper, they were immediately seized upon by conservatives across the globe and translated into "austerity" measures that came down hardest on ordinary citizens. Ironically, Reinhart and Rogoff's result "has been shown to rest…on a simple error, a spreadsheet coding mistake discovered by a 28 year-old graduate student at the University of Massachusetts Amherst named Thomas Herndon."[55] When Herndon tried to replicate this study, he found that it was riddled with both mathematical and data selection errors. He noted, " We did use the terms 'selective' and 'unconventional' to describe the problems we saw with their paper, and we believe these are accurate characterizations…. because the data were 'selected' for exclusion."[56] Somehow Reinhart and Rogoff had miscalculated various percentages and had also selectively left out the data from Canada, Australia, Belgium, Austria, and Denmark. When confronted with Herndon's evidence, Reinhart and Rogoff, as reputable scientists, did acknowledge their errors. But publishing this "selective" study before it was fully vetted and making such definitive claims has done inestimable damage to the economy—to citizens across the globe.

On April 17, 2013, Michael Higgins, President of Ireland, responded to such austerity measures in an address to the European Parliament. He eloquently reviewed the history of European thought and scholarship that had culminated in democratically distributed resources and a safety net for those who needed help. Then, he pointed out that "the Union draws its legitimacy from the support of its citizens...their belief that the European Union is of them and for them."[57] Last, he asserted:

> If we were...to regard our people merely as dependent variables to the opinions of rating agencies, agencies unaccountable to any demos...then instead of being citizens we would be reduced to the status of mere consumers; pawns in a speculative chess board of fiscal moves.[58]

Higgins' answer to every country's economic woes was not to make them worse by imposing austerity measures on those already in trouble, but to realize that the European Union is a complex system that depends on those citizens/components for its legitimacy.

The good news is that despite Wall Street's and the academy's fiascos, in 2013 there are finally pending suits against several Wall Street firms for fraud, and there are also excellent investment advisors who are very realistic about the world as it is today. They know that the economy does not depend on investments sold by the financial sector, but on the resources of our planet, both physical and human. One example is investment guru Jeremy Grantham, cofounder and chief investment strategist for Grantham, Mayo, Van Otterloo, an investment firm overseeing more than $100 billion. Grantham warned his clients about the Japanese, dot-com, and subprime bubbles and advises them on investments that will help sustain, rather than damage, the planet. In 1998, he and his wife funded The Grantham Foundation for the Protection of the Environment, which "tries to raise the public's awareness of environmental issues and promote collaboration within the environmental movement."[59] Most important is his recognition that collaboration is the key to success in our world of complex systems. For the most part, each environmental organization has a seemingly separate cause—save the rainforest, the whales, or the redwoods—and they duplicate efforts while competing for the same funding as if the world were actually made of these separate parts. Grantham "urges us to give up our touching faith in the efficiency of markets and boundless human ingenuity" and promote the planet's well-being by using evidence, not theories.[60] He counsels that our current oil-dependent economy is unsustainable economically and has "enormous environmental consequences that could be quite deadly.... We can get off this terrible trap of expanding as long as the coal and oil is there and then being left high and dry. We have the wherewithal to move fairly seamlessly if we choose to make the effort, to a renewable source of energy that will not run out."[61] In distinction to the stand taken by many Wall Street investment bankers who promote oil stocks and lobby for more drilling and pipelines, Grantham voices his concern about the future of the planet. Although it did not pass the Senate, he "put his own influence and money behind the climate-change bill passed by the house in 2009."[62]

An Alternate Theory of the Economy

When we make our economy a little wheel turning on opposition to what we call "nature," then we set up competitiveness as the ruling principle of our explanation of reality and in our understanding of our economy.... But competitiveness, as a ruling principle, and a virtue, is difficult to control. It explains why... our wastes are toxic.... And why it is so difficult for us to draw the line between "free enterprise" and crime.

—WENDELL BERRY

In this way, Grantham has a lot in common with farmer, writer, and activist Wendell Berry. A poet who lobbies Congress for environmental causes, Berry argues that we have two economies—the perceivable Great economy of soil, water, trees, human capacity, and other planetary resources that we cannot make or duplicate ourselves, and the economists' secretive economy of proprietary industrial processes and financial services.[63] The irony is that while the economists' economy is completely dependent on the Great economy, it acts as if that economy is nothing more than "raw materials" and "labor" that are to be procured at the lowest cost, a cost that may include their disappearance by using them up. In contrast, the Great economy operates on ecological practices that increase capacity by increasing diversity and thus complexity and sustainability. Chapter 10 addresses the disasters that have threatened our planet's large, multicomponent, complex plant-based systems when outside interests manipulate and remove their linchpin components. It also tells how an organic farmer and a nutritionist can show us how to avoid the types of catastrophes that have occurred, when, for example, industrial agriculture and food processors follow theories such as "Bigger is better" and "Food can be partitioned into parts that can be rearranged."

10

Complexity, Components, and Monocultures

Death by Financial Concept

> *Agriculture...had not traditionally engaged the attention of Wall Street bankers, whose riches did not come from the sale of real things like wheat or bread but from the manipulation of ethereal concepts like risk and collateralized debt.... Goldman analysts went about transforming wheat into a concept.*
>
> —FREDERICK KAUFMAN

In 2008, Goldman Sachs invented a "Commodities Index Fund" that, as if by magic, conjured inedible derivatives from edible hard red spring wheat. This latter-day alchemy, coupled with Goldman cornering the wheat market by buying up all the rights to its future crops, removed real wheat from the food economy. It turned a self-organized, self-sustaining, complex system of perceivable crops, growers, buyers, sellers, and eaters that existed in the real world into a speculation spiral spinning out of people's heads that raised the price of real wheat beyond people's ability to pay:[1]

> Within a year, the price of wheat had shot up by 80 per cent....200 million people—mostly children—couldn't afford to get food any more and sank into malnutrition or starvation....Jean Ziegler, the UN Special Rapporteur on the Right to Food, calls it "a silent mass murder."[2,3]

Commodities deregulation not only promoted the same sort of derivatives free-for-all that caused the 2008 financial meltdown, which Brooksley Born and a host of others first warned about in the 1990s, but in this case, replacing real food with invented derivatives and left its victims dead on the streets of Cairo and Mozambique. While investors who had nothing to do with the food economy made enormous profits, the ranks of the malnourished and starving rose to 1 billion.[4,5]

> Until deregulation the price for food was set by the forces of supply and demand for food itself....After deregulation, it was no longer a market in food. It became... a market in food contracts based on theoretical future crops...speculators drove the price through the roof...and the starvation began.[6]

The lesson to be learned from the ranks of the starving is that food economies, like most things in our universe from the tiniest cells to the entire cosmos, normally function as multicomponent, complex systems, many of whose operations are observable. But the derivatives sold through Goldman Sachs' Commodities Index Fund were not like the perceivable components of the real food economy that people can make informed decisions about. Instead, they were like hidden viruses that infiltrated, disrupted, and controlled that economy by replacing wheat—one of its linchpin components—with theoretical bets on the future prices of not-yet-in-existence wheat. As a result, the information people have come to depend on to make economic decisions was no longer available. Within that murky situation the value of derivatives was leveraged up to alarming proportions—not on the value of wheat from which they were supposed to be derived, but solely on a mathematical model's probability predictions of the possible price of wheat futures. One bewildered wheat broker, Austin Damiani, opined, "We're trading wheat, but it's wheat we're never going to see. It's a cerebral experience."[7] In 1936 John Maynard Keynes explained one cause of Damiani's bewilderment:

> Recent mathematical economics are mere concoctions, as imprecise as the initial assumption they rest on, which allows

the author to lose sight of the complexities and interdependencies of the real world.[8]

Keynes points out that using mathematical models to reduce reality to representations fails to reflect the interdependencies and complexities of real-world systems and cannot be relied on to predict real-world outcomes. When asked about the effect of these Wall Street strategies on the wheat market, a shocked Jeff Voge, chairman of the Kansas City Board of Trade, told the *Washington Post*: "We have never seen anything like this before. This isn't just any commodity. It is food, and people need to eat."[9] The idea that the value of real items could be converted to guesses about the future, which then could be leveraged up so much higher than the worth of the original item, bears a striking resemblance to pulling rabbits out of hats. This trick only works because *our minds, with their penchant for theories and magical thinking, pull the wool over our eyes.*

Viral Components and Complex Systems

Today the network of relationships linking the human race to itself and to the rest of the biosphere is so complex that all aspects affect all others to an extraordinary degree. Someone should be studying the whole system...because no gluing together of partial studies...can give a good idea of the behavior of the whole.

—MURRAY GELL-MANN

Consider what happens when a simpler complex system such as a basketball team with various players, positions, coaches, referees, leagues, courts, and rules, is undermined by hostile outside interests. Each component of such a system may play a different role, but no component, not even the player who scores the most points, plays the game alone; everyone participates to preserve the whole and keeps their eyes on the game. When an alien factor with a competing agenda infiltrates that system and replaces, disables, or marginalizes one or more of its components—someone bribes a player to throw the game or a player is knocked down and injured—it cripples the team's network of self-sustaining interactions and puts their entire enterprise at risk. Ironically, although it takes the bulk of a system's components to create and sustain it, one bad apple within, or a predator from without who is attempting to turn the system to their own advantage, can disrupt its normal operations and produce a crisis.

Without seeing, touching, or relocating a single grain, Goldman's traders produced just such a crisis by inserting a rogue component, the derivative, into the food economy and creating a market that mentally abstracted wheat from its sheaths and silos and hid it in warehouses out of anyone's sight. With this sleight of mind, Goldman replaced the concrete reality of wheat with derivatives that promised profits for some and produced starvation for others. The Wall Street attitude toward those who had traditionally subsisted on bread seemed to be, "Let them eat cash."[10]

By 2008 the entire food economy was faltering. Global food prices had risen 217% to the highest price levels since 1845. Millions could no longer afford to eat. Riots broke out in over thirty countries across the globe, including Egypt, Senegal, and Bangladesh. Because wheat was nowhere to be found and people were starving, the government of Madagascar was overthrown.[11]

Since most people consider the world from a parts perspective, each food riot could be dismissed as an isolated incident, not the result of one rogue factor that undermined the entire food economy. It was not until the food riots reached a critical mass that their global reach was noticed. In 2011, food scarcity and its accompanying injustices spilled out onto the streets of Cairo and we watched, fascinated, as a self-organized protest erupted in Tahrir Square, took down Egypt's President Mubarak, and then rapidly spread across the region. No one seemed to realize that this seemingly spontaneous demonstration arose from the shards of the destabilized food economy.[12]

Ironically, in 2008 there was actually plenty of wheat to feed everyone because the wheat harvest was one of the largest in recorded history. However, the information that normally would have revealed this fact and lowered the price of wheat accordingly was unavailable due to the lack of transparency of the derivatives market. Despite the record size of the 2008 wheat crop, not one grain was visible. No one knew where the wheat was, or if it even existed. In fact, it was languishing in private storage facilities, with an uncertain future, in much the same way that many houses existed after the housing bubble burst—in the limbo of foreclosure, boarded up, its former occupants often remanded to the streets, and its neighborhood in decline. As writer John Lanchester noted in *IOU: Why Everyone Owes Everyone and No One Can Pay,* "Finance… underwent a change in the 20th century…a turn toward self-referentiality and abstraction….With derivatives there is a profound break between the language of finance and that of common sense."[13] There is also an abyss between what was once perceivable and understandable and what now is not.

To recap, the price of wheat was not based on the value of real wheat, but solely on paper contracts involving theoretical wheat crops of the future, and the escalating price of those theoretical crops began to generate its own demand. Even though wheat futures are not wheat and the price of wheat is not wheat, and in 2008 there was a bumper harvest of wheat, the usual rules of supply and demand were suspended in a mental netherworld where real wheat in the real world could not be bought on normal market terms. Eventually part of the 2008 crop surfaced and 200 million bushels were sold to animal feedlots that could afford to pay the inflated price because beef brought in far higher prices than bread. The remaining 657 million bushels remained unsold after the buying season. By the end of 2008, the bubble burst and wheat prices plummeted. But those who had starved could not be brought back to life. What is most egregious is that much of this would not have happened if Wall Street's theories, which promoted private, untraceable transactions and obscured gaining accurate information, had not captured our collective minds, seduced us into believing things that could not be true, and deflected our attention away from the real events concerning food availability and distribution.

In his prescient 1999 article, *The Market as God,* Harvard divinity professor Harvey Cox pointed out:

> The lexicon of the *Wall Street Journal* and the business sections of *Time* and *Newsweek* turned out to have a striking

resemblance to *Genesis, The Epistle to the Romans,* and *St. Augustine's City of God....* Theologians call these myths of origins, legends of the fall, and doctrines of sin and redemption. But here they were again, in only thin disguise: chronicles about the creation of wealth.... And ultimately, salvation through the advent of free markets.[14]

In effect, Wall Street's theories became an overarching theology of the economy that took on the cloak of omniscience as if their policies were ordained by some unassailable, extrahuman power. But as Cox also wrote:

Divine omnipotence means the capacity to define what is real. It is the power to make something out of nothing and nothing out of something…there is no conceivable limit to its inexorable ability to convert creation into commodities.[15]

But while Wall Street was replacing wheat with derivatives, there was a companion process in play in the fields of Kansas and Iowa, where agribusiness was replacing biodiverse complex methods of producing food with simplistic and vulnerable monoculture crops.

Turning Sustainable Complexity Into Unsustainable Simplicity

Get big, or get out.
—EARL BUTZ, US Secretary of Agriculture

Industrial agriculture is largely conducted using one-trick ponies called monocultures. Monocultures are like derivatives in that they are single, contrary components in a world made for multicomponent complex systems that depend on their many components' cooperative interactions. The monoculture crops that get the most press are corn and soy because of concerns that most of these crops are genetically modified and used in the preparation of almost all processed foods. But agribusiness also grows our flagship American vegetable, the potato, using the same strategy. Consequently, 99% of industrial potato farming in America is limited to one type of potato, the Russet Burbank, because it makes French fries that fit best into McDonald's packaging.[16] With no other potato varieties to fill in if the one variety planted were to falter, monocultures like these have no protection against failure—as in the 1840s, when, with monoculture potato production the rule, potato blight ruined crops all over Europe and then crossed the sea to devastate Ireland.

The Irish catastrophe started when a windblown oomycete, *Phytophthora infestans*, crossed over from Europe and turned Ireland's entire monoculture potato crop rotten overnight. A million people died of starvation.[17] This tragedy was yet another instance of a failure to perceive the complexities of a natural system and instead replace it with an unworkable, theory-based strategy. What led to that susceptible monoculture potato crop? It's a story of Spanish conquistadors seeking silver who were introduced to many biodiverse Andean potatoes but chose just a few to carry back to Europe (creating the basis for monoculture production), and two misguided agricultural activists who ignored the perceivable conditions where the Irish grew potatoes and, instead, managed to impose a misconceived theory on the Irish farmland.

As far as we know, the potato originated in the Andes, where sophisticated indigenous farmers maintained the biodiversity of their five hundred varieties of this tuber because they knew that strategy gave them the flexibility that protected their crops from all sorts of predators and diseases. Because each variety has different susceptibilities to blight, each one also has the potential to substitute for a variety that has succumbed to disease. The Andean farmers clearly perceived the difficult conditions they faced and developed methods that cleverly mitigated those problems. They terraced the steep slopes of their mountains in order to manage water distribution and erosion. On the flatter, wetter lands that surrounded Lake Titicaca, they built raised earth hummocks that measured several yards across and up to hundreds of yards long to increase drainage, warm the soil earlier in the spring to promote faster growth, and provide deeper layers of topsoil for better root systems. In more confined spaces, they constructed smaller "wachos," two-foot-wide turned earth piles that they separated with furrows to carry off the excess water. The Andean farmer's comprehensive perceptions took in the entire complex system that growing potatoes entailed. They even included the guano droppings of the seabirds and bats that lived on the shores of the islands off the coast at the base of their mountains because it was an excellent fertilizer. The farmers collected the guano by boat and carried it up their mountains on donkey chains to feed their plants.[18] In sum, the Andean farmers perceived, understood, and acted upon how the many components of their complex system of farming worked together. They shared what they saw with one another, and made their decisions based on the sum their informed perceptions.

The story takes a very different turn with the Spanish conquistadors who brought the potato back to Europe. They ignored the fact that an enormous variety of potatoes were grown in the Andes to helped buffer potato crops from disease, and chose instead to bring back only a few types out of the many available. They also failed to import the raised-bed farming system that was critical to the Andean farmer's success. As a result, European farmers replicated the method that they had used for their traditional European crops. They planted huge, flat, open fields containing only one type of potato plant. From genetically diverse Andeans' tubers planted in elevated soil that could resist various forms of blight, the typical potato plantings in Europe had become vast fields of monoculture crops. No one realized that this situation was a catastrophe waiting to happen.

In 1845, *P. infestans*, a devastating potato blight that had been controlled in the Andes by biodiversity, hitched a ride on a ship that sailed from Peru to Belgium, bringing guano fertilizer to the largely monoculture European market. As a result,

in July 1845 the west Flanders town of Kortrijk, six miles from the French border, became the launch pad for Europe's first widespread epidemic of potato blight. Carried by windblown spores…blight was first reported in Ireland on September 13, 1845, by mid-October the British prime minister was privately describing the epidemic as a national disaster.…In two months *P. infestans* wiped out the equivalent of between half and three-quarters of a million acres in every corner of the nation....*P. infestans* swept across the country, striking with a remorselessness not seen anywhere else.[19]

Since all of Europe suffered greatly from the blight, why was Ireland affected far more than any other country? In his fascinating book, *1493*, Charles Mann offers several suggestions.[20] First, in distinction to other countries that also had wheat and a variety of vegetables, Ireland's farmers were much poorer, and they subsisted on nothing more than potatoes and milk. The meat and grains produced in Ireland at that time were the province of wealthier Irish farmers who, despite the starving population around them, exported the bulk of these foodstuffs to England. Second, while the people of the Andes grew many varieties of potato, some of which might have resisted the blight, the Irish grew only one variety, the "Lumper," which unfortunately succumbed to *P. infestans* on contact. Third, many tenant farmers lived clustered close together, surrounded by tightly packed communal farmland that invited the blight to jump from one plant to the next and take over an entire field in record time.

A further problem for the traditional Irish farmer was a new theory promulgated by agricultural activists Andrew Wight and Jethro Tull. This theory held that "flat open fields were better than the Irish farmer's traditional method of 'lazy-bed planting.' "[21] Recall that in order to deal with drainage problems the Andean people had built wachos of raised earth and deep furrows. When they perceived similar boggy conditions, the Irish farmers developed a similar method. They cut sections of sod and piled them on top of one another, leaving what amounted to furrows in between. The Irish raised-bed method provided all the benefits of the wachos—good drainage, resistance to erosion, and the ability to keep the grass's root system intact so the grass regrew quickly and restored nutrients to the soil.

Regardless of the observable benefits of lazy-bed farming in wet soils, Wight and Tull traveled all over Ireland convincing the farmers that the furrows between the beds were a waste and they should switch to simple, flat, open fields that easily accommodated industrial machinery and had space for far more plants. They were proposing a theory based completely on ideas that involved imagined efficiency and possible increased profit, but that had little to do with the ecology of the area. Instead, it helped bring on a disaster.

Michael Myers at the University of Texas at Austin tested Wight and Tull's theory. He planted three lazy-beds and three level fields in Northern Ireland and discovered that "the simple ridges and furrows created a complex geography, with surprisingly sharp temperature and humidity differences between the top of the ridge and the bottom the furrow."[22] Plant-disease experts have calculated the "blight units" from temperature and moisture measures that promote *P. infestans*. Meyers found that his lazy-beds had only half the number of blight units as his level-field plantings. Here again, a theory imposed by outsiders unfamiliar with the land convinced local farmers to replace their traditional method that was far more favorable for growing potatoes in Northern Ireland, and the experiment ended badly. Myers believes that Wight and Tull's misguided theory could be implicated in Ireland's blight epidemic.

One might infer from our preoccupation with our minds that Spanish conquistadors and the agricultural activists in Ireland had to have prior knowledge of plants and planting methods in order to notice, and take advantage of, the biodiversity and strategies that the local Andean and Irish farmers traditionally used. That view lacks logic because it dismisses the role of our perceptual systems. We have perceptual systems so that we are able to notice the structural information that specifies new things that we might want to adopt or that we may need to adapt to increase our successes. It is our minds, with their theories and preconceptions, that get in the way of our attending to the perceivable information that specifies items such as boggy land drained by raised beds that created furrows that were right in front of these theorists' noses. But this shortsighted practice is still in play. Despite our current knowledge of the downside of planting monocultures, little has changed since the days of the conquistadors. Rather than taking such catastrophes seriously, and building protective complexity into its operations, industrial agriculture today plants bigger and bigger fields of monoculture crops. Today large-scale farms in the United States grow only Russet Burbank potatoes in flat fields because they meet the requirements of our current mechanized means of agriculture and because McDonald's with their restrictive packaging dominates the buying market.

Food Economies as Complex Systems

The ideal art, the noblest art: working with the complexities of life, refusing to simplify, to "overcome" doubt.

—JOYCE CAROL OATES

Complex systems are dynamic and nonlinear in that they continually change in ways that are not necessarily predictable and thus require constant tracking. But there are good reasons why most of us fail to do such tracking. John Sterman, director of the Systems Dynamics Group at MIT's Sloan School of Management and co-faculty at The New England Complex Systems Institute, works on the complex boom and bust cycles of commodities. His explanation for fiascos that bear some similarity to the potato blight revolves around "how difficult it is for our mental models to grasp and develop an intuition for non-linear dynamics."[23] One might translate that into how difficult it is for our minds to track the evolving relations among various plant varieties, planting strategies, climate, rainfall, and soil type in order to make decisions that avoid spreading blight or attracting predators. In contrast, the Andean farmer has the benefit of years of perceptual learning of the ways of the potato under various conditions. His eyes are tuned to track the patterns that emerge from those relationships and substitute one variety of potato for another when there is danger of disease. Due to our penchant for following agricultural theories such as Wight and Tull's, which advocated machine-friendly fields and monocultures, we do not have the large-scale complex system of plant varieties in America that allows us to have such options.

In a sense, Sterman's insight corroborates this book's thesis that *our minds and the simulations and models they construct are ill equipped to help us understand the properties of the dynamic, nonlinear complex systems that constitute our world. Rather, structural information in the form of nonlinear dynamic patterns that emerge from operations of complex systems is the province of our perceptual systems.* To improve our cognitive reach on complex systems, we need to base our mental strategies on our perceptions, not our deductions. In addition, consider that complex systems are nature's normal unit of analysis. When we simplify that unit by reducing its components to a monoculture, we eliminate its ability to evolve and adapt to change. That is what happens when we convert a critical component of Earth's complex operating system, such as a mixed forest with its multiple roles—managing water supplies, tempering climate, preventing erosion, providing building materials and habitat for many species, and sequestering carbon—to a human-managed system such as industrial farming, which reduces the forests' many interactive and critical components to one component that is far more vulnerable to disease. To maintain a farm's sustainability, we need to mimic, not discard, Earth's natural processes.

A Sustainable Complex System: Polyface Family Farm

All things are connected. Whatever befalls the earth befalls the sons of the earth. Man did not weave the web of life, he is merely a strand in it. Whatever he does to the web, he does to himself.

—CHIEF SEATTLE

Polyface Farm in Virginia is a family farm that is a prime example of a dynamic complex system that produces food with maximum nutritional value and minimal environmental and energy costs. All its processes are perceivable because they do not originate in someone's mind, but are "built on the efficiencies that come from mimicking the relationships found in nature and layering one farm enterprise over another on the same base of land...farming in time as well as space.... The idea is to model a natural ecosystem in all its diversity and interdependence."[24] Many of these layered relationships, such as sequential-pasture grass sharing first by cows and then by chickens, provides fertilizer for the grass from the cow's manure, which the chickens then pick apart, spread around, and eat the often dangerous insect larvae.

The primary components that constitute a complex, self-sustaining farm are a woodlot, natural grass pastures, a carefully husbanded water source, adequate sunlight, different varieties of rotated row crops, and several animal species and types of fowl. All the farm's components interact and support one another. The woodlot tempers the local climate, protects the water supply, and provides habitat to birds that eat harmful insects. It keeps predators out of the hen house by sheltering smaller wild creatures for the foxes and coyotes to eat. It also offers shade to the farm animals during hot weather.

In contrast to industrial feedlots, where cows require antibiotics to ward off the diseases caused by their unnatural diet of corn and hormones, the animals at Polyface Farm feed on self-renewing pasture grasses, both fresh and baled, that their stomachs evolved to digest. The cows' manure fertilizes the grasses, requires no cleanup, and causes no residual pollution as it disappears into and enriches the soil. Nothing on this farm goes to waste. Composted chicken manure, winter barn bedding, and plant wastes replenish the soil's organic matter and feed the microbes, earthworms, and various microelements that are critical to its fertility. Compost is also used to fertilize vegetable row crops. Animal stock and chickens are moved from pasture to pasture to allow newly grazed grasses to recover and renew.

In *The Omnivore's Dilemma*, Michael Pollan reports that the complex operation of Polyface Farm produces 25,000 pounds of beef, 50,000 pounds of pork, 12,000 broilers, 800 turkeys, 500 rabbits, and 360,000 eggs each season from 100 acres of manure-fertilized pasture that sustains the animals, backed by a 450-acre protective woodlot. The farm produces this amount with one yearly purchase: a moderate amount of chicken feed. Few permanent investments are needed except for the material for the portable electric fencing that is used to confine the cows or chickens to whatever grazing pasture is on their rotation schedule. Joe Salatin, who owns Polyface Farm, tows a prairie-schooner mobile chicken house from pasture to pasture so that the birds can peck their own measure of grasses and eat the ever-present insects before they damage his crops.

Instead of living off government subsidies for grain and oil, as agribusiness industrial farms do, and having to plant annual grains each year, Joel Salatin says that he's actually a sun farmer. All plants produce carbohydrates through photosynthesis. "Grass is just the way we capture solar energy....These blades are our photovoltaic panels."[25] In a complex system, where everything influences everything else, pasture grass is itself a self-sustaining complex system that is composed of many perennial plants that renew themselves. In one square foot you can find orchard grass, foxtail, fescues, bluegrass, and timothy; legumes like red and white clover; lupines; and forbs such as plantain, dandelion, and Queen Anne's lace. You also find several beneficial insect varieties, undergirded by helpful earthworms, bacteria, phages, nematodes, rotifers, and fungi.[26] The pasture grasses' multicomponent complexity assures that its consumers always have something to eat and that, if one plant fails, others immediately fill in the gap. Its deep root system, a response to constant surface grazing, and its ground-hugging crown, allow the grass to recover from drying winds and brush fires as well as from the grazing of their animal clients. Polyface farmers use many of earth's ecological rules that we have discovered through patient observation and pragmatic practices over the centuries.

Unfortunately, industrial agriculture's economies of scale break all of Earth's ecological rules and convert millions of acres of farmland to soil-depleting, single-component monoculture crops. If you were to circle the globe in an airplane and look down, you would see 300 million acres of cloned fields of corn and soy crops located in Iowa, South America, Indonesia, and Africa, as if local climates and conditions were irrelevant to agricultural choices. A large percentage of these monocultures have been planted with proprietary seeds that are engineered to self-destruct once their host plant matures. Farmers who contract with large chemical companies that produce proprietary seeds must bear the expense of buying seeds anew each year instead of collecting them from this year's crops. Rather than farmers adding the diversity of new methods and plant varieties to the complex system of world agriculture, only one variety of each crop is rapidly becoming the rule, and it costs the farmer more to grow than would otherwise be the case. This expanding practice sets a dangerous precedent, because farmers are held hostage to monoculture crops that are often unreliable because they lack the diversity necessary for sustainability.

One outcome of proprietary interventions in the world's complex agricultural system is that one corporation's genetically modified monoculture cotton seeds have triggered the evolution of a resistant pink bollworm that is munching its way through India's cotton crop.[27] From 1997 to 2010, over 197,000 farmers in India committed suicide due to unsupportable debt, much of it incurred when their genetically modified crops succumbed to insects and failed.[28] Propaganda aimed at luring poor farmers into growing cash crops for export has not resulted in more cotton; it has ended up producing less cotton and enormous numbers of landless, fatherless families. Instead of producing more for less, as its promoters claim, the monoculture's biotech assault on biodiversity—an abstract, profit-driven idea that ignores perceivable natural processes—produces negative outcomes on a global scale. At planting time, self-destructing, often pesticide-infused seeds blow on the wind into adjacent fields, producing crops that overtake traditional varieties and essentially poison that land and remove it from use in sustainable agriculture.

In addition to undermining the planet's biodiversity, industrial farming's open fields are an invitation to rapidly spreading insect and fungal predators. As I write this, deadly wheat rust has been killing crops all over Africa and has jumped over to Iran and Yemen. All it takes is one pesticide-resistant, newly hatched predator or fungus gaining access to agribusinesses' unprotected, huge open fields, to destroy a crop in record time. Plant pathologist Yue Jin of the U.S. Department of Agriculture states, "When we cultivate wheat, it is genetically uniform, spatially uniform and temporally uniform— those uniformities favor certain things to blow up rapidly.... You hardly ever see the disease really killing a native plant stand."[29] Unlike industrial wheat fields that are the result of particular agricultural theories, native wheat grows in clumps that are genetically distinct, do not all sprout simultaneously, and are surrounded by other plants that block alien wind-blown spores.

In addition, monoculture farming uses petroleum-based fertilizers, pesticides, and inefficient transport systems, which, combined with the animal feedlots they service, are the primary contributors to the world's carbon, methane, and nitrous oxide emissions. These effluents are the major contributors to global warming; water, air, and land pollution; and chronic disease. "If the sixteen million acres now being used to grow corn to feed cows in the United States became well-managed pasture, that would remove fourteen billion pounds of carbon from the atmosphere each year, the equivalent of taking fourteen million cars off the road."[30]

Since agribusiness food products are replete with hidden costs, have far lower nutritional value (which adds to people's medical costs), and are subject to total crop failure from newly evolved insects and fungi, such crops actually cost more than traditionally grown crops to produce. Even more to the point, when indigenous farming methods are properly employed, any advantage claimed by corporate biotech strategies evaporates. In fact, yields from agribusiness farms recently have started to decline.[31]

Sadly, many of the possibilities for indigenous farming are at risk. In an October 2010 interview on Democracy Now, Olivier De Schutter, the special rapporteur for the "Right to Food" for the UN General Assembly, reported the latest devastating strategy that Wall Street investment firms are using to gain control of the normally bottom-up food economy. They are arranging for foreign governments and large corporations in developed countries to acquire farmland in poor countries. The land being put up for grabs presently belongs to subsistence farmers. It is a strategy aimed at ensuring the future food security of those in developed countries at the indigenous farmers' expense.[32] One example, reported by Smila Narula at NYU Law School, is that in 2010, under a cloak of secrecy, Pakistan's government targeted 2.4 million hectares of farmland for foreign corporate investors to buy. Selling this land threatens the continued existence of twenty-five thousand traditional farming villages.[33]

There is also a more worrisome backstory. In the past few years, one corporation has been quietly buying up the other seed companies in the world, giving themselves even more power over what can be planted. Ironically, that company, Monsanto, is a primary funder of the "doomsday" world seed vault in Svalbard, Norway, which gives them privileged access to these seed stocks in the event of a global disaster.[34]

From Complexity to Simplicity: Whole Grains to Empty Calories

A diet based on quantity rather than quality has ushered a new creature onto the world stage: The human being who manages to be both over-fed and undernourished.

—MICHAEL POLLAN

To add injury to injury, large-scale corporate farms typically sell their subsidized, monoculture crops to large corporate manufacturers that "process" originally complex, natural foods into simpler packaged products. The chemists who work in this industry typically take intact, whole grains with a modicum of nutritional value and slice and dice them into various components that have no counterparts in nature. The complex grains' once-healthy components—fiber, minerals, vitamins, and protein—virtually disappear in the process. Thus whole wheat ends up even more despoiled in a brightly colored box of highly processed air-filled puffs coated with high-fructose corn syrup and infused with chemical preservatives that have unpronounceable names. Since our brains are overly susceptible to sweets, one might think that in adding corn syrup to almost everything, and targeting advertising to small children, agribusiness food processors are deliberately attempting to create an addicted and thus permanently undernourished client base that has no idea what is happening to them.

The partitioning of whole complex foods into processed products has been aided and abetted by the atomistic protocols of nutrition science that isolate, study, and insert single nutrients back into processed foods to supposedly make up for the deficiencies caused by the parts-oriented manufacturing process. The problem is that while certain individual nutrients—perhaps calcium, folic acid, and omega-3 oils—can have important positive effects on the health of some people when taken alone, most nutrients act synergistically because they are interacting components of complex foods. If you isolate and add one component, it does not provide the same benefit as a whole food with the same nutrient built in. The M. D. Anderson Cancer Center at the University of Texas has shown that daily curcumin supplements may help lower the inflammation that causes cancer, but in India, where people's traditional diet includes cooking curries daily using whole curcumin, there is a much lower incidence of cancer than in the United States.[35]

In another classic study, University of Minnesota epidemiologists David Jacobs and Lyn Steffen showed that eating whole grains reduces mortality from all causes when compared to eating processed grains along with the same level of nutrients added to the diet.[36] But since nutrition scientists typically study only one nutrient at a time, their findings are like serial marriages in which they mate with one food element until its proves unworthy, and then they divorce it and try another. The resulting academic food fights pit fats against carbohydrates, carbohydrates against proteins, mono against polyunsaturated fats, and omega-3 fats against omega-6 fats, as if nutrition were an either/or proposition as opposed to being a field that has been decimated by our atomistic worldview.[37]

Remember the hullaballoo when scientists came up with the "lipid hypothesis," that if you ate fat, it immediately migrated to your middle and made you fat, causing your cholesterol to rise, your heart to weaken, and your pancreas to battle diabetes. At that time, doctors and nutritionists advised us to replace fats with carbohydrates. As if by magic, enormous quantities of low-fat products with added sugar to enhance their flavor filled the supermarket shelves. The result was that people may have eaten less saturated fat, but they also ate far more sugar and became much fatter (as well as increasingly diabetic). In 2001, the lipid hypothesis was refuted by Frank Hu and his colleagues at the Harvard School of

Public Health, but not before this unsubstantiated theory had influenced the diets of millions and done considerable damage.[38] Those low-fat, high-sugar products are still on the shelves, and as a result, many of us are mainlining sugar in the belief that we are making healthy choices.

New York University nutritionist Marion Nestle points out, "The problem with nutrient by nutrient science is that it takes the nutrient out of the context of food, the food out of the context of diet, and the diet out of the context of a lifestyle."[39] This practice trashes the synergy available from a nutrient's interactions with the other components in a complex whole food. In other words, a complex food is more than the sum of its parts. The problem with the deductive reasoning that gave birth to the lipid hypothesis is that it has little to do with the reality of how our bodies work. It may seem sensible to think that eating fat will make you fatter, but the evidence proves otherwise, as the Inuit (who traditionally ate a great deal of blubber) and the Argentine gauchos (who subsisted on beef) show. Since 1950, the United States Department of Agriculture has tracked forty-three different crops and found that due to agribusinesses' depleted soil, they all have significantly lower nutrient content today.[40] One dreadful outcome of eating such foods is that "at a health clinic in Oakland, California, doctors report seeing overweight children suffering from old-time deficiency diseases such as rickets."[41]

From Nutritional Simplicity to Obesity

The correlation between poverty and obesity is now the number-one preventable cause of death in this country.

—MICHAEL POLLAN

A fascinating study done by Professor Kerin O'Dea, Director of the Sansom Institute for Health Research at the University of South Australia, compared the outcomes of eating either a modern fast food diet or an indigenous Aborigine diet. She recruited a group of middle-aged Australian Aborigines who had moved from the rural out-back into town.[42] When they relocated, the group members changed their native hunting and gathering diet of whole, complex, wild food to modern reconstituted and refined carbohydrates, packaged prod-ucts, powdered milk, carbonated sodas, beer, potatoes, onions, and fast foods. Within a few years, they had all gained a great deal of weight, developed full-blown type 2 diabetes, and were at risk for heart disease.

To see if she could help reverse these conditions, O'Dea recruited several Aborigines to return to the bush for seven weeks to hunt and gather their native foodstuffs without access to any other food. Their outback diet consisted largely of seafood, plus birds, kangaroo, insect larvae, yams, figs, and bush honey. After seven weeks, tests showed that they had lost an average of 17.9 pounds each, significantly low-ered their blood pressure, normalized their triglycerides, and either eliminated their diabetes or improved their glucose tolerance signifi-cantly. Meanwhile, in school lunchrooms across America, children are eating the equivalent of the Aborigines' city diet and are becom-ing increasingly obese and diabetic.

The theories and strategies we create in our minds and loose upon the world—from Wall Street's Commodities Index Fund to monocultures and processed foods—often produce negative out-comes because they fly in the face of the basic way the world works and how it sustains us. *All these practices manipulate long-term, real complex systems into short-term, simplistic solutions that have over the years caused soil depletion, pollution, crop failures, starvation, farmer suicides, malnutrition, obesity, heart disease, and diabetes across the globe.* The good news is that the fastest growing sector of the agri-cultural economy today is organic farming and direct food buying through farmer's markets and cooperatives—both enterprises that support the diversity and complexity needed for a sustainable food system and a well-functioning planet.

The Epilogue considers how we came to have the ecological prob-lems we now face, and proposes that they are rooted in the theory that we humans have dominion over the Earth and everything on it, which has led to our partitioning and privatizing what was once the Earth's largest complex system, the "commons."

Epilogue: A Cautionary Tale

First hand knowledge about nature...can be the irreducible imprint of experience, inaccessible to rational dissection, the sensual contact of our physical selves with the real world....This kind of knowledge is what intuition is made of.

—CHARLES WOHLFORTH

WHEN WE HUMANS walked out of Africa, the Earth was a seamless commons. Our eyes saw a world of patterns—branching trees, rippling grasses, meandering rivers, and spiraling galaxies that told of the Earth's endless forests, verdant pastures, pristine oceans, and multitudes of creatures. Crystalline ice capped the mountains and sea ice circled the poles—floating deep into the water from the edge of the land out to the horizon over the Arctic seas. The world writ large was a complex, global ecosystem based in fire, water, air, and land, and across the globe that system was tempered by the perceivable presence of far-away ice.

At that time, we had little understanding that these seemingly diverse places and the patterns that revealed their differences and similarities originated from the same source—the laws that govern space, the press of evolution, and the energy of the sun. But we did know that nature's ways and the factors that brought them forth were precious, and we invented creation myths to explain their origins. In some cases we worshipped the Earth or the sun for the bounty they provided. In other cases we took on the visage of the eagle, the raven, or the lion to gain their protection or wisdom. The only rule was, and still is, ecological—everything that exists, including behaviors such as cooperation, altruism, and predation, as well as disastrous events, did so in a matrix of reciprocity. That rule did not come from our imaginations or our theories. It came from the way our planet and everything on it is structured and the way it all works. Like the lilies of the field, we lived off the largesse of the land, and our lives were possible because we perceived and understood the informative patterns that revealed the lay of that land and the resources that ensured our survival. While some of us took advantage of other people, and others wasted resources, there was so much available and so few people, that we had little need for theories to justify our actions.

But as time passed and populations grew larger, some of us began to feel the press of such numbers. They began to override the patterned information they perceived that revealed things as they were. Instead, they began to construct theories in their minds that reframed those things as they wanted them to be. In their mind's eye, the world appeared to be made of separate parts that could be enclosed and exploited. The world—once a shared commons with resources that were available to all—was reframed by some as pieces of property, a source of commodities that could be bought and sold, rather than a source of common sustenance. The reality that the Earth was an intact complex system that required all of its components working together to sustain the whole receded. The components of such systems were wrongly conceived of as separate from one another—forests were clear-cut, animals were hunted to extinction, and sometimes whole groups of people were killed to gain possession of their land.

Where both pagan and Christian religions once believed that taking things from beneath the land violated Mother Earth, we replaced those beliefs with ones that promoted such activities. Theories such as the idea that using raw materials to make products gave them added value and justified mining for everything, especially coal and oil, to run our newly minted machines. We reveled in our new scientific and technological knowledge and our belief that we were rational beings who would not act against our own self-interests. We believed the theory that our advances would make a better life for all and that the problems that did arise could be solved with new technological inventions. In many cases those inventions were beneficial, but not in others. One problem was that most of our inventions required that we keep mining the commons for its ever-lessening resources; and the combination of our theory of infinite progress, and our failure to consider the consequences that this theory produced, left us with black smoke belching into the air, rising temperatures, and—most critical—melting ice. As the population continued to grow and a profit-driven mindset became more prevalent, more and more of the components that constituted our world were siphoned off for private uses or were actually used up and disappeared. The fabric of our world began to fray.

Many indigenous peoples who lived close to the land understood this situation. They continued to rely on their eyes and were informed by their sense of place. Instead of theories that rationalized plundering the Earth, they created metaphors and legends that incorporated the occurrence of natural events and that preserved the Earth's inherent meaning as one self-sustaining system. They honored the interconnections among all things and clarified the place we humans hold in the great chain of being. Their tales claim us as children of the Earth, parts of the whole, where the trees are our brothers; "standing people in whom the winged ones build their lodges and raise their families and who have equal rights to the land" is how Black Elk put it.[1] They understood Chief Seattle's counsel that "humankind has not woven the web of life. We are but one thread in it. Whatever we do to the web, we do to ourselves. All things are bound together. All things connect."[2] Chief Seattle's insights were not a different, gentler type of theory. His counsel was grounded in conditions as they actually were without the overlay of our inventions and interventions.

Centuries ago, there were European thinkers who emphasized these points as well. They challenged the theories that promoted the exploitation of what were once common lands and counseled us to be wary of the ideas we created in our minds. In 1623, British scientist and father of the scientific method Sir Francis Bacon wrote, "All depends on keeping the eye steadily fixed on the facts of nature, and so receiving their images as they are. For God forbid that we should give out a dream of our own imagination, for a pattern of the world."³ In the preface to his major work *Novum Organum*, Bacon fleshed out this view:

> Being convinced that the human intellect makes its own dif-ficulties...whence follows manifold ignorance of things, and by reason of the ignorance mischiefs innumerable...because the primary notions of things which the mind accumu-lates...are false, confused and overhastily abstracted from the facts...whence it follows that the entire fabric of human rea-son which we employ in the inquisition of nature is...like some magnificent structure without any foundation. For while men are occupied in admiring and applauding the false powers of the mind, they pass by and throw away those true powers...to wait upon nature instead of vainly affecting to overrule her.⁴

Going back even further, in the fourteenth century, William of Ockham, whose realistic "razor" urging parsimony in thinking we still use today to judge and constrain our scientific enterprises from flights of excess, distinguished between "intuitive" and "abstractive" cognition. He warned that "human reasoning should start with our direct perception of reality...one should not call on hypothetical entities to explain empirical evidence unless there is no alternative."⁵ Like Galileo, who also used what he saw with his eyes to challenge the unrealistic geocentric theory of his day, William of Ockham was excommunicated for heresy.⁶

A burgeoning theory of the day that Ockham challenged was that of property and enclosure. He wrote, "There was no prop-erty in the Garden of Eden. Instead, Adam and Eve had a natural right to use anything at hand."⁷ Cherokee Jimmie Durham echoed Ockham's view in the twentieth century when he testified before a Congressional committee about a proposed dam that was about to obliterate his ancestral homelands:

> We cannot separate our place on earth from our lives on earth, nor from our vision, nor our meaning as a people. We are taught from childhood that the animals and even the trees and plants...are our brothers and sisters. So when we speak

of the land, we are not speaking of property … or even a piece
of ground upon which our houses sit and are crops are grown.
We are talking of something truly sacred.[8]

Today in our fragmented world, countries are separated by boundaries created in people's minds. These artificial barriers encapsulate
theories of nationalism or ethnicity that pit one group of people
against another and obscure their actual connections. We seem to
believe that we cannot perceive such distant connections because
our eyes cannot see that far. But consider the way of the Kogi people
of Colombia, who see their mountaintop-to-ocean lands of glacial
peaks, cloud forests, rainforests, deserts, river valleys, and shorelines
as a microcosm of the Earth, a mirror that reflects what is happening
across the globe.[9] The Kogi know that as the clouds disappear from
their mountain, they are also disappearing from many other places.
Although they never leave their lands, they see the global patterns,
which include their waning cloud cover, their lessening rain, and
their melting ice. They know that their land is connected to every
other land by the currents that run beneath the sea and high in the
atmosphere, and that it echoes those same patterns in other places.
They understand that their clouds and other clouds across the globe
are one system, and so they *see the whole in the part.*

In the 1980s, the Kogi elders recruited a BBC film crew and came
down off their mountain to send us a message. They said, "Younger
Brothers are looting the world. They have sold the clouds."[10] Now,
the Kogi have retreated back into their high mountain lands. They
have taken up the rope bridge that connects their city to the outside
world. They say that we, the younger brothers, do not listen.

Just as the ice on the Kogis' mountain is gone, we can see the consequences of our not looking and our not listening most clearly in
the disappearance of the ice that tempers our global ecosystem. But
we seem to be dismissing its silent demise. In his prescient book *The
World Without Ice*, ice expert Henry Pollack tells us,

Nature's best thermometer, perhaps its most sensitive and
unambiguous indicator of climate change, is ice. When ice

gets sufficiently warm, it melts. Ice asks no questions, presents no arguments, reads no newspapers, listens to no debates. It is not burdened by ideology and it carries no political baggage as it crosses the threshold from solid to liquid. It just melts.[11]

But while our newspapers and politicians ignore the example set by the ice, and instead debate whether climate change exists, scientists tell us that our glacial, sheet, and sea ice are all melting at an alarming rate. In Glacier National Park in Montana only 30 of the 150 glaciers present in 1850 are still visible. The mountains in East Africa, Alberta, Canada, South America, Europe, and Asia all tell the same story. Mt. Kilimanjaro is bare.[12] Between 1994 and 1996 two sections of the Larsen Ice Shelf that equaled the size of Luxembourg and Rhode Island, respectively, split off and disintegrated.[13] Between 2008 and 2009 the Wilkins Ice Shelf collapsed. It covered an area about half the size of Scotland.[14]

If the West Antarctic land-based ice sheet goes the way of the Larsen Ice Shelf, Pollack predicts that sea levels will rise ten feet.[15] The Antarctic ice shelves buttress the land and block the exit of glacier melt from the interior. Once those shelves disintegrate, glacier melt will have a free run to the sea, adding to its rising level. Pollack warns us that "ice plays a critical and major role in setting the temperature of Earth's atmosphere and oceans, governing major weather patterns, regulating sea-level and dramatically impacting agriculture, commerce and even geopolitics...our history and future are inextricably linked to the world's ice."[16]

Although ice loss is linked to fossil fuel use, today there is still talk of drilling for oil in the land of the ice. But there are people today who know firsthand that such an enterprise would be a folly. The most knowledgeable of those people, the Iñupiat, have lived for the last thousand years near Barrow, Alaska, hunting whales out on the sea ice. Their ability to parse the ever-changing structure of that ice and its relationship to the climate and the future of the Earth is legendary.[17] Sea ice forms beautiful crystalline patterns through the interactions of water, temperature, and brine. These perceivable patterns are precisely organized configurations of diagonal and vertical lines that tell observers the story of its structure and strength and of the many world systems that contributed to its formation. Each structural layout the ice adopted and a whaler then perceived was shared with others and then passed on to the next generation. As a result, each individual whaler came to know every type of ice and the situation in which it was found. The whaler's perceptions were not of a part here and a part there, but of the complex Arctic system as a whole as it changed over both space and time.

When Iñupiat Richard Glenn returned to Barrow as a young PhD candidate studying ice at university to collect data, he was shocked at how much the ice had changed. The tribal elders told him facts about the ice of which the scientists he worked with at school had no knowledge. Glenn began to understand that

> [Iñupiat] knowledge existed as part of a person living in the environment, a whole world constructed from experience, and couldn't be extracted and rationalized with data points…and that "scientists know a collection of facts about ice, Eskimos know ice itself."[18]

When they go out on a hunt, they know "the shape of the ocean bottom, the water and currents, the underside of the ice, and the atmosphere, and how each factor varied through the year to build the shore-fast structure of the ice they used for whaling in the spring."[19] That knowledge comes from living close to the land, not from abstract theories about the land. In contrast, when the theories about ice that scientists use to make sense of this world partition it into separate parts, which they hope can be measured with extrinsic indices, they lose sight of their subject of study. The Iñupiat have no need of such measuring strategies because they perceive the Arctic as a complex whole. Their perceptual systems immediately recognize each different incarnation that ice takes because they parse its structure and the relationship of that structure to the conditions of the complex system that constitutes their world and the world beyond.

Unlike the Kogi, who have the understanding and patience to see the whole in the part but keep themselves aloof from the world, those of us in the modern world now have many eyes, both citizen and scientist, on every part of the world. We can record the effects of climate warming locally and put together our many perceptions to understand it globally. As we saw in chapter 8, we can combine satellite images in real-time using computer programs that reveal the dynamic configurations that emerge from all the complex systems on our planet—the ocean currents, the wind and rainfall patterns, the cloud cover, the biomass growth, and how they are all related to one another. These indicators of climate and its changes are laid out before us like a geometric lexicon that is visible around the world across space and time.[20] All these methods are enhanced strategies for perceiving the world as it is and require little theorizing to understand the information they offer. These overarching images also show the effects of our activities—mountaintop removal that has buried adjacent valleys, oil spills that have despoiled ocean populations, "fracking" for natural gas that has polluted water supplies and sickened families, and oil plumes stretched out beneath the surface of the Gulf of Mexico's waters— and offer us an opportunity to mitigate these situations from a base of evidence, not ideology.

Our economic theories of production, consumption, and investment have put us on a collision course with the laws of physics, chemistry, and biology. We have ignored the requirements of complexity and reciprocity that keep the world sustainable. But the 1964 Alaskan tsunamis taught a fascinating lesson—all the property lines that had made a commercial patchwork of this Arctic Eden disappeared beneath the roiling waters, leaving the land to reinstate itself on its own seamless terms. Our Western atomistic worldview with its partitioning perspective, made-up boundaries, and tunnel vision is no match for Earth's own reality. The world exists in its own right and its dynamic structure is even more perceivable today with our ability to extend our eyes with scientifically precise instruments. Theories couched in words that include *partition* and *privatization,* that today the "unseen hand" has etched deeper and deeper into the landscape of our minds, have minimal meaning in the larger scheme of things. But will the perceivable messages written in the dying trees, the diminishing clouds, and the melting ice keep our attention and energize our actions for long enough to restore the commons we need in order to survive? It is said that the ancient Chinese sage Laotzu warned, *if we do not change direction, we will end up where we are heading.*

Notes

INTRODUCTION

1. Yellowstone National Park. (2011, June 21). Reintroduction changes ecosystem [Blog post]. Retrieved from http://www.yellowstonepark.com/2011/06/yellowstone-national-park-wolf-reintroduction-is-changing-the-face-of-the-greater-yellowstone-ecosystem/
   Estes, J. et al. (2011). Trophic downgrading of planet earth. Science, 303, 301–306.
   Scheffer, M. (2009). Critical transitions in nature and society. Princeton, NJ: Princeton University Press.
2. Chase, A. (1986). *Playing God in Yellowstone Park: The destruction of America's first national park.* Boston. MA: Atlantic Monthly Press.
3. ScienceDaily. (2003, October 29). Wolves are rebalancing Yellowstone ecosystem. Retrieved from http://www.sciencedaily.com/releases/2003/10/031029064909.htm
   Hobbes, N.T. & Cooper, D. J. (2013). Have the Wolves Restored the Riparian Willows in Northern Yellowstone? In White, P.J., Garrott, R.A & Plumb, G.E. (eds) Yellowstone's Wildlife in Transition (179–194), Cambridge, MA: Harvard University Press.
4. Libet, B. (2005). *Mind time: The temporal factor in consciousness.* Cambridge, MA: Harvard University Press.
5. Farmington, B. (1951). Temporis partus masculus (The masculine birth of time), the untranslated writing of Francis Bacon (1605). *Centaurus, 1,* 93–125. doi:10.1111/j.1600-1498.1951.tb10507.x
6. Goldberg, N. (2009). *Old friend from far away: The practice of writing memoir.* New York, NY: Free Press.
7. Uppsala University. (2013, June 28). History of the department and the psychology subject at Uppsala University. Retrieved from http://www.psyk.uu.se/organization/historia/?languageId=1

8. Tanaka, J. W., & Farah, M. J. (2003). Parts and wholes in face recognition. *Quarterly Journal of Experimental Psychology, 46A*(2), 225–245.

9. Chabris, C., & Simon, D. (2010). *The invisible gorilla*. New York: Crown.

10. Kahneman, D. (2011). *Thinking, fast and slow*. New York: Farrar, Straus and Giroux.

11. Mlodinow, L. (2012). *Subliminal: How your unconscious mind rules your behavior*. New York, NY: Pantheon.

12. Mlodinow, "Subliminal," 45.

13. Mlodinow, "Subliminal," 45.

14. Mlodinow, "Subliminal," 45.

15. Myers, D. G. (2002). *Intuition: Its powers and perils*. New Haven, CT: Yale University Press.

16. Chomsky, N. (1969). *Aspects of the theory of syntax*. Cambridge, MA: MIT Press.

17. McCarthy, G., Puce, A., Gore, J. C., & Allison, T. (1997) Face-specific processing in the human fusiform gyrus. *Journal of Cognitive Neuroscience, 9*(5), 605–610.

18. Carramazza, A., & Shelton, J. R. (1998). Domain-specific knowledge systems in the brain: The animate-inanimate distinction. *Journal of Cognitive Neuroscience, 10*(1), 1–34.

19. Gazzaniga, M. (2011). *Who's in charge? Free will and the science of the brain*. New York, NY: HarperCollins.

20. Boyer, P., & Barrett, H. C. (2005). Domain specificity and intuitive ontology. In D. M. Buss (Ed.), *The handbook of evolutionary psychology* (pp. 96–118). New York, NY: Wiley.

21. Eagleman, D. M. (2001, December). Visual illusions and neurobiology. *Nature Reviews Neuroscience, 2*, 920–926.

22. Kahneman, "Thinking, fast and slow."

23. Goodale, M. A, & Milner, A. D. (2004). *Sight unseen: An exploration of conscious and unconscious vision*. Oxford, UK: Oxford University Press.

24. Carroll, S. B. (2005). *Endless forms most beautiful: The new science of evo devo*. New York: W. W. Norton.

25. Sole, R., & Goodwin, B. (2000). *Signs of life: How complexity pervades biology*. New York: Basic Books.

26. Few, A. (1975, July). Thunder. *Scientific American, 233*(1), 80–90.

27. Bower, B. (2012). Babies lip-read before talking, *Science News, 181*(3), 9.

28. Inman, V. T., Ralston, H. J., & Todd, F. (1983). *Human walking*. Baltimore, MD: Williams & Wilkins.

29. Wohlforth, C. (2004). *The whale and the supercomputer: On the northern front of climate change*. New York, NY: North Point Press.

30. Jacobellis v. Ohio, 378 U.S. 184 (1964).

31. Proust, M. (1999). *Remembrance of things past: The captive* (Vol. 5). New York, NY: Random House/Modern Library Classics. (Original work published 1923)

CHAPTER I

1. Barry, J. (1992, July 12). Sea of lies. *Newsweek Magazine*. Retrieved from http://www.the dailybeast.com/newsweek/1992/07/12/sea-of-lies.html

2. http://airdisaster.com/cgi-bin/aircraft_detail.cgi?aircraft=Airbus+A300

3. Barry, "Sea of lies," 4.

4. Klein, G. A. (1998). *Sources of power: How people make decisions*. Cambridge, MA: MIT Press.

5. Klein, "Sources of power."

6. Evans, D. (n.d.). Naval Science 304: Navigation and Naval Operations II. Lesson 20, Crisis decision making: *USS Vincennes*. Retrieved from http://www.unm.edu/~nrotc/ns304/lesson20.htm

7. Koppel, T. (1992, July 1). The USS *Vincennes*: Public war, secret war. *ABC News Nightline*. Retrieved from http://homepage.ntlworld.com/jksonc/docs/ir655-nightline-19920701.html

8. Koppel, "The USS *Vincennes*."

9. Gordon, M. R. (1992, July 2). U.S. account of downing of Iran jet criticized. *The New York Times*. Retrieved from http://www.nytimes.com/1992/07/02/world/us-account-of-downing-of-iran-jet-criticized.html

10. Barry, "Sea of lies," 4.

11. Koppel, "The USS *Vincennes*."

12. Nisbett, R. E. (1993). *Rules for reasoning*. Hillsdale, NJ: Lawrence Erlbaum Associates.

13. Evans, "Naval Science 304."

14. Wilson, G. C. (1988, July 4). Navy missile downs Iranian jetliner. *The Washington Post*. Retrieved from http://www.washingtonpost.com/wp-srv/inatl/long-term/flight801/stories/july88crash.htm

15. Tanaka & Farah, "Parts and wholes."

16. Lakoff, G. (2006). Thinking points: Communicating American values and vision. New York, NY: Farrar, Strauss and Giroux.

17. Haidt, J. (2012). The righteous mind: Why good people are divided by politics and religion. New York, NY: Pantheon.

18. Klein, "Sources of power," 78.

19. Huth, G. (2009, July 31). *A primer of geometry and vision*. Retrieved from http://www.ghuth.com/2009/07/31/a-primer-on-geometry-and-vision/

20. Huth, G. (2010). *A new physics-based model for light interaction with the retina of the human eye and the vision process*. Retrieved from http://www.ghuth.com/a-new-physics-based-model-for-light-interaction-with-the-retina-of-the-human-eye-and-the-vision-process/

21. Haken, H. (1979). *Pattern formation by dynamic systems and pattern recognition*. Berlin: Springer-Verlag. As quoted in Kelso, J. A. S. (1995, p. 89). *Pattern dynamics*. Cambridge, MA: MIT Press.

22. Kelso, J. A. S. (1995). *Pattern dynamics* (pp. 20, 27). Cambridge, MA: MIT Press.

23. Sin, W. C., Hass, K., Ruthazer, E. S., & Cline, H. T. (2002). Dendrite growth increased by visual activity requires NMDA receptor and Rho GTPases. *Nature*, *419*(6906), 475–480.

24. Klein, "Sources of power."

25. Klein, "Sources of power."

26. Klein, "Sources of power."

27. Wickens, T. (2002). *Introduction to signal detection theory*. New York, NY: Oxford University Press.

28. Lindsay, P. H., & Norman, D. A. (1977). *Human information processing* (2nd ed.). New York, NY: Academic Press.

29. Gregory, R. L. (1978). *Eye and brain: The psychology of seeing* (2nd ed.) New York: McGraw-Hill.

30. Hochberg, J. E. (1978). *Perception* (2nd ed.). Englewood Cliffs, NJ: Prentice Hall.

31. Gibson, J. J. (1979). *The ecological approach to visual perception* (p. 253). Boston, MA: Houghton Mifflin.

32. Reid, T. (1785). *Essays on the intellectual powers of man*. Edinburgh, Scotland: Printed for John Bell and J. Robinson. As quoted in Gibson, J. J. (1966). *The senses considered as perceptual systems* (p. 319). Boston, MA: Houghton Mifflin.

33. Yaffe, G., & Ryan, N. (2009, Winter). Thomas Reid. *The Stanford encyclopedia of philosophy*. The Metaphysics Research Lab, Center for the Study of Language and Information. Retrieved from http://plato.stanford.edu/archives/win2009/entries/reid/

34. Gibson, "The ecological approach," 253.

35. Heft, H. (2001). *Ecological psychology in context: James Gibson, Roger Barker, and the radical empiricism of William James*. New York: Taylor and Francis

36. Gibson, "The ecological approach," 253.

37. Gibson, "The ecological approach," 253.

38. Gibson, "The ecological approach," 217.

39. Gibson, "The ecological approach," 197, 258

40. Gibson, "The ecological approach," 223.

41. Gibson, "The ecological approach," 253.

42. Reed, E. (1996). *The necessity of experience*. New Haven, CT: Yale University Press.

43. Heft, H. (1998). Comment on Gergen, K. (1997). Review of Reed, E. (1996). *The necessity of experience*. *Contemporary Psychology*, *43*, 450–451.

44. Reed, E. (1996). *Encountering the world: Toward an ecological psychology* (pp. 70, 82). New York, NY: Oxford University Press.

45. Edelman, G. (1987) *Neural Darwinism*. New York, NY: Basic Books.

46. Mitchell, M. (2009). *Complexity* (p. 4). New York, NY: Oxford University Press.

47. Christopherson, R.W. (2003). *Geosystems: An introduction to physical geography*. Upper Saddle River, NJ: Prentice Hall.

48. Collins UK Staff. (2006). *Fragile earth: Views of a changing world* (p. 50). London: HarperCollins.

49. Pretor-Pinney, G. (2010). *The wave watchers companion* (p. 108). New York, NY: Penguin.

50. Laughlin, R. (2005). *A different universe: Reinventing physics from the bottom down* (pp. 208–209; 218–219). New York: Basic Books.

51. Allport, G., & Postman, L. (1947). *The psychology of rumor*. New York: Holt, Rinehart and Winston.

52. Gazzaniga, M. S., Ivrey, R. B., & Mangun, G. R. (2002). *Cognitive neuroscience* (2nd ed., p. 137). New York: W. W. Norton.

CHAPTER 2

1. Chun, S., & Osier, D. (2004, March 3). Mom finds kidnapped daughter six years later. Retrieved from http://www.cnn.com/2004/US/Northeast/03/01/girl.found.alive/

2. Tanaka & Farah, "Parts and wholes."

3. Enlow, D. H. (1968). *The human face: An account of the postnatal growth and the development of the craniofacial skeleton*. New York, NY: Harper & Row, Hoeber Medical Division.

4. Burton, A. M., & Jenkins, R. (2008). 100% accuracy in automatic face recognition. *Recognition Science, 319*(5862), 435.

5. Haig, N. D. (1984). The effect of feature displacement on face recognition, *Perception, 13*(5), 104–109.

6. Young, A. W., Hellawell, D., & Hay, D. C. (1987). Configural information in face perception. *Perception, 16*(6), 747–759. doi:10.1068/p160747

7. Cooper, E. E., & Wojan, T. J. (2000). Differences in the coding of spatial relations in face identification and basic level object recognition. *Journal of Experimental Psychology: Learning, Memory, & Cognition, 26*(2), 470–488.

8. Alley, T. R. (1983). Infantile head shape as an elicitor of adult protection. *Merrill- Palmer Quarterly, 29*, 411–427.

9. Lorenz, K. (1971). *Studies in human and animal behavior*. Cambridge, MA: Harvard University Press.

10. Thompson, D. W. (1959). *On growth and form* (2 vols.). Cambridge U.K.: Cambridge University Press. (Original work published 1917)

11. Dixon, A., & Sarnat, B. (Eds.). (1983). *Factors and mechanisms influencing bone growth*. New York, NY: Alan R. Liss.

12. Enlow, "The human face."

13. McCabe, V. (1984) Abstract perceptual information for age level: A risk factor for maltreatment, *Child Development, 55*(1), 267–276.

14. Thompson, "On growth and form."

15. Enlow, "The human face," 27.
16. Enlow, "The human face," 34.
17. Enlow, "The human face," 58.
18. Finklestein, S. (Producer), & Stahl, L. (Correspondent). (2012, March 18). Face blindness [Television series episode]. In *60 Minutes*, New York, NY: CBS Television. Retrieved from http://www.cbsnews.com/8301-18560_162-57399118/face-blindness-when-everyone-is-a-stranger/
19. Finklestein & Stahl, "Face blindness."
20. Tanaka & Farah, "Parts and wholes."
21. McCabe, V. (1982). The direct perception of universals: A theory of knowledge acquisition. *Synthese, 52*(3), 495–513.
22. Cotton, R., & Thompson-Cannino, J. (2009). *Picking Cotton: Our memoir of rape and redemption*, New York: St. Martin's Press.
23. Loftus, E. F. (1996). *Eyewitness testimony* (pp. v–vi). Cambridge, MA: Harvard University Press.
24. Booksamillion.com. (1996). Overview to Elizabeth F. Loftus's *Eyewitness testimony*. Retrieved from http://www.booksamillion.com/p/Eyewitness-Testimony/ Elizabeth-F-Loftus/9780674287778#overview
25. Thompson-Cannino, J. (2007, September 28). I sent the wrong man to jail. *Seeing the Forest*. Retrieved from http://www.seeingtheforest.com/archives/2007/09/i_sent_the_wrong.htm
26. The Innocence Project. (n.d.). "Eric Sarsfield." Retrieved from http://www.innocenceproject.org/Content/Eric_Sarsfield.php
27. Vedantam. S. (2010, pp. 9–14). *The hidden brain: How our unconscious minds elects presidents, control markets, wage wars, and save our lives*. New York, NY: Spiegel & Grau.
28. Loftus, E.F. quoted in on line review for Cannino, J.T., Cotton, R. & Toneo, E. (as told to) (2010). *Picking Cotton*. New York: St Martin's Griffin. Retrieved from http://macmillan.com.academictrade/Picking Cotton
29. Miller, G. (1956). The magical number seven, plus or minus two: Some limits on our capacity for processing information. *Psychological Review, 63*(2), 81–97.
30. Kay, H. (1955). Learning and retaining verbal material. *British Journal of Psychology, 46*(2), 81–100. doi:10.1111/j.2004-8295.1955.tb00527.x
31. Whipple, G. M. (1909). The observer as reporter: A survey of the psychology of testimony. *Psychological Bulletin, 6*(5), 153–170.

CHAPTER 3

1. Abrams, D. (2006, January 30). Good Samaritan act saves young girl [Television series episode]. In *The Abrams Report*. Retrieved from http://www.nbcnews.com/id/11101039/ns/msnbc-the_abrams_report/t/good-samaritan-act-saves-young-girl/

2. Dittrich, W. H., Troscianko, T., Lea, S. E. G., & Morgan, D. (1996). Perception of emotion from dynamic point light displays represented in dance. *Perception, 25*(6), 727–738.

3. Johansson, G. (1973). Visual perception of biological motion and a model for its analysis. *Perception and Psychophysics, 14*(2), 201–211. doi:10.3758/BF03212378

4. Runeson, S., & Frykholm G. (1983). Kinematic specification of dynamics as an informational basis for person and action perception: Expectation, gender recognition and deceptive intention. *Journal of Experimental Psychology: General, 112*(4), 585–615.

5. Grossman, E. D., Jardine, N. L., & Pyles, J. A. (2010). fMRI-adaptation reveals invariant coding of biological motion on the human STS. *Frontiers in Human Neuroscience, 4*(15), 1–18. doi:10.3389/Neuro.09.015

6. Inman et al., "Human walking."

7. Cutting, J., Proffitt, D. R., & Kozlowski, L.T. (1978). A biomechanical invariant for gait perception. *Journal of Experimental Psychology: Human Perception and Performance, 4*(3), 357–372.

8. Bardi, L., Regolin, L., & Simon, F. (2010). Biological motion preference in humans at birth: Role of dynamic and configural properties. *Developmental Science, 14*(2), 38–59.

9. Ichikawa, H., Kanazawa, S., Yamaguchi, M. K., & Kagigi, R. (2010). Infant brain activity while viewing facial movement of point-light displays as measured by near-infrared spectroscopy. *Neuroscience Letters, 482*(2), 90–94.

10. Grossman et al., "fMRI-adaptation reveals invariant coding."

11. Pavlova, M., Bidet-Ildel, C., Sokolov, A. N., Braun, C., & Krageloh-Mann, I. (2009). Neuromagnetic response to body motion and brain connectivity. *Journal of Cognitive Neuroscience, 21*(5), 837–846.

12. Saey, T. H. (2010). Body and brain: Protein clumps like prion: slug study hints that molecular "misbehavior" has a purpose. *Science News, 177*(5), 13.

13. Bailey, C. H., Kandel, E. R., & Si, K. (2004). The persistence of long-term memory: A molecular approach to self-sustaining changes in learning-induced synaptic growth. *Neuron, 44*(1), 49–57.

14. Si, K., Giustetto, M., Etkin, A., Hsu, R., Janisiewicz, A. M., Miniaci, M. C., ...Kandel, E. R. (2003). A neuronal isoform of CPEB regulates local protein synthesis and stabilizes synapse-specific long-term facilitation in aplysia. *Cell, 115*(7), 893–904.

15. Leopold, D. A., Bondar, I. V., & Giese, M. A. (2006). Norm-based face encoding by single neurons in the monkey inferotemporal cortex. *Nature, 442*(7102), 572–573.

16. Heyman, K. (2006). The map in the brain: Grid cells may help us navigate. *Science, 312*(5774), 680–681. doi:10.1120/science.312.5774.680

17. Tolman, E. C. (1948). Cognitive maps in rats and men. *Psychological Review, 55*(4), 189–208. doi:10.137/h0061626

18. Sargolini, F., Fyhn, M., Hafting, T., McNaughton, B. L., Witter, M. P., Moser, M. B., & Moser, E. (2006). Conjunctive representation of position, directions,

and velocity in entorhinal cortex. *Science, 312*(5774), 758–762. doi:10.1126/science.1125572

19. Langston, R. F., Ainge, J. A., Couey, J. J., Canto, C. B., Bjerknes, T. L., Witter, M. P., Moser, E. I., & Moser, M. (2010). Development of the spatial representation system in the rat. *Science, 328*(5985), 1576–1580. doi:10.1126/science.1188210

20. Wills, T. J., Cacucci, F., Burgess, N., & O'Keefe, J. (2010). Development of the hippocampal cognitive map in preweaning rats. *Science, 328*(5985), 1773–1776. doi:10.1126/science.1188224

21. Lewontin, R. (1983). The organism as the subject and object of evolution. *Scienta, 18,* 68–32.

22. Midgeley, M. (1979). *Beast and man.* London: Harvester.

23. Pribram, K. H. (1977). The nature of the perceived universe. In R. E. Shaw & J. Bransford (Eds.), *Perceiving, acting, and knowing: Toward an ecological psychology* (pp. 83–101). Hillsdale, NJ: Lawrence Erlbaum Associates.

24. Rizzolatti, G., Fogassi, L., & Gallese, V. (2006). Mirrors in the mind. *Scientific American, 295*(5), 54–62.

25. Gallese, V., Fogassi, L., & Rizzolatti, G. (2002). Action representation and the inferior parietal lobule. In W. Prinz & B. Hummel (Eds.), *Common mechanisms in perception and action: Vol. 19. Attention and performance* (pp. 334–355). Oxford, UK: Oxford University Press.

26. Rizzolatti et al., "Mirrors in the mind," 61.

27. Gallese, V., Keyers, C., & Rizzolatti, G. (2004). A unifying view of the basis of social cognition. *Trends in Cognitive Science, 8,* 396–403. doi:10.1016/j.tics.2004.07.002

28. Gallese et al., "A unifying view," 401.

29. Myers, "Intuition."

30. Hadhazy, A. Think twice: How the gut's "second brain" influences mood and well-being. *Scientific American.* Feb. 12, 2010. http://www.scientificamerican.com/article.cfm?id=gut-second-brain

31. Lipps, T. (1907). Das wissen von fremden ichen. In T. Lipps (Ed.) *Psychologische untersuchungen (Band 1)* (pp. 694–722). Leipzig, Germany: Englemann.

32. Carr, L., Iacoboni, M., Dubeau, M. C., Mazziotta, J. C., & Lenzi, G. L. (2003). Neural mechanisms of empathy in humans: A relay from neural systems for imitation to limbic areas. *Proceedings of the National Academy of Sciences, 100*(9), 5497–5502.

33. Chartrand, T. L., & Barge, J. A. (1999). The chameleon effect: The perception-behavior link and social interaction. *Journal of Personality and Social Psychology, 76*(6), 893–910.

34. Carr et al., "Neural mechanisms."

35. Meltzoff, A. N., & Moore, K. M. (1977). Imitation of facial and manual gestures by neonates. *Science, 98*(4312), 75–78.

36. Hatfield, E., Cacioppo, J. T., & Rapson, R. L. (1994). *Emotional contagion.* Paris, France: Cambridge University Press.

37. Richardson, M. J., Marsh, K. L., & Schmidt, R. C. (2005). Effects of visual and verbal interaction on unintentional interpersonal coordination. *Journal of Experimental Psychology: Human Perception and Performance, 31*(1), 62–79.

38. Carr et al., "Neural mechanisms."

39. Ekman, P., & Rosenberg, E. L. (1998). *What the face reveals.* New York, NY: Oxford University Press.

CHAPTER 4

1. Penland, S. (2005, February). Taming the river to let in the sea. *Natural History, 114*(1), 42–47.

2. Stokstad, E. (2005). Louisiana's wetlands struggle for survival. *Science, 310*(5752), 1264–1266.

3. McQuaid, J., & Schleifstein, M. (2002, June 23–27). Special report: Washing away. Part 1—In harm's way. *The New Orleans Times-Picayune*, p. 3. Retrieved from http://www.nola.com/hurricane/content.ssf?/washingaway/harmsway_1.html

4. McPhee, J. (1990). The Atchafalaya. In *The control of nature* (pp. 38–39). New York, NY: The Noonday Press.

5. McPhee, "The control of nature," 41.

6. Leopold, L. B., & Langbein, W. B. (1979). River meanders. In *The physics of everyday life—Readings from* The Scientific American (pp. 28–38). San Francisco: W. H. Freeman. (Original work published 1966)

7. Rodrigues-Iturbe, I., Rinaldo, A., Rigon, R., Bras, R. L., Ijasz-Vasquez, E., & Marani, A. (1992). Fractal structures as least energy patterns: The case of river networks. *Geophysical Research Letters, 19*(9), p. 889.

8. McPhee, "The control of nature."

9. McPhee, "The control of nature."

10. McPhee, "The control of nature," 20.

11. McPhee, "The control of nature," 13.

12. McPhee, "The control of nature," 30.

13. Stokstad, "Louisiana's wetlands."

14. Van Heerden, I., & Bryan, M. (2006). *The storm: What went wrong and why during Hurricane Katrina—The inside story from one Louisiana scientist.* New York, NY: Viking.

15. Grunwald, M., & Glasser, S. B. (2005, September 21). Experts: Faulty levees caused floods. *The Seattle Times.* p. A18.

16. Warrick, J., & Grunwald, M. (2005, October 24). Design flaws may have doomed levees. *The Seattle Times* p. 6.

17. Azcona, B. (2005). Hurricane Katrina: Natural disaster or public policy. *Z Magazine, 18*(10), 5–7.

18. Headden, S. (2007, January 15). Down on the bayou, slip sliding away. *U.S. News & World Report, 142*(2), 22.

19. Surface Water Management Division. (2009). *Project effectiveness monitoring Program: North Meander Channel Reconnection Project, Stillaguamish River, 3- year Monitoring Results.* Everett, WA: Snohomish County Public Works Department, pp. 1, 5.

20. Stevens, P. (1974). *Patterns in nature.* Boston: Little, Brown.

21. Thompson, "On growth and form."

22. Mattheck, C., & Breloer, H. (1994). *Body language of trees: A handbook for failure analysis (Research for amenity trees).* London: Her Majesty's Stationery Office.

23. McMahon, T. A., & Bonner, J. T. (1987). *On size and life.* New York, NY: Scientific American Library.

24. Hove, J. R., Koster, R. W., Forouhar, G. A .B., Fraser, S. E., & Gharib, M. (2003). Intracardiac fluid forces are an essential epigenetic factor for embryonic cardio-genesis, *Nature, 421*(9), 172–177.

25. Dabiri, J. O., Colin, S. P., & Costello, J. H. (2007). Morphological diversity of medusan lineages constrained by animal-fluid interactions. *Journal of Experimental Biology, 210*(1), 1868–1873.

26. Lock, C. (2005). Ocean envy. *Science News, 166*, 154–156.

27. Summers, A. (2005, October). Boxed up to go. *Natural History*, pp. 38–39.

28. Vesilind, P. L. (2004). Chasing a tornado. *National Geographic, 205*(4), 2–37.

29. Leopold & Langbein, "River meanders."

30. Holden, C. (2005). Random samples. *Science, 310*(5751), 1114.

CHAPTER 5

1. Christensen, D. (2002, November). The great Alaska earthquake of 1964. Alaska Earthquake Information Center. Retrieved from www.aeic.alaska.edu/quakes/Alaska_1964_earthquake.html

2. Stover, C. W., & Coffman J. L. (1993). Historic earthquakes, USGS Earthquake Hazards Program. Abridged from *Seismicity of the United States 1568–1989* (Revised). (U.S. Geological Survey Paper 1527, p. 1). Washington, DC: U.S. Government Printing Office.

3. Wohlforth, C. (2010). *The fate of nature: Rediscovering our ability to rescue the earth* (pp. 204–205). New York: St. Martin's Press.

4. Denly, C. (2007, January 1). Bacteria talk. NOVA scienceNow [Blog post]. Retrieved from http://www.pbs.org/wgbh/nova/sciencenow/3401/04-bact.html

5. Klarreich, E. (2006). The mind of the swarm. *Science News, 170*(22), 347–349.

6. Mitchell, M. (2009). *Complexity: A guided tour* (p. 9). New York, NY: Oxford University Press.

7. Mitchell, "Complexity," 173.

8. Glaser, A., & von Hipple, F. N. (2006, January 22). Intrigue at the immune synapse. *Scientific American, 294*(2) 48–55.

9. Hines, P. J. (2006). The invisible bouquet. *Science, 311*(5762), 803.

10. Baldwin, I. T., Halitschke, R., Paschold, A. Dahl, C. C., & Preston, C. A. (2006). Volatile signaling in plant-plant interactions: "Talking trees" in the genomics era. *Science, 311*(5672), 812–813.

11. Goff, F. A., & Klee, H. J. (2006). Plant volatile compounds: Sensory cues for health and nutritional value? *Science, 311*(5762), 815–819.

12. Baldwin et al., "Volatile signaling."

13. Lund, S. T., & Bohlman, J. (2006). The molecular basis for wine grape quality—A volatile subject. *Science, 311*(5672), 804–807.

14. Milius, S. (2002). Frogs play tree. *Science News, 162*(23), 356.

15. Ingle, D. (1973). Spontaneous shape discrimination by frogs during unconditioned escape behavior. *Physiological Psychology, 1*(1), 71–73.

16. Attenborough, D. (1998). *The life of birds.* Princeton, NJ: Princeton University Press.

17. Lorenz, "Studies in human and animal behavior."

18. Tinbergen, N., & Kuenen, D. J. (1939). Über die auslösenden und die richtunggebenden Keiz-situationen der Sperrbewegung von jungen Drosseln (*Turdus m. merula* L. und *T. e. ericetorum* Turton) *Zeitschrift für Tierpsychologie, 3*(1), 37–60. doi:10.1111/j.1439-0310.1939.tb00603.x

19. McCabe, V. (1982). Invariants and affordances: An analysis of species-typical information. *Ethology and Sociobiology, 3*(2), 79–91.

20. Eibl-Eibesfeldt, I. (1975). *Ethology: The biology of human behavior* (2nd ed.). New York, NY: Holt, Rinehart and Winston.

21. Emlen, S. T. (1970). Celestial rotation: Its importance in the development of migratory orientation. *Science, 170*, 1198–1201. doi:10.1120/science.170.3963.1198

22. Emlen, S. T. (1970). The influence of magnetic information on the indigo bunting, Passerina cyanea. *Animal Behavior, 18*, 215–224. doi:10.1016/S0003-3472(70)80031-8

23. Emlen, S. T. (1971). Celestial rotation and stellar orientations in migratory warblers. *Science, 173*, 1460–1461. doi:10.1126/science.173.3995.459

24. Tolman, E. C. (1932). *Purposive behavior in animals and men.* New York, NY: Century Company.

25. Mouritsen, H., & Ritz, T. (2005). Magnetoreception and its use in bird navigation. *Current Opinions in Neurobiology, 15*(4), 406–414.

26. Heyers, D., Manns, M., Luksch, H., Guntukkum, O., & Mourtisen, H. (2007). A visual pathway links brain structures active during magnetic compass orientation in migratory birds, *PLoS One, 2*(9), 937. doi:10.1371/journal.pone.0000937.

27. Wiltschko,W., & Wiltschko, R. (2002). Magnetic compass orientation in birds and its physiological basis. *Naturwissenschaften, 89,* 445–452. doi:10.1038/nature0098

28. Ritz, T., Adem, S., & Schulten, K. (2000). A model for photoreceptor-based magnetoreception in birds. *Biophysiology Journal, 78*(2), 707–718.

29. Shulten, K., & Weller, A. (1978). Exploring fast electron transfer by magnetic fields. *Biophysiology Journal, 24*(1), 295–305.

30. Mouritsen, H., Janssen-Bienhold, U., Liedvogel, M., Feenders, G., Stalleicken, J., Dirks, P., & Weiler, R. (2004). Cryptochromes and neuronal-activity markers colocalize in the retina of migratory birds during magnetic orientation. *Proceedings of the National Academy of Sciences, USA, 101,* 14294–14299.

31. Baker, R. R., Mather, J. G., & Kennaugh, J. H. (1983). Magnetic bones in human sinuses. *Nature, 301*(5895), 78–80.

32. Gibson, "The ecological approach."

33. Michaels, C. F., & Carrello, C. (1981). *Direct perception* (p. 42). Englewood Cliffs, NJ: Prentice Hall.

34. Kelso, "Pattern dynamics," 145.

35. Warren, W. (1984). Perceiving affordances: Visual guidance of stair climbing. *Journal of Experimental Psychology: Human Perception and Performance, 10,* 683–703.

36. Meltzoff & Moore, "Imitation of facial and manual gestures."

37. Meltzoff, A. N., & Brooks, R. (2007). Eyes wide shut: The importance of eyes in infant gaze-following and understanding other minds. In R. Flom, K. Lee, & D. Muir (Eds.), *Gaze following: Its development and significance* (pp. 217–241). Mahwah, NJ: Lawrence Erlbaum Associates.

38. Rosenblum, L. (2010). *See what I'm saying.* New York, NY: W.W. Norton.

39. Mandelbrot, Benoit. (1982). *The fractal geometry of nature.* San Francisco: W. H. Freeman.

40. Taleb, N. N. (2007). *The black swan: The impact of the highly improbable.* New York, NY: Random House.

41. Peitgen, H. O. (2010). Retrospective: Benoit Mandelbrot (1924–2010). *Science, 330,* doi:10.1126/science.1199947

42. West, G. B., Brown, J. H., & Enquist, B. J. (1997). A general model for the origin of allometric scaling laws in biology. *Science, 276,* 122. doi:10.1126/science.276.5309.112

43. West et al., "A general model."

44. Bassett, D., Meyer-Lindenberg, A., Achard, S., Duke, T., & Bullmore, E. (2006). Adaptive reconfiguration of small world human brain functional networks. *Proceedings of the National Academy of Sciences, 103*(51), 19518–19523.

45. Watts, D. J., & Strogatz, S. (1998). Collective dynamics of small world networks. *Nature, 393*(6684), 440–442.

46. Freeman, W. J. (2000). *How brains make up their minds*. New York, NY: Columbia University Press.

47. Barnesley, M. F. (1988). Fractal modeling of real world images. In H. O. Peitgen & D. Saupe (Eds.), *The science of fractal images* (pp 221–242) New York, NY: Springer Verlag.

48. Jurgens, H., Peitgen, H. O., & Saupe, D. (1990, August). The language of fractals. *Scientific American*, pp. 60–67.

49. Briggs, J., & Peat, D. F. (1989). *The turbulent mirror*. New York, NY: Harper & Row.

50. Barrow, J. D. (1995). *The artful universe*. Oxford, UK: Clarendon Press.

51. Carroll, S. (2005). *Endless forms most beautiful*. New York: W. W. Norton.

52. Garner, W. (1970). Good patterns have few alternatives. *American Scientist*, *58*, 34–42.

53. Bak, P. (1996). *How nature works*. New York, NY: Copernicus/Springer Verlag.

CHAPTER 6

1. Bernstein, N. A. (1996). On dexterity and its development (M. L. Latash, Trans.). Mahwah, NJ: Lawrence Erlbaum Associates.

2. Woods, E., & McDaniel, P. (1997, p. 140). *Training Tiger*. New York, NY: Harper Collins pg. 140.

3. Woods & Daniel, "Training Tiger," 145.

4. Bernstein, "On dexterity."

5. Hatsoulas, N. (1996) Coupling the neural and physical dynamics in rhythmic movements. *Neural Computation*, *8*, 567–581.

6. Ward, P., Williams, M. A., & Bennet, S. J. (2002). Visual search and biological motion in tennis. *Research Quarterly for Exercise and Sport*, *73*(1), 107–112.

7. Williams, M. A., & Ward, P. (2003). Perceptual expertise: Development in sport. In J. L. Starkes & K. A. Ericsson (Eds.), *Expert performance in sports: Advances in research on sport expertise* (pp 219–250). Champaign, IL: Human Kinetics.

8. Abernathy, B. (1993). Searching for the minimal essential information for skilled perception and action. *Psychological Research*, *55*(2), 131–138.

9. Huys, R., & Beek, P. J. (2002). The coupling between point-of-gaze and ball movements in three-ball cascade juggling: The effects of expertise, pattern and tempo. *Journal of Sports Sciences*, *20*(3), 171–186.

10. Post, A. A., Daffertshofer, A., & Beek, P. J. (2000). Principal components in three-ball cascade juggling. *Biological Cybernetics*, *82*(2), 143–152.

11. Klein, G. A., & Hoffman, R. R. (1988). Seeing the invisible: Perceptual-cognitive aspects of expertise. In M. Y. H. Chi, R. Glaser, & M. J. Farr (Eds.), *The nature of expertise* (pp. 203–226). Hillsdale, NJ: Lawrence Erlbaum Associates.

12. Ste.-Marie, D. (2003). Expertise in sports: Judges and referees. In J. L. Starke & K. A. Ericsson (Eds.) *Expert performance in sports* (pp. 170–189). Champaign, IL: Human Kinetics.

13. Hatsoulas, N. (1996). Coupling the neural and physical dynamics in rhythmic movements. *Neural Computation, 8*(3), 567–581.

14. Cutting, J., & Proffitt, D. R. (1982). The minimal principle and the perception of absolute, common, and relative motions. *Cognitive Psychology, 14*, 211–246.

15. Keller, E. (1983). *A feeling for the organism: The life and work of Barbara McClintock* (p. 118). New York: W. H. Freeman.

16. Mikki Townshend, interview with the author.

17. Mikki Townshend, interview with the author.

18. Mikki Townshend, interview with the author.

19. Moseley, G. L. (2005). Distorted body image in complex regional brain syndrome type 1. *Neurology, 65*(5), 773. doi:10.1212/01.wni.0000174515.07205.11

20. Butler, D. & Moseley, L. (2003). *Explain pain* (p. 96). Adelaide, Australia: Noigroup Publications.

21. Butler & Moseley, "Explain pain," 82–83.

22. Moseley, G. T., Butler, D. S., Beames, T. B., & Giles, T. J. (2012). *The graded imagery handbook* (pp. 24–25). Adelaide, Australia: Noigroup Publications.

23. Ploghaus, A., Narain, C., Beckmann, C. F., Clare, S., Bantick, S., Wise, R., . . . Tracey, I. (2001). Exacerbation of pain by anxiety is associated with activity in a hippocampal network. *Journal of Neuroscience, 21*(24), 9896–9903.

24. Moseley, G. L. (2004). Graded motor imagery is effective for long-standing complex regional pain syndrome. *Pain, 108*(1–2), 192–198.

25. Moseley, G. L. (2006, October). *Pain and the brain. Training class outline for medical professionals.* Seattle: WA: UW Medicine Northwest Hospital and Medical Center.

26. Butler & Moseley, "Explain pain," 76–77.

27. Butler & Moseley, "Explain pain," 22–23.

28. Moseley et al., "The graded imagery handbook," 63–78.

29. Moseley et al., "The graded imagery handbook," 86–94.

30. Ramachandran, V. S., & Rogers-Ramchanran, D. (1996). Synaethesia in phantom limbs induced with mirrors. *Proceedings of Biological Science, 263*(1369), 377–386.

31. Brent Wood, MD, PhD, interview with the author.

32. Ibid.

33. Douglas Tanaka, interview with the author.

34. Holland, J. S. (2005, April). Tsunami update: Saved by knowledge of the sea. *National Geographic.* Retrieved from http://ngm.nationalgeographic.com /2005/04/sea-gypsies/holland-text

35. Simon, B. (Correspondent). (2007, June 11). Sea gypsies see signs in the waves [Television series episode]. In M. H. Gavshon & S. Granatstein (Producers), *60 Minutes*. New York, NY: CBS Television. Retrieved from http://www.cbsnews.com/video/watch/?id=2909732n

36. Holland, "Tsunami update."

37. Winchester, S. (2003). *Krakatoa. The day the world exploded: August 27th 1883*. New York, NY: HarperCollins.

38. Wohlforth, "The fate of nature."

CHAPTER 7

1. Mukherjee, S. (2011, p. 64). *The emperor of all maladies*. New York, NY: Scribner's.

2. Mukherjee, "The emperor of all maladies," 64.

3. Mukherjee, "The emperor of all maladies," 64.

4. Mukherjee, "The emperor of all maladies," 65.

5. Mukherjee, "The emperor of all maladies," 68.

6. Saporito, B. (2013). The conspiracy to end cancer. *Time, 181*(12), 32

7. Saporito, "The conspiracy," 31.

8. Saporito, "The conspiracy," 32.

9. Gazzaniga, "Who's in charge?"

10. Gazzaniga, M. S. (1989). Organization of the human brain. *Science, 245*(4921), 947–952.

11. Gazzaniga, "Who's in charge?", 103.

12. Libet, B. (2002). The timing of mental events: Libet's experimental findings and their implications. *Consciousness and Cognition, 11*, 291.

13. Libet, "The timing of mental events."

14. Libet, B. (2004, p. 90). *Mind time: The temporal factor in consciousness*. Cambridge, MA: Harvard University Press.

15. Libet, "Mind time," 91.

16. Jeannerod, M. (1997). *The cognitive neuroscience of action*. Oxford, UK: Blackwell.

17. Soon, C. S., Brass, M., Heinze, H. J., & Haynes, J. D. (2008). Unconscious determinants of free decisions in the human brain. *Nature Neuroscience, 11*(5), 543–545.

18. Gazzaniga, M. S. (1998, p. 3). *The mind's past*. Berkeley: University of California Press.

19. Retrieved from www.Kochblog.com/?p=789

20. MaryRenee. (2010, July 14). Funny quotes from kids [Blog post]. Retrieved from http://maryrenee.hubpages.com/hub/Kids-Say-The-Darndest-Things-Funny-Kid-Quotes

21. "My daddy had a hysterectomy" and fun other things kids say. (2010, April 7). Retrieved from www.parentdish.com/2010/04/07/my-daddy-had-a-hysterectomy-and-other-things-kids-said/

22. Allport, G. (1979). *The nature of prejudice*. Reading, MA: Addison-Wesley.

23. Ramachandran, V. S. (1995). Asagnosia in parietal lobe syndrome. *Consciousness and Cognition, 4*(1), 22–51.

24. Ramachandran, V. S., Blakeslee, S., & Sacks, O. (1998). *Phantoms in the brain: Probing the mysteries of the human mind*. New York: William Morrow.

25. Ramachandran et al., "Phantoms in the brain," 136.

26. Gazzaniga, "Who's in charge?", 94.

27. Gazzaniga, "Who's in charge?"

28. Gibson, E., & Walk, R. D. (1960). The "visual cliff." *Scientific American, 202*(4), 64–71.

29. El Baradei, M. (2003, March 7). The status of nuclear weapons inspections in Iraq: An update. Retrieved from http://www.iaea.org/newscenter/statements/2003/ebsp2003n006.shtml

30. Blix, H. (2003, February 14). Hans Blix's briefing to the Security Council. *The Guardian*. Retrieved from http://www.guardian.co.uk/world/2003/feb/14/iraq.unitednations1

31. DeYoung, K. (2007, April 28). Tenet details efforts to justify invading Iraq. *The Washington Post*. Retrieved from http://www.washingtonpost.com/wp-dyn/content/article/2007/04/27/AR2007042700550.html

32. Kleck, R., & Strenta, A. (1980). Perceptions of the impact of negatively valued physical characteristics on social integration. *Journal of Personality and Social Psychology, 39*(5), 861–873.

33. Wolford. G., Miller, M. B., & Gazzaniga, M. S. (2000). Split decisions. In M. S. Gazzaniga (Ed.), *The cognitive neurosciences III* (pp. 1189–1199). Cambridge, MA: MIT Press.

34. Gazzaniga, "Who's in charge?", 84.

35. Gazzaniga, "Who's in charge?", 85.

36. Lakoff, G. (2006). *Thinking points: Communicating American values and vision*. New York, NY: Farrar, Strauss and Giroux.

37. Haidt, J. (2012). *The righteous mind: Why good people are divided by politics and religion*. New York, NY: Pantheon.

38. Feygina, I., Jost, J., & Goldsmith, R. E. (2010). System justification, the denial of global warming, and the possibility of "system-sanctioned change." *Personality and Social Psychology Bulletin, 36*(3), 326–338. doi:10.1177/0146167209351435

39. Feygina et al., "System justification."

40. Lewandowsky, S. L., Ecker, U. K. H., Seifert, C., Schwarz, N., & Cook, J. (2012). Misinformation and its correction: Continued influence and successful

debiasing. *Psychological Science in the Public Interest, 13*(3), 106–131. doi: 10.1177/1529100612451018

41. Etcoff, N. L., Ekman, P., Magee, J. J., & Frank, M. G. (2000). Lie detection and language comprehension: People who can't understand words are better at picking our lies about emotions. *Nature, 405*(6783), 139. doi:10.1038/35012129

42. Anderson, A. K., & Phelps, E. (2000). Perceiving emotion: There's more than meets the eyes. *Current Biology, 10,* R551–R554.

43. Sacks, O. (1985). *The man who mistook his wife for a hat.* New York, NY: Summit.

44. Sacks, "The man who mistook."

45. Sacks, "The man who mistook."

46. Sacks, "The man who mistook."

47. Sacks, "The man who mistook," p. 80.

48. Edwards, P. (Ed.). (1967). *The encyclopedia of philosophy* (Vol. 4). New York, NY: Macmillan and The Free Press.

49. Ghiselin, M. (1974). A radical solution to the species problem. *Systematic Zoology, 23*(4), 536–544.

50. Hull, D. L. (1978). A matter of individuality. *Philosophy of Science, 45*(3) 335–360.

51. Bohm, D. (2002, p. 82). *Wholeness and the implicate order.* London: Routledge Classics. (Original work published 1980)

52. McLaughlin, R. (2005, p. 209). *A different universe: Reinventing physics from the bottom down.* New York, NY: Basic Books.

53. Derman, E. (2011). *Models. Behaving. Badly: Why confusing illusion with reality can lead to disaster, on Wall Street and in life.* New York: Free Press.

54. Mayer, J. (2010, August 30). Covert operations: The billionaire brothers who are waging a war against Obama. *The New Yorker.* Retrieved from http://www.newyorker.com/reporting/2010/08/30/100830fa_fact_mayer

CHAPTER 8

1. Sobel, D. (2005). *Galileo's daughter* [Audiobook, CD 8, track 17]. New York, NY: Random House.

2. Sobel, "Galileo's daughter."

3. Galileo, G. (1610) *Sidereus nuncius.* In *Opere* III, 95. Quoted in W. R. Shea & M. Artigas (2003), *Galileo in Rome* (pp. 22–23). New York, NY: Oxford University Press.

4. Hawking, S., quoted in White, M. (1999), *Galileo Galilei: Inventor, astronomer, and rebel* (p. 55). Woodbridge, CT: Blackbirch Press.

5. Klemke, E. D., Hollinger, R. K., & Kline, A. D. (1980). *Introductory readings in the philosophy of science.* Amherst, NY: Prometheus.

6. Planck, M. (1949). *Scientific biography and other papers* (F. Gaynon, Trans.). New York, NY: New York Philosophical Library.

7. Hallam, A. (1975). Alfred Wegener and the theory of continental drift. In *Scientific genius and creativity: Readings from* Scientific American (pp. 76–85). New York, NY: W. H. Freeman.

8. Wegener, A. (1922). *The origins of continents and oceans.* New York, NY: E. P. Dutton. (Original work published 1915)

9. Wegener, "The origins of continents and oceans," 814.

10. White, "Galileo Galilei," 77.

11. Ramachandran, V. S. (2006). Creativity versus skepticism within science. *Skeptical Inquirer: The Magazine for Science and Reason, 30*(6), 48–51.

12. Hallam, "Alfred Wegener," 83–84.

13. Stent, G. (1975). Prematurity and uniqueness in scientific discovery. In *Scientific genius and creativity: Readings from* Scientific American (pp. 95–104). New York, NY: W. H. Freeman.

14. Wegener, "The origins of continents and oceans."

15. Kuhn, T. R. (1996). *The structure of scientific revolutions* (3rd ed.). Chicago, IL: University of Chicago Press.

16. Kuhn, "The structure of scientific revolutions."

17. McClintock, B. (1950). The origin and behavior of mutable loci in maze. *Proceedings of the National Academy of Sciences, 36*(6), 344–355.

18. Crick, F. H. C. (1957). On protein synthesis. *Symposium of the Society of Experimental Biology, 12*, 138–163.

19. Creighton, H., & McClintock, B. (1931). A correlation of cytological and genetic crossing over in Zea Mays. *Proceedings of the National Academy of Sciences, 17*(8), 492–497.

20. U.S. National Library of Medicine. (n.d.). The Barbara McClintock papers. Breakage-fusion-bridge: The University of Missouri, 1936–1941. *Profiles in science.* Retrieved from http://profiles.nlm.nih.gov/ps/retrieve/Narrative/LL/p-nid/48

21. Kass, L. B., & Bonneuil, C. (2004). Mapping and seeing: Barbara McClintock and the linking of genetics and cytology to maize genetics, 1928–1935. In H. J. Rheinberger & J. P. Gaudilliere (Eds.), *Classical genetic research and its legacy: The mapping cultures of 20th century genetics* (pp. 91–118). London: Routledge.

22. U.S. National Library of Medicine. (n.d.). The Barbara McClintock papers. Controlling elements: Cold Spring Harbor, 1942–1967. *Profiles in science.* Retrieved from http://profiles.nlm.nih.gov/ps/retrieve/Narrative/LL/p-nid/49

23. Keller, E. F. (1983, p. 44). *A feeling for the organism: The life and work of Barbara McClintock.* New York, NY: W. H. Freeman.

24. Keller, "A feeling for the organism," 101.

25. Keller, "A feeling for the organism," 125.

26. Jacob, F., & Monod, J. (1961). Genetic regulatory mechanisms in the synthesis of proteins. *Journal of Molecular Biology, 3*(3), 318–355.

27. Keller, "A feeling for the organism."

28. McClintock, B. (1953). Induction of instability in selected loci in maize. *Genetics, 38*(6), 579–599.

29. Keller, "A feeling for the organism."

30. Keller, "A feeling for the organism."

31. Comfort, N. C. (1999). The real point is control: The reception of Barbara McClintock's controlling elements. *Journal of the History of Biology, 32*(1), 133–162.

32. Orgel, L. E., & Crick, F. H. C. (1980). Selfish DNA: The ultimate parasite. *Nature, 284,* 604–607. doi:10/1038/284604a0.

33. Federoff, N. (2012). Transposable elements, epigenetics, and genome evolution. *Science, 338*(6108), 758–767.

34. Federoff, "Transposable elements," 760.

35. Ramachandran, "Creativity versus skepticism."

36. Riddick, I. (Writer and Director). (2013). Earth from space. In I. Riddick, A. Handel, & B. Bowie (Executive Producers), *NOVA.* Boston, MA: WGBH.

37. Riddick, "Earth from space."

38. Richardson, D. B., Volkow, N. D., Kwan, M. P., Kaplan, R. N., Goodchilde, M. F., & Croyle, R. T. (2013, March 22). Spatial turn in health research. *Science, 339*(6126), 1390–1391.

39. Richardson et al., "Spatial turn in health research."

40. Wesolowsi, A., Eagle, N., Tatem, A. T., Smith, D. L., Noor, A. M., Snow, R. W., & Buckee, C. O. (2012, October 12). Quantifying the impact of human mobility on malaria. *Science, 338*(6104), 267–270.

41. Fang, B. T., & Lu, Y. (2012, May). Personal real-time air pollution exposure assessment methods promoted by technological advances. *Annals of GIS: Health and Place, 18*(2), 321–329.

42. Godfrey-Smith, P. (2002). Environmental complexity and the evolution of cognition. In R. Sternberg & J. Kaufman (Eds.), *The evolution of intelligence* (pp. 233–249). Mahwah, NJ: Lawrence Erlbaum Associates.

43. Thiffault, P., & Bergenon, J. (2003). Monotony of road environment and driver fatigue: A simulator study. *Accident Analysis and Prevention, 35*(3), 381–391.

44. Garder, P. (1995). Rumble strips or not along wide shoulders designated for bicycle traffic? *Transportation Research Record,* No. 1502, 1–7.

45. Wohlwill, J. F. (1973, August). *Factors in the differential response to the natural and the man-made environment.* Symposium held at the meetings of the American Psychological Association, Montreal, Quebec.

46. Lorenzo, E. (1992). Visual needs in urban environments and physical planning. In J. L. Nasar (Ed.), *Environmental aesthetics: Theory, research, and application* (pp. 393–421). New York, NY: Cambridge University Press.

47. Schjeldahl, P. (2009, November 16). Bauhaus rules. *The New Yorker*. Retrieved from http://www.newyorker.com/arts/critics/artworld/2009/11/16/091116craw_art_world_schjeldahl

48. Russell, R. L., & Gaubatz, M. D. (1995). Contested affinities: Reaction to Gergen's and Smith's postmodernisms. *American Psychologist, 50*, 389–390.

49. Jacobs, J. (1993). *The life and death of great American cities*. New York, NY: Random House.

CHAPTER 9

1. Kirk, M. (Producer). (2009, October). The warning. *Frontline*. Retrieved from www.pbs.org/wgh/pages/frontline/warning/

2. Partnoy, F. (2003). *Infectious greed: How deceit and risk corrupted the financial markets*. New York, NY: Times Books/Henry Holt.

3. Morris, C. R. (2008). *The trillion dollar meltdown*. New York, NY: PublicAffairs Books.

4. *In the matter of BT securities corporation*. (1994, December). SEC Release Nos. 33-7124, 34-35136, 3-8579, p. 3.

5. Morris, "The trillion dollar meltdown."

6. Jacque, L. L. (2010, p. 219). *Global derivatives debacles: From theory to malpractice*. Singapore: World Scientific.

7. Partnoy, "Infectious greed," 53.

8. Jacque, "Global derivatives debacles," 219, 220.

9. Jacque, "Global derivatives debacles," 219.

10. Holland, K., Himelstein, L., & Schiller, S. (1995, October). The Bankers Trust tapes. Retrieved from http://www.businessweek.com/1995/42/b34461.htm

11. Jacque, "Global derivatives debacles," 203.

12. Kirk, "The warning."

13. Jacque, "Global derivatives debacles," 219.

14. Posner, R. A. (2005). Hayek, law, and cognition. *NYU Journal of Law & Liberty, 1*(0), 147–166.

15. Morison, S. T. (2005). A Hayekian theory of social justice. *NYU Journal of Law and Liberty, 1*(0), 225–248.

16. Hayek, F. A. (1976). *Law, legislation, and liberty, Volume 2: The mirage of social justice*. Chicago, IL: University of Chicago Press.

17. Posner, "Hayek, law, and cognition."

18. Rivkin, J. (2011). *The third industrial revolution: How lateral power is transforming energy, the economy, and the world*. New York, NY: Palgrave MacMillan.

19. Rivkin, "The third industrial revolution."

20. Hedges, C. (2009). *Empire of illusion*. New York, NY: Nation Books.

21. Camerer, C., Lowenstein, G., & Rabin, M. (Eds.). (2003). *Advances in behavioral economics*. Princeton, NJ: Princeton University Press.

22. Ariely, D. (2008). *Predictably irrational: The hidden forces that shape our decisions.* New York, NY: HarperCollins.

23. Schiller, R. J. (2000). *Irrational exuberance.* Princeton, NJ: Princeton University Press.

24. Ingrao, B., & Israel, G. (1990, p. 87). *The invisible hand.* Cambridge, MA: MIT Press.

25. Walras, L. (2003). *Elements of pure economics: Or, the theory of social wealth.* New York, NY: Taylor & Francis. (Original work published 1872)

26. Ingrao & Israel, "The invisible hand," 88.

27. Beinhocker, E. R. (2006, p. 48). *The origin of wealth: Evolution, complexity, and the radical remaking of economics.* Boston, MA: Harvard Business School Press.

28. Beinhocker, "The origin of wealth," 49.

29. Graham, B. (2009, pp. 564, 570). *The intelligent investor: The definitive book on value and investing* (Rev. ed.). New York, NY: HarperCollins.

30. Beinhocker, "The origin of wealth," 32.

31. Cassidy, J. (2009, p. 20). *How markets fail.* New York: Farrar, Straus and Giroux.

32. Lynn, B. (2011). *Cornered: The new monopoly capitalism and the economics of destruction.* Hoboken, NJ: Wiley.

33. Lewis, M. (2010, pp. 75–77). *The big short.* New York: W. W. Norton.

34. Kirk, "The warning."

35. Lanchester, J. (2010). *IOU: Why everyone owes everyone and no one can pay.* New York, NY: Simon & Schuster.

36. Audet, J. R. (2002, February 15). An octopus of greed: The Enron financial web of corruption. *The Quarterly Report.* Retrieved from http://www.quarterly-report.com/energy/enron.html

37. McCoy, P. A. (2009, March 3). Hearing on "Consumer protections in financial services: Past problems, future solutions" before the U.S. Senate Committee on Banking, Housing, and Urban Affairs: Prepared statement of Patricia A. McCoy. Retrieved from http://www.banking.senate.gov/public/index.cfm?FuseAction=Files.View&FileStore_id=40666635-bc76-4d59-9c25-76dafo784239

38. Kirk, "The warning."

39. Scheer, R. (2010, pp. 101–102). *The great American stickup: How Reagan Republicans and Clinton Democrats enriched Wall Street while mugging Main Street.* New York: Nation Books.

40. Scheer, "The great American stickup," 246, 269, 273.

41. Scheer, "The great American stickup," 105, 107.

42. Scheer, "The great American stickup," 103.

43. Story, L., & Morgenson, G. (2010, April 16). SEC accuses Goldman of fraud in housing deal. *The New York Times.* Retrieved from http://www.nytimes.com/2010/04/17/business/17goldman.html?pagewanted=all&_r=0

44. Lowenstein, R. (2008, April 27). Triple-A failure. *The New York Times*. Retrieved from http://www.nytimes.com/2008/04/27/magazine/27Credit-t.html?pagewanted=all.

45. Lewis, "The big short," 75–77.

46. Lewis, "The big short," 75–77.

47. Hurley, L., & Stempel. J. (2013, March 18). Supreme Court refuses to hear Goldman Sachs' appeal to financial crisis lawsuit. *Huffington Post Business*. Retrieved from http://www.huffingtonpost.com/2013/03/18/goldman-sachs-supreme-court_n_2900929.html

48. Brooksley Born, in Kirk, "The warning."

49. Arthur Levitt, in Kirk, "The warning."

50. Brooksley Born, in Kirk, "The warning."

51. Gelinas, N. (2009, pp. 121, 139). *After the fall: Saving capitalism from Wall Street and Washington*. New York, NY: Encounter Books.

52. Galbraith, J. K. (2012). *Inequality and instability: A study of the world economy just before the great crisis*. New York, NY: Oxford University Press.

53. Lynn, B. (2010). *Cornered: The new monopoly capitalism and the economics of destruction*. Hoboken, NJ: Wiley.

54. Reinhart, C. M., & Rogoff, K. S. (2010). Growth in a time of debt. *American Economic Review, 100*(2), 573–578. doi:10.1257/aer.100.2.573. Retrieved from http://www.aeaweb.org/articles.php?doi=10.1257/aer.100.2.573.

55. Murphy, E. (2013, April 19). Math in a time of Excel: Economists' error undermines influential paper. *Daily Finance*. Retrieved from http://www.dailyfinance.com/on/reinhart-rogoff-debt-GDP-spreadsheet-error/

56. Kim, C. (2013, April 24). Debunked: The Harvard study that Republicans used to push austerity. *The Last Word with Lawrence O'Donnell*. Retrieved from http://tv.msnbc.com/2013/04/24/debunked-the-harvard-study-that-republicans-used-to-push-austerity/.

57. Higgins, M. D. (2013, April 17). Formal address by Michael D. Higgins to the European Parliament, Strasbourg, Alsace. Retrieved from http://www.europarl.ie/en/News_Events/Events_Activities/Events_Activities_2013/President_Higgins_in_Plenary.html

58. Higgins, "Formal address."

59. Rotella, C. (2011, August 11). Can Jeremy Grantham profit from ecological mayhem? *The New York Times Magazine*. Retrieved from http://www.nytimes.com/2011/08/14/magazine/can-jeremy-grantham-profit-from-ecological-mayhem.html?pagewanted=all

60. Rotella, "Can Jeremy Grantham profit?"

61. Rotella, "Can Jeremy Grantham profit?"

62. Conversation with Jeremy Grantham: America and its economic future (2013, March 10). *Charlie Rose*. Retrieved from http://www.charlierose.com/watch/60191122

63. Berry, W. (1987). Two economies. In *Home economics* (pp. 54–75). San Francisco, CA: Northpoint Press.

CHAPTER 10

1. Kaufman, F. (2010, July). The food bubble. *Harper's, 321*(1922), 27–34. Retrieved from http://harpers.org/archive/2010/07/the-food-bubble/

2. Hari, J. (2010, July 2). How Goldman gambled on starvation. *The Independent.* Retrieved from http://www.independent.co.uk/voices/commentators/johann-hari/johann-hari-how-goldman-gambled-on-starvation-2016088.html

3. Food price rises are "mass murder": U.N. envoy. (2008, April 20). Retrieved from http://www.reuters.com/article/2008/04/20/us-un-hunger-idUSL2069830020080420

4. Blaser, T. (2012, October 5). We let them starve. *Guardian Africa Network.* Retrieved from http://www.guardian.co.uk/world/poverty-matters/2012/oct/05/jean-ziegler-africa-starve

5. U.N. Chief: Hunger kills 17,000 kids daily. (2009, November 17). Retrieved from http://edition.cnn.com/2009/WORLD/europe/11/17/italy.food.summit/

6. Hari, "How Goldman gambled on starvation."

7. Kaufman, "The food bubble," 29.

8. Keynes, J. M. (1964, p. 272). *The general theory of employment, interest, and money.* New York, NY: Harvest/Harcourt.

9. Kaufman, "The food bubble," 28.

10. Kaufman, F. (2009, June). Let them eat cash: Can Bill Gates turn hunger into profit? *Harper's, 318*(1909), 51–59. Retrieved from http://harpers.org/archive/2009/06/let-them-eat-cash/

11. Hari, "How Goldman gambled on starvation."

12. Ahmed, N. (2013, March 6). Why food riots are likely to become the new normal. *The Guardian.* Retrieved from http://www.guardian.co.uk/environment/blog/2013/mar/06/food-riots-new-normal

13. Lanchester, "IOU," 45, 49.

14. Cox, H. (1999, March 1). The market as God. *The Atlantic*, 18–24. Retrieved from http://www.theatlantic.com/magazine/archive/1999/03/the-market-as-god/306397/

15. Cox, "The market as God."

16. McDonald's the holy grail for potato farmers. (2009, September 23). Retrieved from http://www.nbcnews.com/id/32983108/ns/business-us_business/t/mcdonalds-holy-grail-potato-farmers/#.UZWgmRk

17. Mann, C. (2011). *1493: Uncovering the new world Columbus created.* New York, NY: Knopf.

18. Mann, "1493."

19. Mann, "1493," 223, 227.

20. Mann, "1493."

21. Mann, "1493."

22. Myers, M. D. (1998). *Cultivation ridges in theory and practice: Cultural ecological insights from Ireland* (Master's thesis, University of Texas at Austin). Retrieved from http://www.openthesis.org/documents/Cultivation-ridges-in-theory-practice-397264.html

23. Beinhocker, E. D. (2006, p. 114). *The origin of wealth: Evolution, complexity, and the radical remaking of economics.* Boston MA: Harvard Business School Press.

24. Pollan, M. (2009 p. 215). *The omnivore's dilemma.* New York, NY: Penguin.

25. Pollan, "The omnivore's dilemma," 188-189.

26. Pollan, "The omnivore's dilemma."

27. Bagla, P. (2010). Hardy cotton munching pests are latest blow to GM crops. *Science, 327*(5972), 1439.

28. Sainath, P. (2010, December 28). 17,368 farm suicides in 2009. *The Hindu.* Retrieved from http://www.hindu.com/2010/12/28/stories/2010122861950100.htm

29. Ehrenberg, R. (2010, September 25). Rust never sleeps. *Science News, 178*(7). Retrieved from http://www.sciencenews.org/view/feature/id/63187/description/Rust_Never_Sleeps

30. Pollan, "The omnivore's dilemma," 188–189.

31. Edwards, S., Asmelash, A., Araya, H. & Egziabher, T. B. G. (2009). *The impact of compost use on crop yields in Ethiopia 2000–2006 inclusive* (Environment and Development Series No.10). Penang, Malaysia: TWN.

32. The right to food: Corporate, foreign gov't land grab causing hunger in poor countries. (2010, October 28). *Democracy Now!* Retrieved from http://www.democracynow.org/2010/10/28/un_special_rapporteur_on_the_right

33. Narula, S. (2013). The global land rush: Markets, rights and the politics of food. *Stanford Journal of International Law, 49*(1), 101.

34. Engdahl, F. W. (2007, December 4). "Doomsday seed vault" in the Arctic—Bill Gates, Rockefeller and the GMO giants know something we don't. *Global Research.* Retrieved from http://www.globalresearch.ca/index.php?context=va&aid=7529

35. De Leon, D. (2008, September). Curcumin temporarily slows pancreatic cancer. *CancerWise.* Retrieved from http://www.mdanderson.org/publications/cancerwise/archives/2008-september/cancerwise-september-2008-curcumin-temporarily-slows-pancreatic-cancer.html

36. Jacobs, D. R., & Steffen, L. M. (2003). Nutrients, foods, and dietary patterns as exposures in research: A framework for food synergy. *American Journal of Clinical Nutrition, 78*(3, Suppl.), 508S–513S.

37. Pollan, M. (2008). *In defense of food: An eater's manifesto.* New York, NY: Penguin

38. Hu, F. B., Manson, J. E., & Willett, W. C. (2001). Types of dietary fat and risk of coronary heart disease: A critical review. *Journal of American College of Nutrition, 20*(1), 5–19.

39. Nestle, M. (2002). *Food politics: How the food industry influences nutrition and health.* Berkeley: University of California Press.

40. Halweil, B. (2007 September). Still no free lunch: Nutrient levels in U.S. food supply eroded by pursuit of high yields. Retrieved from Worldwatch Organic Center website: http://www.organiccenter.org/reportfiles/YieldsReport. pdf

41. Pollan, "The omnivore's dilemma," 119.

42. O'Dea, K. (1984). Marked improvement in carbohydrate and lipid metabolism in diabetic Australian Aborigines after temporary reversion to traditional lifestyle. *Diabetes, 33*(6), 596–603.

EPILOGUE

1. Griffiths, J. (2006, p. 60). *Wild: An elemental journey.* New York, NY: Tarcher.

2. Chief Seattle. (n.d.). Retrieved from http://www.brainyquote.com/quotes/quotes/c/chiefseattle104989.html

3. Bacon, F. (1863). The great instauration. In *The works, volume VIII* (J. Spedding, R. L. Ellis, & D. D. Heath, Trans.). Boston, MA: Taggard and Hammond. (Original work published 1620)

4. Bacon, F. (1863). Proem. In *Organum novum* (J. Spedding, R. L. Ellis, & D. D. Heath, Trans.). Boston, MA: Taggard and Hammond. (Original work published 1620).

5. Wohlforth, "The whale and the supercomputer," 247–248.

6. Spade, P. V. (2008). William of Ockham. In E. Zalta (Ed.) *Stanford Encyclopedia of Philosophy.* Retrieved from http://plato.stanford.edu/archives/fall2008/entries/ockham

7. Taylor, S. (2005). *The fall: The insanity of ego in human history and the dawning of a new era.* Oakland, CA: O Books.

8. Wright, R. (2005, p. 304). *Stolen continents: Five hundred years of conquest and resistance.* New York, NY: Mariner Books.

9. Ereira, A. (Producer). (1988). *From the heart of the world: The elder brothers' warning.* London: BBC Films.

10. Ereira, "From the heart of the world."

11. Pollack, H. (2009, p. 114). *A world without ice.* New York, NY: Penguin.

12. Pollack, "A world without ice."

13. Pollack, "A world without ice."

14. Pollack, "A world without ice."

15. Pollack, "A world without ice."

16. Wolfson, R. (2007, p. 35). *The great courses: Earth's changing climate.* Washington, DC: The Teaching Company.
17. Gore, A. (2009). Foreword. In H. Pollack, *A world without ice* (p. ix–xii). New York, NY: Penguin.
18. Wohlforth, "The whale and the supercomputer," 128.
19. Pollack, "A world without ice," 186.
20. Riddick, "Earth from space."

Index